REGIONAL DEVELOPMENT IN A
MODERN EUROPEAN ECONOMY:
The Case of Tuscany

REGIONAL DEVELOPMENT IN A MODERN EUROPEAN ECONOMY:
The Case of Tuscany

Edited by
Robert Leonardi
and
Raffaella Y. Nanetti

PINTER
PUBLISHERS
LONDON, NEW YORK

Distributed in the USA and Canada by St. Martin's Press

Pinter Publishers
25 Floral Street, Covent Garden, London, WC2E 9DS, United Kingdom

First published in Great Britain, 1994

Distributed Exclusively in the USA and Canada by St. Martin's Press, Inc., Room 400, 175 Fifth Avenue, New York, NY10010, USA

British Library Cataloguing in Publication Data
A CIP catalogue record for this book is available from the British Library
ISBN 1 85567 1557

Library of Congress Cataloging-in-Publication Data
A CIP catalog record is available from the Library of Congress

Research for this volume has been funded with the generous assistance of the Tuscan Regional Government

Typeset by Mayhew Typesetting, Rhayader, Powys
Printed and bound in Great Britain by Biddles Ltd of Guildford and King's Lynn

Contents

List of contributors

Ash Amin, senior lecturer, Center for Urban & Regional Development Studies (CURDS), University of Newcastle upon Tyne.

Giacomo Becattini, professor of political economy, Department of Economics, University of Florence.

Marco Bellandi, researcher, Department of Economics, University of Florence.

Reginaldo Cianferoni, professor of agrarian economics, University of Florence.

Gabi Dei Ottati, researcher, Department of Economics, University of Florence.

Antonio Florida, researcher, Tuscan Regional Institute for Economic Planning (IRPET).

Shari Orris Garmise, PhD, candidate in the Department of Government, London School of Economics.

Robert Leonardi, Jean Monnet lecturer in European Community politics and policy, London School of Economics.

Raffaella Y. Nanetti, professor of urban planning and policy, University of Illinois, Chicago.

Marco Romagnoli, director of Social Policy Research Institute (IRIS), Prato.

Fabio Sforzi, researcher, Tuscan Regional Institute for Economic Planning (IRPET) and professor of economic geography, University of Modena.

Part I

Tuscany in the European Union

1 Introduction: the role of Tuscany in the European Community

Robert Leonardi

1.1 Introduction

Ever since the creation of the Italian regional administrative and political structure in 1970 and during the course of its subsequent reforms, Tuscany has taken an active part in the political debate on the regions and played a crucial role in the experimentation of economic and social policies at the regional level. In the past, the ability of Tuscany to carry out this leadership role was attributed to a series of diverse factors: for example, the vivacious nature of its cultural tradition and institutions, the historical record of citizen participation in local affairs, and its mercantile traditions.

The Tuscan economy has also received a considerable amount of scrutiny from scholars, but the results of the analysis have been ambiguous due to the mixed nature of its economic base and the dispersed structure of its production facilities. The course of development followed by Tuscany in the postwar period does not fit well into the traditional models of economic growth. In comparison to the industrialized areas of northern Italy and other parts of Europe, Tuscany lacks an historically dominant industrial sector; its urbanization pattern remains fairly balanced from one end of the region to the other; it still conserves a vigorous and specialized agricultural sector; and it preserves a robust service sector based on tourism and high-quality services.

Alongside the developed areas around Florence, Prato, Pistoia, Livorno, Pisa, and Arezzo the region has a series of underdeveloped rural areas (Monte Amiata, Grossetano and Garfagnana) that have been designated as Objective 5B areas by the European Community and industrial zones undergoing restructuring. These are the Objective 2 areas (Prato, Piombino, Massa Carrara) which have received special consideration and aid from the Community in an attempt to reverse the course of industrial decline.[1]

Aside from a few heavy industrial plants in Piombino (steel), Pistoia (railway cars) and Florence (high-tech optical equipment), Tuscany is strongly identified with a system of diffused forms of small and medium-sized enterprises. A good many of the large industries are in the public sector while the small and medium-sized enterprises are heavily involved in the textile (Prato), leather (Santa Croce sull'Arno), fashion (Florence), mechanical (Pontedera) and jewellery (Arezzo) industries.

Abroad, Tuscany is probably best known for its robust tourist industry in the cities (Florence, Siena, Pisa, Arezzo) as well as the interior (Chianti area) and along the coastline (Viareggio, Forte dei Marmi, Argentario, Punta Ala, etc.) and its world renowned agriculture products (fine wines and olive oil) along with its exquisite cuisine. However, in recent years tourism in Tuscany has been on the decline due to a variety of factors. Some of the reasons given for the decline of tourism have been tied to the inability to make significant investments in the region's infrastructure, the steep rise in prices, and the difficulty in accessing the region's cultural and artistic resources.[2] The region still lacks a coastal highway linking Pisa–Livorno with upper Lazio and easy access to the Roman metropolitan area. The difficulty in providing adequate high-speed access along the coast and laterally between the coast and the 'Autostrada del Sole', which is the major north–south highway running along the interior, serves to limit the region's development potential in tourism and other productive sectors in southern Tuscany, despite the fact that this area contains in the province of Grosseto, a significant natural park and bird reserve (Uccellina Park in the Orbetello Basin) and some of the major historical and artistic centres of Etruscan civilization in the area around Viterbo and Grosseto.

Tuscany has historically lacked an adequate east–west highway system linking the region with complementary areas in Marche and Emilia-Romagna. For many years the 'Autostrada del Sole' has provided access for Arezzo and Florence southward to Rome and Naples and northward to Bologna and Milan, but the section crossing the Apennine mountain range has always been risky, under constant repair, and congested. The need to double the highway – or create a separate section for trucks – has fallen victim to the constant bickering between, on the one hand, the two regions (Tuscany and Emilia-Romagna) and, on the other, the state over the control of the planning process and by the fierce opposition on the part of environmental groups to any further extension of the Apennine highway system. Aside from the highway linking Florence to Pisa via Prato and Pistoia, the realization of other east–west highways has proceeded with difficulty. A case in point is the Perugia–Cesena 'super strada' which was completed recently, but which now is saturated with commercial traffic. Other highways running across the region linking the Tyrennian and Adriatic coasts have remained on the drawing boards of regional transportation planners. Inadequate cross-regional road networks exist in linking, south of Florence, the cities and major tourist centres of the Val d'Elsa area with the coastal city of Cecina, or Grosseto in the Maremma area with Città del Pieve and the Lake Trasimeno area around Perugia and with Arezzo and Sansepolcro.

A similar situation exists in relation to air transportation in the region. At the present time, Tuscany's major airport is located in Pisa (Galileo Galilei airport) which in 1992 serviced 1,070,286 passengers (a 6 per cent increase over the previous year) with regularly scheduled airline and charter flights connecting the region to the major commercial and financial centres in Europe (London, Paris and Frankfurt). The role of Pisa as the region's main airport is being challenged by Florence where the number of flights servicing the city has been constantly increasing and where in 1992 the number of passengers rose by 50 per cent to a total of 399,989 – two-fifths of the number serviced by Pisa.[3] However, the capacity of the Florence airport is limited by a lack of adequate space to lengthen the runway. Thus, despite flights to other European centres such as London, Munich, Brussels and Barcelona, the prospects of expanding the capacity of the airport are limited in the struggle to become the dominant regional airport in central Italy.

Given the infrastructure limitations present in the region, what is striking to an outside observer is how much it has developed during the last four decades. In the past, periodic analyses of the economic performance of the region have stressed the 'precariousness' of its development. However, Tuscany's continued growth in comparison with other regions in Italy and in the European Community has suggested that, though the composite and diffused nature of the Tuscan economy may seem precarious, in reality it provides the region with an internal compensatory mechanism for the overcoming of periodic downturns connected to international and local economic cycles.

There is a growing awareness among scholars that the structure of the Tuscan economy and its growth patterns are not in any way unique to the region; similar phenomena have been identified in Emilia-Romagna, Veneto, Marche, Umbria and elsewhere in Italy and other parts of newly industrialized southern and central Europe.[4] Diffused industrialization structured on the basis of industrial districts composed of small and medium-sized enterprises is part and parcel of the phenomena that characterize Italy's less traditional manufacturing centres concentrated in what has been termed 'the Third Italy' and even some parts of the south and those found in other parts of Europe that have been undergoing rapid economic growth starting from the foundations of a mixed economy (e.g., Rhône–Alpes, Valencia, Baden–Württemberg, etc.). In other words, Tuscany's pattern and level of economic development is not unique to the region but has its counterparts in other areas of Italy and Europe in alternative modes of production that began to emerge in earnest after the major restructuring of Italian and European firms in the post-1970 period.

During the 1980s the pattern of economic development in Tuscany has been characterized by two forms of internal organization – flexible specialization and industrial districts. The causes of Tuscany's diffused form of industrialization pattern have been attributed to a variety of developments: horizontal networking, communitarian bases of economic growth, market niche production, and perpetual product innovation. In the postwar period Tuscany's economic development was never strongly tied to the presence of large, heavy industry (or the Ruhr model of industrialization) or the large extractive enterprises which have dominated certain parts of northern England, Wallonia and the Lorraine areas. Changes which have become highly visible during the last decade of severe de-industrialization and restructuring of large plants suggest that any understanding of the Tuscan pattern of growth or prospects for the future requires a profound rethinking of the factors and the mix of elements which promote economic growth. Economic performance in Tuscany clearly raises the question of what is the optimum combination of the traditional economic factors (e.g., levels of investment, product innovation, unemployment rates, rates of entrepreneurial reproduction) tied to non-traditional factors (such as the nature of sub-regional networking structures, quality of institutional infrastructures, presence of strong traditions of associationalism, and productive political institutions) in spurring and perpetuating development. Attention also needs to be paid to the interconnection between regional, national, and supranational economic and political factors. Local economic conditions are dependent upon a mix of local and international trends as well as the role of strictly non-economic factors.

Based on previous empirical work on the relationship between economic development and political productivity,[5] it is our conviction that it is no longer possible to ignore the role of political institutions in promoting positive economic outcomes. The role of institutions is important at the regional as well as at the national and European levels of decision making and implementation. Institutions have vital roles to play in the structuring of societal priorities and creating incentives for the pursuit of particular lines of development.

1.2   The structure of the study

In order to take into account the role of economic, social, political and institutional factors in determining the level and quality of regional economic performance, we have adopted a multi-disciplinary approach. This volume brings together a group of researchers from the London School of Economics, the University of Florence, and the University of Illinois at Chicago who have been working for a number of years on economic, social, and political issues related to Tuscan developments from a variety of disciplinary perspectives. The common objective of the group has been to peel away the veneer of localism and peculiarity which in the past presented Tuscany as a unique case. The approach adopted here is both comparative and transregional; it focuses its analysis on the performance of Tuscany within the context of the Single Market in which Tuscany currently finds itself along with the other 156 regions of the European Community.

The volume begins with a discussion of Tuscany within the context of other regions in the European Union (Chapters 1 and 2) and then proceeds toward an evaluation of the region's economic and institutional history (Chapters 3, 4 and 5). Particular attention is paid to the evolution of the region's economic and social policies (Chapter 3) and industrial districts (Chapters 4 and 5). To illustrate different trends and aspects of the regional economy, five case studies are presented on the region's two best-known industrial districts: the Prato industrial district (Chapters 6 and 7) and Santa Croce sull'Arno (Chapter 8). The next two chapters analyse, respectively, the role of Tuscany's agriculture and physical environment (Chapter 9) and historical-cultural patrimony (Chapter 10) as strategic economic assets. The volume concludes with a consideration of the role of Tuscany within the Single Market and the search for a proper role within the EC's Mediterranean area through a conscious strategy of European networking capable of taking advantage of the opportunities offered by the advent and expansion of Europe-wide economic growth and development strategies (Chapter 11).

1.3 Tuscany within the European context

Any consideration of Tuscany's role in the European Union is based on the assumptions that are made in relation to the major forces at work in Europe. During the last two decades, three basic changes have taken place in European integration which have impacted on Tuscany and other European regions: (1) the pace and ramifications of European economic integration; (2) regional political institutions have come into existence in a variety of European nation-states from which they were traditionally absent; and (3) the nation-state's prerogatives in formulating socio-economic, political and international policies can no longer be considered exclusive rights of the national government.

With regard to the first change, the realization of the Single Market is only the last of a series of events that have led to constant convergence of European economies (Leonardi, 1993) and integration of markets, and as part of the integration process traditional regional markets have been opened up to internationalization. Products and processes that previously had only a local dimension have either gradually achieved an international position or have simply disappeared from the local market. Thus, single entrepreneurs as well as associations and organizations providing services to manufacturers have had to face the growing presence of competitors from outside both the region and the country. To survive, the response of regional entrepreneurs has had to be one focused at a European level rather than a merely regional one.

The second basic change is tied to the growing presence of regional political institutions in a wide variety of member states in the European Community. Regional governments were not only introduced in Italy in 1970; they were also inaugurated in other member states at the same time or shortly thereafter. Belgium created its three regional groupings during the same year. Seven years later, regions were incorporated into the Spanish constitution and twelve years later they were inserted in the state reforms inaugurated by François Mitterrand during the first term of his presidency in France. The experience of the Italian regions as well as their European counterparts during these two decades has shown that the regionalization of previously centralized nation-states is not only a means of devolving the administration of socioeconomic policies from the national to the regional level, but it is also a means of fundamentally restructuring the policy-making process with regard to policies that are of important concern to citizens and interest groups in society and in providing a major economic stimulus to alternative forms of production.

Today, intergovernmental relations in regionalized states do not look so radically different from those in federal states. The *Länder* in Germany have similar problems of making their voices heard at the federal and Union levels as is the case with the Spanish or Italian regions, and they share similar problems of conflicting attributions of policy responsibilities combined with inadequate revenue bases. In the European Community context it is obvious that for the regions and *Länder* to maintain a positive role they must coordinate their actions and advance a common set of objectives in order to maintain their active role in economic and social policy.

The third change is connected to the growing role of the European Union in the general definition and implementation of economic policies. The economic role of nation-state structures has been weakened by the allocation of key decisions in economic, fiscal, monetary and international trade policies to the European level. The EC as a political and economic entity conditions the actions of individual member states. National governments are no longer free to determine exclusively their own national monetary policies or their approaches to international issues such as the former Yugoslavia or the Middle East. More and more, these decisions are being taken in concert with European partners and within the context of European institutional arrangements.

What do these three trends imply for the evaluation of a region such as Tuscany? Is the political leadership cognizant of the developments taking place in the most developed regions in Europe, and do the leaders have a strategy to maximize the opportunities for Tuscany's entrepreneurs and population presented by the process of European integration and the creation of new European markets?

We cannot, of course, answer all of these questions in this chapter. It will suffice here to answer the first. However, it is imperative that later chapters respond to the other two queries proposed above. What is learned about Tuscany can help us in clarifying our ideas and theories about what has been and will be happening at the European level during the next decade.

1.4   Regional disparities and centre–periphery relations in the European Union

The literature on regional disparities in Europe has a long history and is intertwined with the expectations tied to theories used to understand economic trends and the development of certain disciplines, such as applied economics and regional sciences (Isard and Maclaren, 1982). Rather than taking up one model and trying to argue the applicability of that model to the European context, our review of the literature will be based on the discussion of the economic and political literature on the trend of economic development in Europe in relation to the southern European member states. The predictions will then be tested on the basis of an analysis of data drawn from European level data for the period between 1970 and 1990.

The ratification of the Maastricht Treaty brought to light a contradiction existing within the literature on southern Europe. In the past, southern European states – such as Italy, Greece, Spain and Portugal – were described as peripheral or semiperipheral countries which only with difficulty could insert themselves into a greater European and international context. Observers also noted that, despite early membership in the European Community (in Italy's case as a founding member of the European Coal and Steel Community in 1951 and European Economic Community in 1957), these southern European states remained economically, and in many cases politically, subordinate to their northern European partners. From the perspective of southern Europe, the European Community was basically a rich states' club to which the southern European nations were reluctantly admitted through a sense of political solidarity (consolidate the roots of democracy and spur the tendency in these countries to slip back into authoritarian forms of government) and historical ties (the city-state tradition, the Renaissance, the sharing of religious practices, etc.). Economics was not part of the reasoning for their membership because in all cases the other EC member states had to engage in significant transfer of resources to the poorer southern periphery.

In contrast, the northern European states had as a part of their national patrimony a long tradition of democratic institutions and strong economic bases which only with difficulty could ever be approximated by the southern European states. This line of argumentation would suggest that the northern Europeans should be the most ardent supporters of European integration given that it helps to consolidate the control of Europe's core industrial and financial centres over a vast economic area. Southern European states and populations should, on the other hand, only be reluctant supporters of economic and political integration because they have the most to lose in terms of transferring to the European level control over economic, fiscal and financial decisions affecting their own welfare.

However, when we look at the Maastricht ratification process, we note exactly the opposite to be the case. It is the more northern European countries which express the greatest reluctance at both the governmental and mass level in taking the step towards full economic integration personified by European monetary union and to full political integration as represented by the goal of European political union. In contract, southern European states and populations have continued to exhibit widespread support for the European integration process. Why is this so?

The theoretical literature on centre–periphery relations posits the view that economic and political integration is not necessarily in the best interest of peripheral countries and regions. This dichotomy is present in both the economics and political science literature. In the latter the emphasis of centre–periphery relations has been mainly expressed in terms of the activities within the nation-state while in the economics literature there is a greater tendency to generalize at the European level.[6]

Interest in political and economic conditions in southern Europe received a big boost in the 1980s due to the coming together of two phenomena: the creation in the late 1970s and early 1980s of socialist governments from Portugal to Greece and the rapid development of southern European economies. As observed by Hudson and Lewis (1985, p. 35), for the last two decades growth rates in southern Europe 'exceeded those in most major advanced capitalist nations, particularly in manufacturing, as Southern Europe assumed greater significance within the changing international division of labour'.

In the 1980s the combination of economic and democratic growth in southern Europe and the membership of Italy, Greece, Spain and Portugal in the European Community placed into question the applicability of a number of theories derived from the experience of Third World countries, such as dependency and surplus extraction,[7] which had been common before in attempting to explain the relative low rates of development of Western Europe's periphery.

Given the contrast between the pessimism that characterized considerations on southern Europe in the pre-1980s period and the political and economic changes which we have witnessed during the last decade, what happened to change so radically the course of development? Our contention is that during the last two decades the individual member states, and the European Community as a whole, have witnessed an economic and social change which has yet to be accounted for in the theoretical literature.

The work of Rokkan and Urwin (1982, 1983) sought to look at centre–periphery relations within nation-states with an overall consideration of the changes taking place across Europe over the centuries. Rokkan and Urwin defined the centre on the basis of a series of structural characteristics. The authors point out that the location of major military-administrative, economic and cultural institutions (or the 'command centres') gives the first and most obvious clue to the identification of territorial centres. However, their subsequent analysis of nation-state systems in Europe shows that there is a significant amount of variation among individual countries in the concentration of political, administrative, military, economic and cultural decision-making centres.

The authors identify three types of territorial structures in describing the degree of concentration of key decision-making bodies: monocephalic, mixed and polycephalic.[8]

Given that there is a variety of cores, it is also logical for a variety of peripheries to exist. Rokkan and Urwin, in fact, point to the existence of two basic types of peripheries: *interface* and *external*. The former describes peripheries located in central European areas which have the possibility of interfacing with other peripheral territories.[9] The term 'external periphery' is, instead, used to describe peripheral areas which do not find other economic interlocutors across their political borders due to their island, peninsular, or external territorial status. This is the case, for example, of the regions in the periphery of Greece, Ireland, Italy and the UK.

In either case, though, the periphery finds itself at a disadvantage vis-à-vis the core. According to Rokkan and Urwin the key characteristics of the periphery are physical distance from the centre; a difference and inferiority in the allocation of economic, political, and cultural resources; and, finally, a dependence on the centre for its livelihood and well-being. The attributes of the periphery are in most cases not the result of random events but rather of a specific policy of subjugation undertaken by the centre. The periphery is described as territory penetrated, absorbed and dominated by the centre.

The Rokkan and Urwin characterization of the periphery goes beyond a mere geographical definition of peripherality. As recognized by the two authors, their definition of periphery proposes an ideal-type which may not be applicable in all cases. They do, however, draw attention to the fact that peripherality as a structural characteristic of a particular area or country may exist in three distinctive domains of social life: politics, economics and culture. But whatever the domain, the essential point is that the periphery depends on one or more centres, and its situation, its predicament, and its future cannot be understood in isolation.

Selwyn (1979) describes the economic characteristics of the periphery in similar terms: the periphery is unable to exercise local control over the use of resources, it lacks local innovation, it has weak internal linkages, it is dominated by information flows originating from the centre, and labour migrates from the periphery to the core. As the peripheral economy becomes absorbed into the national economy, its ability to resist structural dependency on the core is weakened and eventually full domination is applied.

In a similar fashion, concepts derived from core–periphery theories have been used to analyse the impact of market integration in the context of the European Community. Seers (1979) poses the question of what does a small, relatively unindustrialized country on the periphery gain from belonging to a system composed of technically advanced core countries? The answer given is that even if in the short run the periphery gains in terms of being able to raise its income levels through a strategy of labour migration and attraction of outside capital, in the long run it subjugates itself to economic, military and cultural hegemony originating from the core (Seers, 1979, p. xviii). The expectation of Seers and other writers on core–periphery economic relations (Seers and Vaitos, 1981) is that membership of the European Community would benefit capitalists and workers linked to multinational corporations operating within the peripheral countries, but the forced opening of peripheral markets 'would destroy many small businesses' and sectors (e.g., textiles and clothing) not prepared to face 'the full competitive power of the giant corporations of the core, despite the difference in wage levels' (ibid., p. 27).

Rokkan and Urwin marshal a variety of studies to make the point that the concepts of centre and periphery describe two empirically distinct phenomenon. However, they fail to make the point suggested by both their political and historical considerations and Selwyn's economic considerations that the differences between centre and periphery grow as the centre supposedly penetrates and exploits the periphery for its own advantage. Instead, Rokkan and Urwin admit that the currents of economic fortunes in Europe have changed on the basis of political/military events, the discovery of new trade routes, and technological/economic change.

Similarly, Arrighi (1985) observes that during the last forty years the position of Europe's peripheral economies in the world economic system has undergone extensive change. Evidence exists pointing to significant shifts in countries such as Italy and Spain which have moved, in Arrighi's terms, from semiperipheral to core status and Portugal and Greece from peripheral to semiperipheral positions (Lange, 1985).

Based on the analysis contained in Rokkan and Urwin (1983) and Arrighi (1985), it is possible to identify three major trends in the history of European development. Up until the sixteenth century, Europe was dominated by the east–west axis of economic and commercial activity founded on the string of important commercial centres along the Mediterranean coast. In this context, the position of Florence and the other city states in Tuscany was central to the revival of economic activity in the Mediterranean and in Europe as a whole. As long as the development axis was centred along the Mediterranean the role of Tuscany was clearly that of a European core area.

However, as a result of a complex series of events tied to the rise of the Muslim presence in the eastern Mediterranean (the fall of Constantinopole) and the expulsion of the Muslims from the western Mediterranean (the fall of Granada) combined with the emergence of the nation-state system in Spain, France and the United Kingdom and the discovery of the New World and the opening of the Atlantic trade routes, the dominance of the east–west, Mediterranean axis and the pivotal role of Mediterranean cities quickly began to decline. Cities in Tuscany began to lose their predominance over cities in the north and especially over capital cities in the major nation-states developing in the northern European interior.

Thus, the second major trend in the subsequent centuries was the movement of the European economic axis towards the north–south dimension, especially above the Alps. This trend was tremendously facilitated by the Reformation in which the links between the state and religion were forged into a national identity and reinforced by the beginnings of the industrial revolution which was grounded on coal as the primary energy source and iron ore as the foundation for the manufacturing of capital goods. The industrial revolution and the introduction of railways as major forms of internal transport added even more emphasis on the core of the nation-state as the centralizing command structure for the conduct of national economic and political affairs and for the protection of the political community from internal as well as external enemies.

Centralization hit its peak in the interwar period as part of the growing political/military tensions among the European nation-states. As a result of domestic as well as international activities, the countries in the European periphery, with Italy in the forefront but quickly followed by Portugal, Spain and Greece, progressively cut themselves off from the rest of Europe and the world economy in the pursuit of nationally inspired goals of political and economic autonomy. In this phase, the national authorities emphasized the predominance of the state over market considerations and greater autarkic provisions to protect national economic activity from the effects of international competition and penetration.

The trend toward autarky and centralization in the European system was sharply reversed in the postwar period as countries were forced to open up their economies and their political systems as part of the underlying structural conditions imposed by the Allies in reorganizing political and economic life in Western Europe. As part of this change, the relationship between the European northern core and southern periphery started to change. In contrast to the interwar period, there was a de-emphasis of the role of the state in being able to manage the economy. The new role of the state was one of supplementing rather than substituting itself for the market, and authoritarian rule began to give way to democratic, parliamentary institutions and procedures.

The opening up of national economies to outside capital, migration of labour, and external trade had a profound impact on the structure of internal and external core–periphery relations. Data cited by Rokkan and Urwin and others show that in the postwar period differences between centre and periphery in nation-states started to decrease (Rokkan and Urwin, 1983, pp. 46–7), and some of the biggest decreases in socioeconomic differences between core and periphery took place in southern European countries (Williams, 1984; Arrighi, 1985).

These findings were not incorporated by Rokkan and Urwin to modify their initial conception of the periphery or the definition of the integration process stressing the conquest of the periphery by the centre and the stripping away of the internal barriers protecting the periphery from central encroachment. Despite the contrary empirical evidence, centre–periphery relations continued to be seen by Rokkan and Urwin as mostly a one-way street; the possibility that the periphery could gain from integration more or to the same extent as the centre was never seriously contemplated. Nor was it fed into the formulation of a more flexible conception of centre–periphery relations taking into account recent trends in southern Europe.

One of the main shortcomings of the centre–periphery literature is that it is strong on theory but it is very weak on data. The analysis of semi-periphery or transformations of the European economic space are handled in a purely descriptive manner. Data are not used to test the hypotheses formulated, and therefore it is not clear what has been happening at the national level to say nothing about what has been happening at the regional level. This type of information is quite important in considering the case of Tuscany because if we were to accept the centre–periphery theorists' notion of the semiperipheral allocation of Italy in the European distribution of countries what are the implications for Tuscany? Is Tuscany part of the core, part of the periphery, or part of the 'Italian semi-periphery'? The answer to this question is important if we are to place the course of economic and political development in Tuscany in proper perspective.

1.5   The findings: Tuscany as a peripherally ascendant region

The data used in the following analysis are derived from Eurostat data sources. The cases to be used in this analysis are distributed accordingly to member states: 20 Italian regions, 22 regions in France, 11 in the UK, 3 in Belgium, 11 in Germany, and 10 in the Netherlands. Ireland, Luxembourg and Denmark are kept as one case each at the national level. Given that alternatives in selecting data for longitudinal analysis were not available, the two measures used here to measure regional government performance over a twenty-year period are gross domestic product (GDP) per capita and PPS (purchasing power standards) to track regional disparities over time.[10]

The analysis of the eighty cases over the past twenty years using the two variables (GDP/per capita in ECU and PPS/per capita) shows two major trends.

First, there has been a significant *reduction* of the gap between the core and the peripheral regions in the Community between 1970 and 1990. The data show that there has been a strong upward convergence of Tuscany and other less developed regions starting in the 1970s which continues in a fairly consistent manner through to the end of the 1980s. At the same time, there has been a downward convergence of the regions which in 1970s found themselves in the upper echelons of the indexes. In other words, the regions in the upper parts of the index fall – i.e., their value on the index falls – while the regions at the bottom experience an upward movement.

Table 1.1 presents the GDP/per capita figures for the eighty regions between 1970 and 1990 at seven points in time. The EC average was calculated on the basis of the data from the eighty cases, and each region's index score was calculated vis-à-vis the EC average. By calculating the gap separating the different groups of developed and underdeveloped regions – i.e., the single, the top five, and the top ten most developed in comparison to their equivalent number among the less developed – and comparing the ratios over the twenty year period, the results show a clear *reduction* of the gap between developed and underdeveloped regions. This is true for both dependent variables: GDP and PPS per capita.

On the GDP per capita variable the gap between the single most developed and the single least developed region fell from the 1970 level of 5:1 to 4.3:1 in 1990. A clearer delineation of the trend is observable in comparing the gap between the five most developed and five least developed regions. In 1970 the difference was 3.5:1, and in 1990 it had

Table 1.1   Regional index scores on GDP/inhabitant in ECU, 1970–90 (EC=100)

Region	1970	1977	1981	1984	1986	1988	1989	1990
Schleswig–Holstein	108	118	101	103	104	104	103	102
Hamburg	211	207	188	200	201	202	195	191
Niedersachsen	111	114	103	105	108	108	105	105
Bremen	174	169	151	155	161	162	159	154
Nordrhein–Westfalen	130	132	117	118	120	120	117	116
Hessen	126	144	130	137	141	142	139	141
Rheinland–Pfalz	109	118	107	109	111	112	108	118
Baden–Württemberg	137	140	125	127	132	132	129	129
Bavaria	114	125	115	121	125	125	123	125
Saarland	106	115	110	112	115	116	111	113
W. Berlin	147	146	130	137	138	138	125	120
Ile de France	179	165	167	163	172	165	171	164
Champagne–Ardennes	122	117	113	103	105	102	104	109
Picardie	109	109	106	96	99	95	97	94
Haute Normandie	137	130	125	111	120	116	117	104
Centre	107	107	105	102	105	102	104	110
Basse Normandie	95	98	95	97	90	87	88	95
Bourgogne	103	102	102	95	99	96	98	98
Nord Pas De Calais	110	99	99	90	91	88	90	89
Lorraine	114	108	105	95	95	92	95	95
Alsace	121	115	119	112	117	113	115	113
Franche–Comte	105	111	106	98	98	95	96	101
Pays de la Loire	99	99	102	95	98	94	96	95
Bretagne	82	91	94	89	92	89	91	91
Poitou–Charentes	90	93	92	89	91	88	90	88
Acquitaine	102	106	108	107	104	100	101	99
Midi-Pyrennes	85	88	94	93	91	88	90	89
Limousin	85	86	88	86	88	85	88	85
Rhône-Alpes	123	114	116	109	114	109	112	108
Auvergne	92	93	92	90	91	88	91	89
Languedoc–Roussillon	85	89	89	88	89	85	87	86
Provence–Alpes C. D'A.	107	108	110	103	104	100	100	100
Corse	–	–	84	75	80	77	77	77
Piemonte	105	88	95	100	104	106	102	115
Valle d'Aosta	110	108	115	111	116	120	113	121
Liguria	115	84	97	103	104	106	107	112
Lombardia	110	92	101	113	120	123	117	131
Trentino-Alto Adige	79	74	86	104	103	105	107	113
Veneto	81	73	81	97	101	104	103	111
Friuli-Venezia Giulia	89	75	89	97	101	104	106	113
Emilia-Romagna	92	86	98	110	111	114	113	123
Toscana	**87**	**76**	**86**	**97**	**101**	**104**	**98**	**108**
Umbria	70	67	79	87	88	88	84	93
Marche	72	68	78	88	92	95	91	98
Lazio	87	71	80	97	101	105	105	111
Campania	55	48	55	61	59	60	57	63
Abruzzi	56	56	65	77	78	79	78	84
Molise	46	46	58	67	69	70	70	75
Puglia	55	49	56	62	63	65	64	69
Basilicata	46	48	56	61	56	57	64	59
Calabria	42	43	49	50	51	52	45	54
Sicilia	54	46	54	61	61	63	64	65
Sardegna	84	53	56	67	67	67	68	71
Groningen	121	251	240	231	181	174	166	129
Friesland	80	105	84	80	84	80	84	78

Region	1970	1977	1981	1984	1986	1988	1989	1990
Drenthe	82	117	110	101	100	96	95	84
East Netherlands	91	111	89	85	86	82	84	82
Utrecht	96	124	104	101	101	97	96	92
North Holland	115	138	118	122	119	114	117	113
South Holland	119	134	110	108	108	104	107	105
Zeeland	108	125	104	104	102	98	104	105
North Brabant (NL)	100	113	92	92	96	92	95	91
Limburg (NL)	87	105	88	87	90	87	90	90
Flanders	106	124	104	95	98	98	88	101
Wallonia	97	104	88	78	80	81	75	81
Brussels	133	188	164	143	149	149	137	157
Luxembourg (GD)	135	125	112	111	114	113	114	119
Northern England	78	66	89	82	72	80	84	76
York and Humberside	87	67	88	83	77	83	87	80
East Midlands	94	68	92	88	79	86	90	85
East Anglia	85	69	93	93	83	90	95	90
Southeast UK	106	82	116	110	100	112	120	106
Southwest UK	85	65	91	88	79	88	93	84
West Midlands	95	68	87	83	75	83	88	81
Northwest UK	95	68	91	86	78	85	94	79
Wales	85	60	80	77	69	76	80	73
Scotland	90	69	94	88	79	86	91	81
Northern Ireland	75	55	74	71	64	69	72	65
Ireland	57	48	57	61	61	59	62	63
Denmark	137	143	120	129	138	134	125	132

declined to 2.5:1! As expected, the trend is in the same direction if one compares larger groups of regions. For example, the gap between the average of the ten most developed and ten least developed regions went from 2.7:1 in 1970 to 2:1 in 1990.

What explains this remarkable set of results? The data show that between 1970 and 1990 the index scores for 'core' regions generally fell. Germany maintained five of its *Länder* in the top ten in the index, but a majority of the German *Länder* (eight out of eleven) experienced a decrease in their index scores. A similar phenomenon characterizes the French regions. Out of the twenty-one regions for which data are available, sixteen French regions saw their index scores drop.[11] In Belgium Flanders and Wallonia fell, as did the countries of Luxembourg and Denmark, while Brussels rose. The British and Dutch regions were almost evenly split between those regions which fell and those which rose on the index.

The main benefactor of the change in index scores is the EC-9 periphery. Ireland and seventeen out of the twenty Italian regions witness significant increases in their index scores. Even the southern Italian regions – long relegated to the bottom of the rankings in the Community of nine or even twelve member states – make strong gains, especially those positioned along the Apennine mountain range. Abruzzi goes from 56 to 78 per cent on the index;[12] Molise from 46 to 70 per cent; and Basilicata from 46 to 64 per cent. Given that in 1970 all five of the weakest regions were located in the Italian Mezzogiorno, their increased index scores combined with the strongest regions' fall during the last two decades help to explain the reduction of the cohesion gap as measured by GDP/per capita and as predicted by the peripheral ascendancy thesis.

The reduction of the gap between strong and weak regions can also be seen in the relative rank of the regions on the GDP/per capita index. There has been a significant drop in rank registered by regions which in the 1970s occupied the middle or upper parts of the rankings such as Champagne–Ardennes, Nord Pas de Calais, Lorraine, Picardie, Flanders, Wallonia, East Netherlands, West Midlands, Basse Normandie, and Sardegna.

The second conclusion drawn from the analysis of our eighty cases is that during the last two decades there has been a significant improvement of the ranking and index scores attributable in the analysis to Tuscany. Using the criteria presented above, we see that there has been a considerable movement upwards in the ranking of Groningen, Lombardia, Southeast UK, Saarland, Trentino-Alto Adige, Emilia-Romagna, Veneto, Friuli-Venezia Giulia, Lazio, East Anglia, Southwest UK, Bretagne, Marche and Toscana.

Tuscany belongs to the group of regions which in 1970 were located in the middle or lower end of the scale which have during the intervening period moved up strongly. The performance of Tuscany and the 'intermediate' regional grouping provides confirmation of the applicability of a peripheral ascendancy model. In 1970 Tuscany was thirteen points below the European mean on the variable while during the last five years it has effectively crossed the EC mean and in 1990 it was eight points above the mean. At the European level, the performance of Tuscany can be compared with some of the most dynamic regions in France (e.g., Rhône-Alpes and Champagne–Ardenne), Netherlands (North and South Holland), and the Southeast UK (including London).

A similar trend is discernible when we look at the other comparative measure of regional performance, PPS (Table 1.2). On this variable the Tuscan region does even better. Since 1977 it has been above the EC mean, and it continues to demonstrate a consistent level of well-being. The regional index scores show that Tuscany is an integral part of that northern and central Italian phenomenon of high levels of economic growth accompanied by high levels of personal consumption within a context not characterized by heavy industrial capacity. Tuscany represents an interesting mix of socioeconomic characteristics that have permitted it to operate as a vanguard region where new forms of industrial structures were experimented with in the postwar period. The changing nature of the Tuscan economy can be clearly seen in comparing the change in the percentage of the region's workforce employed in agriculture and industry. As is illustrated in Table 1.3, in 1950 agriculture accounted for 42 per cent of the region's employed population while in 1990 that figure had declined to a mere 6 per cent. At the same time, industrial employment rose significantly.

What explains the success of Tuscany's development, and what are the

Table 1.2   Regional index score on PPS/inhabitant, 1970–90

Region	1970	1977	1981	1984	1986	1988	1989	1990
Schleswig–Holstein	95	96	92	92	91	93	92	95
Hamburg	185	168	171	179	176	170	169	178
Niedersachsen	97	93	93	94	94	95	95	98
Bremen	152	138	138	138	141	139	138	144
Nordrhein–Westfalen	113	107	107	106	105	105	105	108
Hessen	110	117	118	122	124	126	125	132
Rheinland–Pfalz	95	96	97	97	98	97	96	110
Baden–Württemberg	120	114	113	114	116	116	116	120
Bavaria	100	101	105	108	110	111	110	116
Saarland	93	93	100	100	101	99	99	105
W. Berlin	128	119	118	122	121	110	110	112
Ile de France	158	153	154	158	161	158	159	162
Champagne–Ardennes	107	108	104	100	99	101	101	108
Picardie	96	101	98	93	93	93	93	93
Haute Normandie	121	120	115	108	113	107	107	103
Centre	94	99	97	98	99	98	98	100
Basse Normandie	84	91	88	93	85	91	91	94
Bourgogne	91	94	94	92	93	95	95	97
Nord Pas De Calais	97	92	92	87	85	85	85	88
Lorraine	100	100	97	92	89	89	89	94
Alsace	106	108	110	108	110	110	111	112
Franche–Comte	92	103	98	94	92	97	97	100
Pays de la Loire	87	91	94	92	92	90	91	94
Bretagne	72	85	87	86	86	88	88	90
Poitou–Charentes	79	87	85	86	86	87	87	87
Acquitaine	90	98	100	103	97	98	98	98
Midi–Pyrennes	74	82	87	90	86	89	89	88
Limousin	75	80	81	84	82	82	82	84
Rhône–Alpes	108	106	107	106	107	101	101	107
Auvergne	81	86	85	87	85	87	87	88
Languedoc–Roussillon	75	83	82	85	84	84	84	85
Provence–Alpes C. D'A.	94	100	101	99	97	96	96	99
Corse	–	–	78	73	75	77	78	77
Piemonte	106	118	119	111	115	118	118	117
Valle d'Aosta	112	145	144	124	127	125	125	123
Liguria	117	113	122	115	115	115	115	114
Lombardia	112	124	127	126	132	136	136	133
Trentino-Alto Adige	80	100	108	116	114	116	116	114
Veneto	82	97	101	108	111	115	115	113
Friuli-Venezia Giulia	90	101	112	108	111	116	116	114
Emilia-Romagna	92	116	123	123	122	127	127	125
Toscana	**88**	**102**	**109**	**109**	**112**	**111**	**111**	**110**
Umbria	71	89	99	97	96	96	96	95
Marche	73	92	98	99	101	101	101	100
Lazio	89	96	101	109	111	114	115	112
Campania	56	64	69	68	64	65	65	64
Abruzzi	57	75	81	86	86	87	87	85
Molise	46	62	73	74	76	77	77	76
Puglia	56	66	70	69	69	72	72	70
Basilicata	47	65	70	68	62	61	61	60
Calabria	43	58	62	56	56	56	56	55
Sicilia	55	61	68	68	67	67	67	66
Sardegna	63	71	71	75	73	73	74	72
Groningen	123	216	234	226	179	131	132	131
Friesland	82	90	82	78	83	80	80	79

Region	1970	1977	1981	1984	1986	1988	1989	1990
Drenthe	83	101	107	99	99	86	86	85
East Netherlands	92	95	87	83	85	85	85	83
Utrecht	98	107	102	98	100	98	98	93
North Holland	117	119	116	119	118	116	117	115
South Holland	121	116	107	106	107	107	107	106
Zeeland	109	107	102	102	101	107	108	106
North Brabant (NL)	101	97	90	90	95	94	94	93
Limburg (NL)	88	90	86	85	89	92	93	91
Flanders	95	98	97	99	98	100	100	103
Wallonia	86	82	82	81	80	80	80	82
Brussels	120	148	153	149	149	153	155	160
Luxembourg (GD)	126	110	111	115	119	122	126	120
Northern England	80	93	87	87	86	90	89	84
York and Humberside	89	93	86	88	93	94	91	89
East Midlands	96	95	90	93	95	98	97	94
East Anglia	87	96	90	98	100	102	104	100
Southeast UK	109	114	112	116	121	128	128	118
Southwest UK	87	91	88	93	96	100	101	93
West Midlands	97	96	85	88	91	96	94	89
Northwest UK	97	95	89	92	94	97	95	88
Wales	86	85	77	81	83	87	85	81
Scotland	92	96	91	94	95	99	97	90
Northern Ireland	76	78	72	75	77	78	78	72
Ireland	60	60	62	62	61	63	65	66
Denmark	118	107	102	108	112	107	105	104

Table 1.3 Agricultural and Industrial Employment in Italy, 1950–90

	Agriculture					Industry				
	1950	1960	1970	1981	1990	1950	1960	1970	1981	1990
Piemonte	33	25	12	10	7	43	47	55	43	42
Val d'Aosta	38	23	14	13	8	42	47	47	28	26
Liguria	18	14	8	7	6	41	41	36	26	22
Lombardia	20	11	5	4	3	53	59	60	48	47
Trentino-Alto Adige	42	35	17	15	11	29	30	37	25	26
Veneto	47	30	16	12	7	30	39	46	41	42
Friuli-Venezia Giulia	33	23	12	9	5	37	42	44	33	32
Emilia-Romagna	52	35	21	13	10	24	35	42	37	37
Marche	62	53	30	16	10	20	25	37	39	39
Toscana	**42**	**28**	**13**	**11**	**6**	**33**	**41**	**47**	**39**	**34**
Umbria	58	48	24	15	8	24	29	40	37	34
Lazio	34	22	11	9	6	27	32	32	23	19
Campania	48	36	26	20	11	25	33	35	32	23
Abruzzi	64	51	32	20	11	17	25	32	32	29
Molise	79	71	46	32	21	10	14	26	24	27
Puglia	60	47	35	22	17	21	27	32	27	26
Basilicata	72	59	40	32	21	15	23	31	26	26
Calabria	64	48	34	28	23	19	27	31	23	17
Sicilia	51	38	27	19	15	24	30	34	26	21
Sardegna	53	40	26	16	15	24	29	32	27	24

prospects for the future of other intermediate peripheral areas such as Tuscany in Italy and other regions in the European Union? We will try to analyse these issues in the subsequent chapters in this volume.

Notes

1. Livorno is currently applying for Objective 2 status.
2. The limited hours when the national museums are open reflect a non-commercial, bureaucratic approach to the tourist trade. They seem to reflect more the exigencies of the administrative personnel to maintain intact their part-time schedules rather than satisfying the demand from the clientele to visit some of the world's most precious art treasures. It is important to note that after the 27 May 1993 bomb blast that partially damaged the Uffizi and caused five deaths in via dei Geogofili, the city administration and the Minister of Culture arrived at an agreement permitting the national and local museums to extend their hours through a more effective rotation of personnel and use of volunteers.
3. The large increase in passengers serviced in 1992 is mostly due to the opening of the new air terminal in Florence and the fact that Florence has become one of the major hubs for the Meridiana airline which has developed a strategy of servicing the major regional airports in Italy mostly ignored by the national air carrier such as Florence, Verona and Catania.
4. See Bagnasco (1977); Fuà and Zacchia (1983); Piore and Sabel (1985); Leonardi and Nanetti (1990).
5. See Putnam, Leonardi and Nanetti (1985, 1993); Nanetti (1988, 1992); Leonardi and Garmise (1993).
6. See the interesting discussion contained in Krugman (1991, pp. 93–8) in relation to the comparison of core–periphery in the USA and the EC.
7. The manifestation of these two phenomena has not prevented students of southern Europe applying dependency theories to predict the development of the Mediterranean countries. These attempts were more theoretical than empirical in nature, thereby demonstrating all their limitations in being able to predict the economic take-off of southern Europe during the 1980s. See Seers, Schaffer and Kiljunen (1979).
8. Based on the Rokkan and Urwin distinction one could distribute the countries into the following categories: (a) monocephalic countries: France, UK, Belgium, Austria, Denmark, Greece, Ireland, Portugal; (b) intermediate countries: Sweden, Norway, Finland; and (c) polycephalic countries: Germany, Italy, Netherlands, Switzerland and Spain.
9. This is the classic border areas covered by Article 10 of the 1988 ERDF regulation.
10. The periodic reports spawned a whole series of studies based on secondary analysis of regional trends in the Community that accepted in an uncritical fashion the conclusions that regional disparities were on the increase in Europe.
11. In Denmark and Ireland, going back to 1960 the differences were similar to those of 1970 while the gap between the two countries narrowed even further by 1990. Using data cited in the CEC (1992) (Table 1 in Appendix) the top three countries (Luxembourg, UK and Denmark) had in 1960 levels of GDP per capita 2.9:1 in comparison to the bottom three countries (Ireland, Portugal and Greece). In 1992 the ratio between the same six countries had

declined to 1.9:1. Corsica (Corse) was dropped from the calculation due to the lack of 1970s data. In 1989 it was ranked 69th.
12. For a detailed analysis of the rise of the Abruzzo region, see Leonardi (1991).

References

Arrighi, G. (ed.), *Semiperipheral Development: The Politics of Southern Europe in the Twentieth Century*, London, Sage, 1985.

Bagnasco, A., *Le tre Italie*, Bologna, Il Mulino, 1977.

CEC, *Community Structural Policies: Assessment and Outlook*, COM(92) 84 Final, 1992.

Fuà, G. and Zacchia, C., *Industrializzazione senza fratture*, Bologna, Il Mulino, 1983.

Hudson, R. and Lewis, J., *Uneven Development in Southern Europe: Studies of Accumulation, Class, Migration and the State*, London, Methuen, 1985.

Isard, W. and Maclaren, V.W., 'Storia e stato attuale delle ricerche nella scienza regionale' in M. Bielli and A. Labella (eds.), *Problematiche dei livelli subregionali di programmazione*, Milan, Franco Angeli, 1982, pp. 19–40.

Krugman, P., *Geography and Trade*, Cambridge, MA, MIT Press, 1991.

Lange, P., 'Italy' in G. Arrighi (ed.), *Semiperipheral Development: The Politics of Southern Europe in the Twentieth Century*, London, Sage, 1985.

Leonardi, R., 'Riflessi della riduzione del sostegno comunitario sull'economia regionale, con particolare riguardo al sistema industriale', Presidenza della Regione Abruzzo, L'Aquila, Italy, 1991.

—— 'The State of Economic and Social Cohesion in the Community Prior to the Creation of the Single Market: The View from the Bottom Up', Brussels, Commission of the European Communities, 1993.

Leonardi, R. and Garmise, S.O. in Leonardi, R. (ed.), *Regions and the European Community: The Regional Response to 1992 in the Underdeveloped Areas*, London, Frank Cass, 1993.

Leonardi, R. and Nanetti, R.Y. (eds.), *The Regions and European Integration: The Case of Emilia-Romagna*, London, Pinter, 1990.

Nanetti, R.Y., *Growth and Territorial Policies: The Italian Model of Social Capitalism*, London, Pinter, 1988.

—— 'Coordination in Development Planning: An Evaluation of the Initial Implementation of the Community Support Framework', Bussels, Commission of the European Communities, 1992.

Piore, M. and Sabel, C., *The Second Industrial Divide: Possibilities for Prosperity*, New York, Basic Books, 1984.

Putnam, R.D., Leonardi, R. and Nanetti, R.Y., *La pianta e le radici*, Bologna, Il Mulino, 1985.

—— *Making Democracy Work: Civic Traditions in Modern Italy*, Princeton, Princeton University Press, 1993.

Rokkan, Stein and Urwin, Derek W. (eds.), *The Politics of Territorial Identity: Studies in European Regionalism*, London, Sage, 1982.

—— *Economy, Territory, Identity: Politics of West European Peripheries*, London, Sage, 1983.

Seers, D., 'Preface' in D. Seers, B. Schaffer and L. Kiljunen (eds.), *Underdeveloped Europe: Studies in Core–Periphery Relations*, Hassocks, Harvest Press, 1979.

Seers, D., Schaffer, B. and Kiljunen, L. (eds.), *Underdeveloped Europe: Studies in Core–Periphery Relations*, Atlantic Highlands, NJ, Humanities Press, 1979.

Seers, D. and Vaitos, C., *Integration and Uneven Development*, London, Macmillan, 1981.

Selwyn, P., 'Some Thoughts on Cores and Peripheries' in Seers, Schaffer and Kiljunen (1979).

Williams, A. (ed.), *Southern Europe Transformed: Political and Economic Change in Greece, Italy, Portugal and Spain*, London, Harper & Row, 1984.

2 Convergence in the European Community: the case of Tuscany

Shari O. Garmise

'Real convergence is one of the [European] Community's fundamental objectives and is essential for its cohesion' (CEC, 1987, p. 52).[1] To better understand the problems of regional disparity, the European Community has been actively studying the situation and publishing its findings in 'The Periodic Reports on the Social and Economic Situation of the Regions of the Community'. These periodic reports have based their analysis on a comparison of the differences found between the strongest and weakest regions. However, a comparison between strong and weak, especially if the regions in these categories remain fairly constant over time, lends itself to only a tautological explanation of the differences between the two groups. I argue, instead, that a more suitable approach for studying convergence is to determine which regions are converging with the stronger regions and then investigate what they are doing that supports these changes (Garmise, 1991). This chapter will demonstrate the strength of this approach by examining the process of convergence in a single region: Tuscany.

Section 1 examines the economic indicators of convergence and demonstrates that Tuscany is indeed converging with the strongest European regions. Section 2 then looks in depth at Tuscany's economic, political and social structures to answer the question of how it achieved that convergence. Finally, the conclusion argues that, to achieve convergence, regional institutions matter.

2.1 Tuscany in an interregional comparison

This section examines the changing economic position of Tuscany by comparing it, over time, with a sample of twenty-five European regions.[2] The study uses cluster analysis to identify analogous regions according to shared economic characteristics. The regions were chosen because they covered the range of regional problems in four countries of the European Community (Germany, France, Italy and the UK). The sample means for the variables chosen mirror the means of the Community as a whole indicating that the sample is an appropriate one for the comparison. Furthermore, the inclusion of Calabria and Basilicata in the sample ensures that the lower parameters of the Community's economic spectrum are preserved because these two regions remain at the bottom of the regional rankings even when compared with Greece and Portugal. Finally, Spain, Greece and Portugal were excluded for two reasons. First, I wanted to demonstrate true, not just relative, change in economic rank in countries that have participated in the Common Market for at least a decade. The mere addition of those three countries push many regions from below to above the EC mean. Second, data were not available for those three countries for the decade of the seventies in the data bank employed.

Comprehensive regional statistics for the Community are difficult to find. The only regional data set is REGIO, the Eurostat regional data bank, which is complemented by the annual Eurostat Regional statistical yearbooks. Both these sources suffer from data shortages which limit the years, regions and variables that can be utilized for any study requiring economic data at the regional level. In this regard, the variables, regions and years chosen for this study were determined, to some extent, by data availability. To measure change over time, five cluster runs were carried out for the years 1977, 1981, 1984, 1987 and 1990. The hypothesis being tested is that Tuscany would move from the cluster representing the less-favoured regions to a higher cluster demonstrating convergence with the stronger European regions. The variables used in the cluster runs were: (1) gross domestic product (GDP) at market prices as a measure of economic strength and the degree of development, (2) harmonized unemployment rates and population density[3] which operationalize the present and future labour market, and (3) the percentage of active population employed in agriculture, industry and services which represents the economic structure of the region. Table 2.1 presents the clusters created in the five selected years. Cluster 1 represents the strongest regions, cluster 2 the intermediate regions, and cluster 3 the least-favoured regions.[4]

Table 2.1 demonstrates several significant trends. Overall, the regions in the strongest cluster, particularly the German regions, remain stable over time. Two Italian regions, Lombardy and Emilia-Romagna enter the strongest grouping in 1984 and retain their position. Southeast, the British region which includes London, oscillates between the strongest and intermediate groups despite its status as a capital region and financial centre. The most significant movement is found between the least favoured group and the intermediate cluster. There is a clear steady trend of regions improving in position as the number of regions in cluster 3 shrinks dramatically from eleven members in 1977 to two members in 1987. This exodus suggests that these regions have demonstrated absolute improvement within the European context and not just relative improvement due to the entry of Greece, Portugal and Spain. Only for the case of Wales do we find a vacillation in position.

Looking at Tuscany, it falls in the least-favoured regions' cluster only in 1977 and is grouped in the intermediate cluster in all other years until it enters the strongest cluster in 1990. The hypothesis that Tuscany should ascend into a higher cluster and approach convergence with the strongest regions has been supported. To deepen our understanding of these changes,

Table 2.1   The Clusters

Year	Cluster 1	Cluster 2	Cluster 3
1977	Niedersachsen Nordrhein–Westfalen Hessen Baden–Württemberg Bavaria Saarland Lorraine Alsace	Southeast UK Nord Pas de Calais Midi–Pyrenees Languedoc–Roussillon Lombardy Emilia–Romagna	**Tuscany** Marche Abruzzi Molise Basilicata Calabria East Midlands Southwest UK
1981	Nordrhein–Westfalen Hessen Baden–Württemberg Bavaria Saarland Alsace Southeast UK	Nord Pas de Calais Midi–Pyrenees Languedoc–Roussillon Lorraine Niedersachsen Lombardy Emilia–Romagna **Tuscany** Marche East Midlands Southwest UK West Midlands East Anglia Wales	Abruzzi Molise Basilicata Calabria
1984	Niedersachsen Nordrhein–Westfalen Hessen Baden–Württemberg Bavaria Saarland Alsace Lombardy Emilia–Romagna Southeast UK	Nord Pas de Calais Midi–Pyrenees Languedoc–Roussillon Lorraine **Tuscany** Marche East Midlands Southwest UK West Midlands East Anglia	Abruzzi Molise Basilicata Calabria Wales
1987	Niedersachsen Nordrhein–Westfalen Hessen Baden–Württemberg Bavaria Saarland Alsace Lombardy Emilia–Romagna	Nord Pas de Calais Midi–Pyrenees Languedoc–Roussillon Lorraine **Tuscany** Marche Abruzzi Molise East Midlands Southwest UK West Midlands East Anglia Southeast UK Wales	Basilicata Calabria
1990	Niedersachsen Nordrhein–Westfalen Hessen Baden–Württemberg Bavaria **Tuscany**	Nord Pas de Calais Midi–Pyrenees Languedoc–Roussillon Lorraine	Basilicata Calabria

Year	Cluster 1	Cluster 2	Cluster 3
1990 (cont.)	Saarland	Marche	
	Alsace	Abruzzi	
	Lombardy	Molise	
	Emilia–Romagna	East Midlands	
	Southeast UK	Southwest UK	
		West Midlands	
		East Anglia	
		Wales	

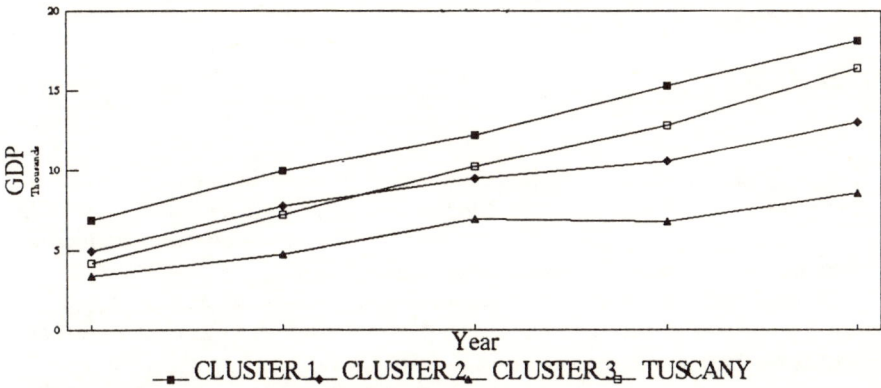

Figure 2.1 Regional GDP per capita (in ecu)

Source: REGIO

Tuscany will be compared with the cluster means for all the economic variables.

Figure 2.1 shows the first variable, economic development measured by regional GDP per capita. Tuscany's growth rate is striking and represents the key to its convergence with the stronger regions. Despite being placed in the weakest cluster in 1977, Tuscany's GDP (4235.53 ECU) was clearly above this cluster's mean (3390.62 ECU). Closer investigation demonstrates that Tuscany had the highest regional GDP in cluster 3 (see Appendix), although it was still below the lowest GDP found in cluster 2, (4551.00 ECU for the Southeast). In 1984, Tuscany, now placed in cluster 2, reflects its group mean GDP. In the later years, Tuscany's GDP is clearly above its cluster mean showing that it is moving towards convergence with the stronger regions. In fact, in 1984 and 1987, Tuscany had the highest GDP in cluster 2 at, respectively, 10,227 ECU and 12,805 ECU although it was still below cluster 1's lowest GDPs (see Appendix). Finally, in 1990, Tuscany enters the cluster containing the strongest regions with a GDP of

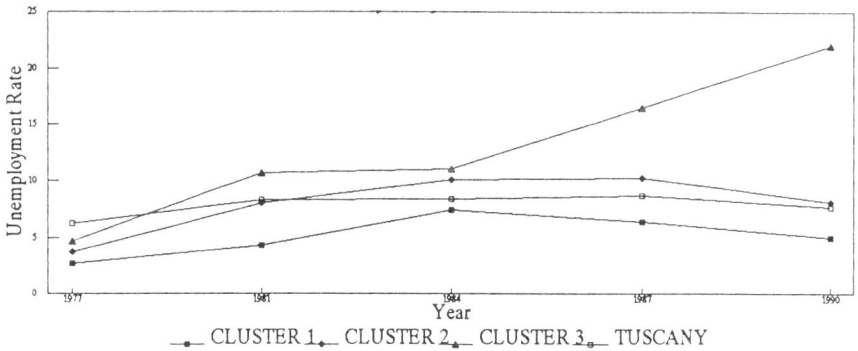

Figure 2.2   Unemployment rates

Source: REGIO

16,397 ECU which is lower than the cluster 1 mean but not the lowest in the cluster. The Southeast and Niedersachsen have lower GDPs. Overall, the evidence is suggestive of Tuscany's continued success and economic growth in both relative and absolute terms.

Despite this steady growth, Tuscany contains several zones designated by the European Community as Objective 2, areas in industrial decline, which indicates that it still has some structural problems. These problems will emerge in the examination of the other variables. Looking at the labour market, measured by unemployment rates and population density, the evidence suggests that there may be limits to prolonged economic expansion. On one hand the unemployment rates in Tuscany, shown in Figure 2.2, are below the mean of its cluster group only in 1984 and 1987 but above the mean in all other years including 1990 (See Appendix 1).[5] Therefore unemployment is a bigger problem for Tuscany than it is for the most favoured regions. In addition, the population density in Tuscany, Figure 2.3, is still rather low relative to the stronger and intermediate regions.

Looking now at regional economic structure, measured by the importance of each sector for overall employment (see Figure 2.4), the findings are somewhat ambiguous. Tuscany slightly resembles the less-favoured regions with a higher than average dependence upon the agricultural sector (10 per cent) for employment until 1990 when it drops dramatically to 6 per cent (panel (a)). The manufacturing sector (panel (b)) tells a different story. In 1977, Tuscany's manufacturing sector was, at 44 per cent, comparable in size to the cluster 1 mean of 44.4 per cent. By 1990 Tuscany has a slightly smaller industrial base (34 per cent) than the stronger regions (38 per cent) but it is higher than the cluster 2 mean (31 per cent). However, the 10 per cent drop in manufacturing employment between 1977 and 1990 is higher than the drop experienced in both cluster

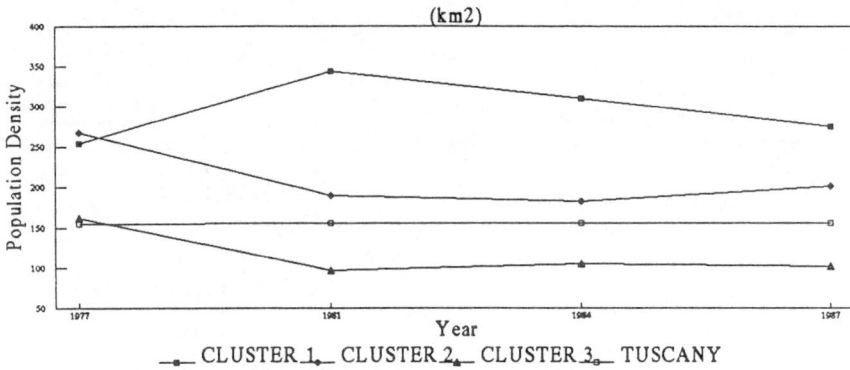

Figure 2.3   Population density

Source: REGIO

1 and cluster 2 (6 per cent). Thus deindustrialization and its consequences present larger problems for Tuscany than for the stronger European regions.[6] This deindustrialization, coupled with high unemployment rates, represent the measurable symptoms of the problems which influenced the Community to designate several Tuscan areas as those in industrial decline. Looking at the less-favoured regions in 1990, they clearly stand apart with a strong dependence on the agricultural sector for employment (22 per cent) and a small industrial base (21 per cent). In sum, these indicators suggest that, despite Tuscany's successful consistent growth, several problems confront the region which must be overcome if it is to maximize the opportunities offered by the single market.

Turning to the service sector (panel (c)), the information available from this variable is also not very instructive. Note that the size of the service sector for all clusters is more or less the same. In all cases, the service sector has increased in importance for the provision of jobs in the economy. However, different stages of development require different types of services (Cappellin, 1990) which cannot be distinguished by this general indicator. So an increase in jobs provided by the service industry cannot lead to the conclusion that development is progressing in a positive fashion. In the case of Tuscany, a strong tourist sector has developed alongside industrialization which can lead to an increase in the low-wage service sector (restaurants, hotels, etc.) as well as to a corresponding increase in higher-wage business services (banking, marketing, information technology) that provide the necessary support structure for industrial expansion and adjustment. A greater breakdown of the service sector and a classification of certain services, especially business services, which are integral to the region as a whole, would help to determine what should be provided to whom at what particular stage of development.

This section has demonstrated that Tuscany has indeed approached

Agricultural Employment
(in percent)

CLUSTER 1 _CLUSTER 2_ _CLUSTER 3_ _TUSCANY

Manufacturing Employment
(in percent)

CLUSTER 1 _CLUSTER 2_ _CLUSTER 3_ _TUSCANY

Service Employment
(in percent)

CLUSTER 1 _CLUSTER 2_ _CLUSTER 3_ _TUSCANY

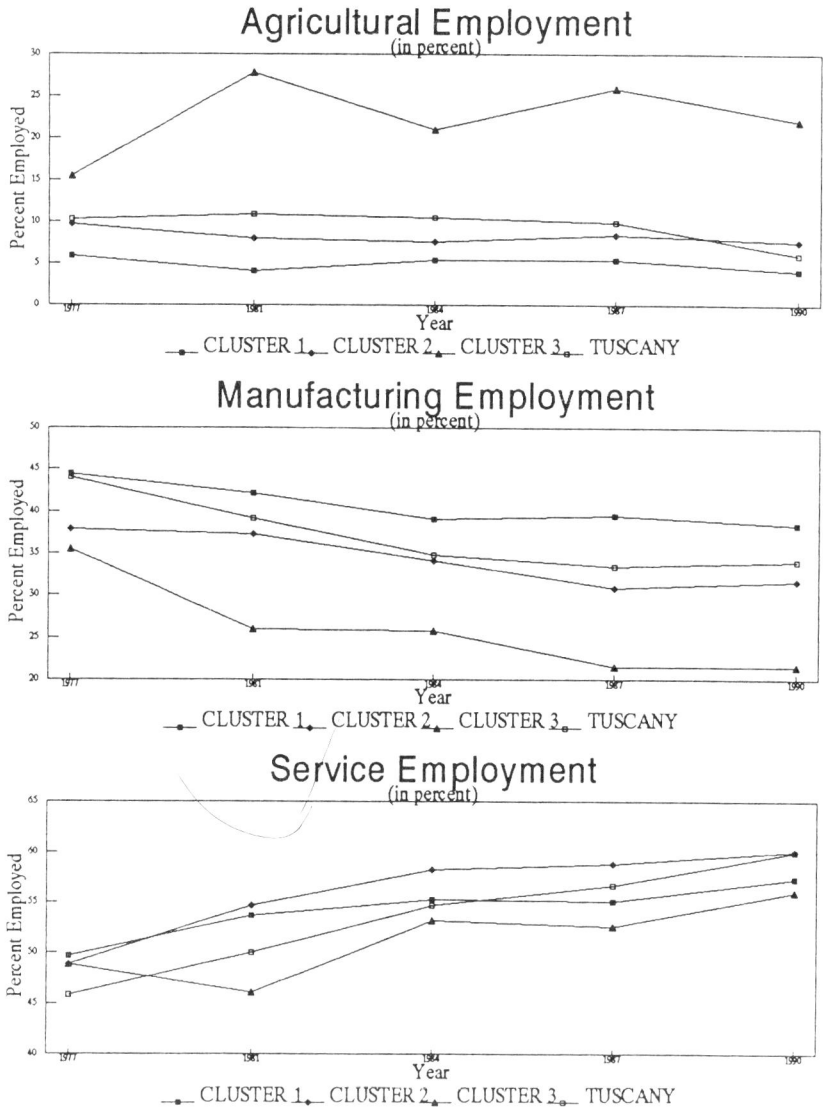

Figure 2.4 Percentage of workforce employed by sector: (a) agricultural,
(b) manufacturing, (c) service

Source: REGIO

convergence with the stronger European regions. Despite certain weak-
nesses that were brought out in the analysis, the Tuscan economy has
grown steadily. What is the secret behind this successful growth? How
determinative is the political and social infrastructure for economic success?
Section 2 attempts to answer these questions.

2.2   Explaining regional economic success

The dynamism of the Tuscan economy rests on three foundation stones: a distinct economic structure based on small firm production, supportive regional institutions, and a strong civic society. This section will examine each of these three elements. The conclusion which emerges from this discussion is that regions do matter. The section below examines the economic foundation, concentrating on the importance of the organization of production into flexibly specialized industrial districts.

The economic foundation: industrial districts and flexible specialization

Before the Second World War, Tuscany was primarily an agricultural region with several small but active urban centres and minimal industrialization.[7] In the postwar period, Tuscany witnessed rapid industrialization assisted by the deterioration of the share-cropping system that encouraged a large migration of agricultural workers to the cities. The exodus of the share-croppers also stimulated a good deal of political discontent which translated into support for the parties of the left. Tuscany is in the Italian red zone, regions in which the parties of the left, especially the Communist Party, have consistently received the largest percentage of the vote, enabling them to form the government. This is in direct contradiction to the national average where the Christian Democratic Party has received the majority of the votes and has had the electoral mandate to form the national coalitions.[8] The political continuity found in Tuscany in the postwar years may be a key explanatory element of its economic success (Trigilia, 1986).

Concurrent with the changes in the agricultural sector, the Tuscan industrial structure also saw the number of artisan enterprises (which had been the traditional foundation of the Tuscan productive sector) greatly increase in the postwar period in response to increased international demand and the expansion of tourism. Population migration, political stability, and the regionally diffused growth of artisan enterprises within concentrated territorial spaces ultimately led to a transformation in Tuscany's socioeconomic structure. This socioeconomic structure is the key to understanding Tuscany's economic dynamism.[9]

Tuscany's socioeconomic structure is rooted in these territorially concentrated, small and medium-sized artisan enterprises. These productive zones, known as industrial districts, represent an alternative form of industrial organization (as opposed to vertically integrated large corporations) that is able to take advantage of fragmenting markets, new technologies and rapidly changing demand.[10]

The comparative advantage of industrial districts emerges from the territorial concentration of several thousand small firms within a single community, each of which specializes in a single manufacturing sector, usually a labour-intensive traditional sector, such as glass (Empoli), textiles (Prato), and extractive industries like marble (Massa Carrara). Geographical proximity allows each small firm to specialize in one phase of the manufacturing process. These firms, and the various phases of production, are brought together through horizontally integrated subcontracting networks. This productive organization supports a just-in-time small-batch work strategy which allows the industrial districts to produce a wide variety of differentiated goods which can be easily changed to meet varying market demand. Because they adapt easily to changes in demand, these districts are flexible (Brusco, 1982, p. 179). Thus, flexibility plus specialization shapes the nature of the production process. As a result, this system of industrial organization has been termed flexible specialization (Piore and Sabel, 1984).[11]

While flexible specialization is founded on interfirm cooperation, firms specializing in the same phase of production are, conversely, highly competitive. Competition, however, is not based on price or wage reductions but on product quality and innovation. The necessary coexistence of cooperation and competition is integral to the logic of this productive system because it keeps the firms innovative. To maintain the appropriate balance of cooperation and competition, industrial districts rely on two reinforcing mechanisms. First, economic relations are heavily embedded in dense community-based social networks creating what Dei Ottati (1991) has termed the 'community market'. Thus, social relations support and enhance economic relations. The second mechanism is the interwoven networks of local and regional institutions that coordinate the allocation of resources to benefit the industrial sector as well as providing many necessary and useful services to small businesses (Piore and Sabel, 1984). Regional institutions include subnational government, business, artisan and trade associations, chambers of commerce, universities and research centres.

Flexible specialization, as a paradigm, does not just challenge our beliefs as to what constitutes competition – price versus quality or small versus large firms – but rather presents its greatest challenge to the realm of ideas particularly regarding the role of government in the economy. It is not, therefore, coincidental that the economic decentralization found in Tuscany and the Third Italy has been paralleled by the political decentralization to the regions over the past twenty years (Nanetti, 1988). The synchronous progress of institutional and economic decentralization results in a growing interdependence of these two dimensions so that increased demands stemming from the economic sphere influences increased economic planning and policy decisions in the political sphere at the subnational level (ibid.). Studies of Italian regions have shown that regional governments have been growing in institutional performance and capability since their inception two decades ago (Putnam, Leonardi and Nanetti, 1985; Leonardi and Nanetti, 1990). Thus, the economic success of Tuscany owes credit to the local and regional governments' supportive activities. The political foundation will now be examined.

The political foundation: subcultures and endogenous development

Two political factors have supported Tuscany's economic growth: a strong leftist subculture and a pragmatic approach to economic development. Each will be examined in turn. Trigilia's (1986) comprehensive study of industrial districts in Tuscany and Veneto demonstrates how the interactive networks of local and regional institutions have encouraged and sustained, respectively, a leftist and a Catholic political subculture. These subcultures found political expression in the continuous electoral majority of the Communist or Christian Democratic Party in these regions. The political continuity furnished by these subcultures has influenced the economic development of these areas, in particular by contributing to the preservation of the traditional social environment and the shaping of a particular orientation regarding economic activities. The political continuity has helped to reproduce the strong consensus found in these regions that has allowed these governments to pursue activities that favour the growth of small businesses. It follows that Tuscan economic development and the origins and transformation of these political subcultures have been mutually reinforcing. Modernization, however, has encouraged a concurrent transformation in the nature of this consensus. It has moved from an implicit social base to explicit forms of political exchange. Local governments must offer more services in exchange for political support that had once been arguably assured given the high degree of political homogeneity. The paradox is that small firms and the preservation of the political subculture have become more interdependent as a result.

While the subcultures have been a crucial variable for explaining the political support given to small firms, they form only one piece of the puzzle. Also important has been the specific development strategies that the regions have followed. The Italian regions have limited constitutional powers to undertake economic development policy. While the region retains full responsibility for the artisan and craft sector, the powers to pursue industrial, employment, credit and banking policy are in the hands of the national government. To cope with these constitutional constraints on their formal powers, Italian regions have only been able to extend their role in these other strategic sectors by working cooperatively with other regional institutions (Nanetti, 1988, pp. 94–7). This collaborative approach to policy-making can be conceptualized as a regional productivity coalition, defined by Garmise and Grote (1990) as 'interorganizational networks of private and public actors [that] manage the economic and social development process in institutional arrangements of jointly shared responsibilities' (p. 75).

As a result of these constraints on their formal powers, Italian regions, no matter what their political inclination, have been compelled to follow a pragmatic approach to economic planning; an approach which has supported a model of endogenous regional development (Nanetti, 1988). According to Nanetti, the heart of this model is based on the provision of advanced business services (*servizi reali*) to small and medium-sized firms (pp. 94–7). These services help to contain the costs of innovation, secure new markets, assist in the restructuring of productive capacity, and expand production activities through the promotion of cultural, environmental and archaeological resources (pp. 102–14).

These advanced business services take four main forms: (i) strategic assistance aimed directly at small businesses through the provision of credit, capital, market research, interpreting governmental and international regulations and other integral business services, (ii) specific education requirements such as vocational schools and management training courses (Leonardi, 1991), (iii) direct regulation of externalities and the labour market, and (iv) the instigation of public–private partnerships to provide the necessary resources for larger development-inspired projects.

Many of these services are often provided by business service centres. These business centres, which primarily collect and supply information in support of the industry as a whole, are semi-public bodies, governed jointly by member companies, local government, and business and trade associations. Thus, these centres also represent another form of collaboration among regional institutions. Service centres allow for economies of scale in information that the market would not provide to small firms. One point cannot be overemphasized, these centres all target the *system* of firms, not the individual firms (Brusco and Righi, 1989).

Table 2.2 shows Italian business service centres by category and by region. The centres fall into four classifications: those that promote the diffusion of innovation, those that strengthen the productive relations among firms, those that strengthen the functions internal to individual firms, and those that improve the efficiency of the territorial system, referred to as external economies (Bellini et al., 1991).

Table 2.2 shows that Tuscany has established the highest number of centres (12) which represents 16 per cent of total Italian centres. Tuscany is also the only region with a balanced distribution between all four types of centre. In the north and south of Italy, the majority of the centres concentrate on innovation diffusion while in the Third Italy, most of the centres are concerned with the reinforcement of interfirm relations.

In addition to business service centres, the regions also use three other methods to promote and sustain regional development: social service provision, political intermediation, and the maintenance of political consensus. First, the delivery of comprehensive social services acts as a social wage to the community at large, provides the infrastructure necessary for a healthy business climate, and improves the overall quality of life for all regional citizens (Nanetti, 1988). Second, the region serves as inter-locutor with both other levels of government and among regional social and economic interests. For example, the regions effectively lobby the central government and the European Community to maximize the resources that can be used to assist small firms (Trigilia, 1989). Finally, the regions help to create and maintain the consensus that supports both the industrial structure and active intervention on the part of the government (Brusco, 1982; Brusco and Righi, 1989). Consensus is also a function of the

Table 2.2   Distribution of Italian business service centres

Region / Category	Diffusion of innovation	Interfirm relations	Functions internal to firms	External economies
Tuscany	4	4	1	3
Emilia-Romagna	1	7	2	1
Veneto	1	0	0	0
Marches	0	3	2	0
Umbria	0	3	2	0
Friuli	2	1	1	2
Trentino	0	0	0	0
Total Third Italy	*8*	*18*	*8*	*6*
Piedmont	1	1	0	1
Liguria	2	0	0	1
Lombardy	3	2	1	0
Val D'Aosta	0	0	0	0
Lazio	3	0	0	0
Total North (excluding Third Italy)	*9*	*3*	*1*	*2*
Abruzzi	1	0	0	0
Molise	1	0	0	0
Campania	2	0	0	1
Puglia	1	0	2	3
Basilicata	0	0	0	0
Calabria	1	0	0	0
Sicily	3	0	0	2
Sardegna	1	0	0	1
Total South	*10*	*0*	*2*	*7*

Source: Nomisma, Industrial Policy Laboratory, 'I Centri di Servizio Reale alle Imprese: Stato dell'arte Repertorio delle Esperienze Italiane', Nomisma, Bologna, 1988 cited in Bellini et al, (1991)

social infrastructure, particularly of the level of development of the civic society found in the region. A strong civic society provides the third foundation stone of the Tuscan economy. Let us now turn to examine this variable.

The social foundation: civic society

Every region possesses a different fabric of social and economic networks. The strongest regions have networks and institutions that are critical inputs to their economic health and weaker regions, as found in southern Italy, may actually have networks, based on personal, clientalistic practices, that work to their economic disadvantage (see Putnam, Leonardi and Nanetti 1993). Tuscany, as well as having proactive regional and local governments, is also endowed with the appropriate social infrastructure for pursuing economic development – a strong civic society. Recent work by

Putnam, Leonardi and Nanetti (1993) demonstrates that areas with strong civic traditions and networks of civic engagement are highly correlated with strong institutional and economic performance. In fact, they found that, although a strong economy does not necessarily predict a strong civic culture, a strong civic culture predicts a strong economy. The Putnam/ Leonardi/Nanetti study determined that the civic society in Tuscany was ranked particularly high, thus predicting economic strength.

According to Putnam, Leonardi and Nanetti, strong civic traditions, characterized by trust, cooperative norms and networks of civic engagement, provide a community with social capital, a resource which facilitates cooperative behaviour among the populace as well as among regional institutions. As social capital can only be accumulated over time, areas with strong civic societies must have a history of civicness. Thus, the prospect for successful collective efforts increases in areas with historical precedents and traditions of cooperation. Past examples of successful cooperation provide actors with a 'culturally-defined template for future collaboration' (p. 174).

Putnam, Leonardi and Nanetti have shown that the civic Italian regions have had such a history of civicness dating from medieval times. Thus, social capital in these regions has 'long been a key ingredient in the ethos that has sustained economic dynamism and government performance' (p. 170). As we saw earlier, cooperation has been a foundation stone of both the economy and the polity in Tuscany. The economy is based on cooperation among small firms while the regional government has only been able to accomplish its development objectives working cooperatively with other local and regional actors. Trust breeds cooperation and cooperation breeds trust. Thus, social capital, as a community resource, increases with use and, conversely, atrophies with disuse. Those communities or regions, like Tuscany, which possess it, will therefore be able to exploit it and increase it more easily than those which do not. Summing up, norms of cooperation, arising from strong historical traditions of cooperation, and dense political and social networks, are important inputs explaining the success of the Tuscan economy and the performance of the Tuscan region.

2.3 Conclusions

Economists can only describe convergence, they do not explain it. Convergence can only be explained by examining the social and political situations in the regions. Social and political configurations of the region are as important (if not more so) as the economic factors for understanding and explaining regional disparities. How each region individually manages the constraints and opportunities offered by the Single European Market is a sociopolitical question. I submit that economic disparity is highly correlated with disparities in the political capabilities of subnational governments. It is no trivial coincidence that the strongest economic regions in the Community, the German regions, have the most extensive political powers while the weakest regions, found in Greece, Portugal and Ireland, have regional bodies in name only – where they exist at all. In other words there is some suggestion here that, at the regional level, economic disparity parallels disparity in political power.

Economic life is embedded in social and political relationships (Granovetter, 1985) that exert a profound influence on the efficiency and effectiveness of production methods. Economics alone does not explain why certain regions rise and fall – the process is too complex. Understanding development means that we must approach it with multidimensional tools that capture the process in its entirety, not one piece at a time. To sum up, the essential components for achieving economic and social cohesion are the presence of capable subnational institutions and social structures that support cooperative behaviour among those institutions and among individuals. Regions can and do make a difference.

Appendix

Table 2A.1 GDP per capita (in ECU) and harmonized unemployment rates (by percentage) by cluster membership, 1977

Cluster member	GDP per capita	Unemployment rates
Cluster 1		
Niedersachsen	6,379	3.2
Nordrhein–Westfalen	7,348	3.4
Hessen	8,014	1.8
Baden–Württemberg	7,824	2.0
Bavaria	6,960	2.7
Saarland	6,391	3.5
Lorraine	6,017	2.7
Alsace	6,422	2.8
Cluster 2		
Nord Pas de Calais	5,530	5.0
Midi-Pyrenees	4,908	4.7
Languedoc–Roussillon	4,984	4.4
Lombardy	5,153	2.0
Emilia-Romagna	4,816	2.4
Southeast	4,551	3.8
Cluster 3		
Tuscany	4,236	3.2
Marche	3,802	2.9
Abruzzi	3,128	6.2
Molise	2,587	4.0
Basilicata	2,703	5.9
Calabria	2,397	9.3
East Midlands	3,783	3.8
East Anglia	3,829	4.5
Southwest	3,639	4.0
West Midlands	3,817	4.5
Wales	3,376	4.8

Table 2A.2 GDP per capita (in ECU) and harmonized unemployment rates (by percentage) by cluster membership, 1981

Cluster member	GDP per capita	Unemployment rates
Cluster 1		
Nordrhein–Westfalen	9,823	4.5
Hessen	10,861	3.0
Baden–Württemberg	10,447	2.2
Bavaria	9,663	3.0
Saarland	9,228	5.7
Alsace	9,950	5.0
Southeast	9,685	6.7
Cluster 2		
Niedersachsen	8,610	4.4
Nord Pas de Calais	8,317	10.7
Lorraine	8,781	8.2
Midi-Pyrenees	7,857	7.8
Languedoc–Roussillon	7,469	9.6
Lombardy	8,469	5.1
Emila-Romagna	8,203	5.9
Tuscany	7,246	6.7
Marche	6,527	4.8
East Midlands	7,730	8.8
East Anglia	7,762	7.0
Southwest	7,590	8.3
West Midlands	7,295	12.0
Wales	6,675	12.2
Cluster 3		
Abruzzi	5,410	8.3
Molise	4,850	8.0
Basilicata	4,689	13.7
Calabria	4,133	12.7

Table 2A.3 GDP per capita (in ECU) and harmonized unemployment rates (by percentage) by cluster membership, 1984

Cluster member	GDP per capita	Unemployment rates
Cluster 1		
Niedersachsen	11,027	8.90
Nordrhein–Westfalen	12,429	8.50
Hessen	14,365	5.70
Baden–Württemberg	13,387	4.30
Bavaria	12,706	5.60
Saarland	11,773	10.50
Alsace	11,773	7.00
Lombardy	11,897	6.60
Emilia-Romagna	11,563	8.70
Southeast	11,517	8.40
Cluster 2		
Nord Pas de Calais	9,472	12.30
Lorraine	10,003	10.90
Midi-Pyrenees	9,751	8.90
Languedoc–Roussillon	9,221	11.90
Tuscany	10,221	8.70
Marche	9,227	7.30
East Midlands	9,216	10.00
East Anglia	9,736	8.30
Southwest	9,241	9.20
West Midlands	8,741	13.50
Cluster 3		
Abruzzi	8,112	8.40
Molise	6,987	7.90
Basilicata	6,445	10.70
Calabria	5,274	14.90
Wales	8,053	13.30

Table 2A.4 GDP per capita (in ECU) and harmonized unemployment rates (by percentage) by cluster membership, 1987

Cluster member	GDP per capita	Unemployment rates
Cluster 1		
Niedersachsen	13,655	7.80
Nordrhein–Westfalen	15,230	8.00
Hessen	17,890	4.70
Baden–Württemberg	16,729	3.50
Bavaria	15,852	4.40
Saarland	14,620	10.10
Alsace	14,214	7.00
Lombardy	15,155	5.70
Emilia-Romagna	14,097	6.40
Cluster 2		
Nord Pas de Calais	11,091	14.00
Lorraine	11,651	10.90
Midi-Pyrenees	11,129	9.10
Languedoc–Roussillon	10,778	14.20
Tuscany	12,804	7.50
Marche	11,738	6.70
Abruzzi	9,789	8.70
Molise	8,714	12.10
East Midlands	9,826	9.90
East Anglia	10,102	8.00
Southeast	12,462	8.20
Southwest	9,903	8.60
West Midlands	9,372	12.30
Wales	8,603	12.80
Cluster 3		
Basilicata	7,057	15.90
Calabria	6,479	17.10

Table 2A.5 GDP per capita (in ECU) and harmonized unemployment rates (by percentage) by cluster membership, 1990

Cluster member	GDP per capita	Unemployment rates
Cluster 1		
Niedersachsen	15,962	6.80
Nordrhein–Westfalen	17,641	6.90
Hessen	21,457	4.10
Baden–Württemberg	19,634	3.00
Bavaria	18,935	3.40
Saarland	17,087	9.20
Alsace	17,152	4.50
Lombardy	19,960	3.40
Emilia-Romagna	18,730	4.30
Tuscany	16,397	7.60
Southeast	16,167	4.30
Cluster 2		
Nord Pas de Calais	13,562	11.80
Lorraine	14,468	8.00
Midi-Pyrenees	13,549	8.70
Languedoc–Roussillon	13,059	12.90
Marche	14,398	6.30
Abruzzi	12,731	10.20
Molise	11,406	12.10
East Midlands	12,900	5.30
East Anglia	13,682	3.90
Southwest	12,794	4.50
West Midlands	12,229	6.30
Wales	11,145	6.90
Cluster 3		
Basilicata	8,954	21.50
Calabria	8,181	22.60

Notes

The research and preparation for this chapter have been supported by the Region of Tuscany and the Central Research Fund of the University of London. I am grateful to Vittorio Bufacchi for comments on earlier drafts. Any errors in the text are, of course, solely my own responsibility.

1. Convergence refers to the equalization of standards of living among all European regions. There is an extensive debate concerning whether European integration encourages increased convergence or divergence. See Leonardi (1993) for a comprehensive analysis of the debate, and evidence that, overall, European integration has promoted convergence.
2. The regions included are Niedersachsen, Nordrhein-Westfalen, Hessen, Baden-Würtemberg, Bavaria, Saarland, Nord-pas-de-Calais, Lorraine, Alsace, Midi-Pyrenees, Languedoc-Roussillon, Lombardy, Emilia-Romagna, Tuscany, Marches, Abruzzi, Molise, Basilicata, Calabria, East Midlands, East Anglia, Southeast, Southwest, West Midlands, and Wales.
3. Population density was not available for 1990 so I used the 1987 statistics for

the 1990 cluster run. The difference across three years is minimal so it does not distort the results.

4. The correspondence between the clusters and the actual EC regional classifications is an approximate one and may not be accurate for certain individual regions.

5. In the case of unemployment rates, lower is better so for this indicator, the region is stronger if it is below the mean.

6. See Bianchi (1992) for a another study, using the most recent 1991 Italian Census Data, that charts deindustrialization in Tuscany.

7. This synopsis of Tuscan postwar economic history was summarized from Pridham (1981).

8. This situation has been changing in the past years as all the traditional mass parties in Italy have been losing their electoral strength.

9. Tuscany is one of the regions in the Third Italy, a term coined by Bagnasco (1977) to differentiate the northeast and central regions from the traditional north–south dichotomy. The regions in the Third Italy were distinguished by the electoral majority of either the Communist or Christian Democratic Party and by their distinct economic structure based on industrial districts.

10. See Dei Ottati (1991) for the development of an ideal-type model of industrial districts.

11. Industrial districts are only one manifestation of flexible specialization. See Piore and Sabel (1984) for other forms.

References

Bagnasco, Arnaldo, *Tre Italie: La problematica territoriale dello sviluppo italiano*, Bologna, Il Mulino, 1977.

Bellini, Nicola, Giordani, Maria Grazia, Magnatti, Piera and Pasquini, Francesca, 'Il livello locale e la politica industriale', pp. 49–79 in Nomisma (ed.), *Strategie e valutazione nella politica industriale: esigenze, proposte esperienze a livello locale*, Milan, FrancoAngeli, 1991.

Bianchi, Giuliano, 'Requiem per la terza Italia, prime considerazioni sui risultati provvisori dei censimenti 1991', paper presented to the thirteenth Italian Conference of Regional Science, the Italian Regional Science Association, Ancona, Italy, October 5–7, 1992.

Brusco, Sebastiano, 'The Emilian Model: Productive Decentralisation and Social Integration', *Cambridge Journal of Economics*, 6, pp. 167–84, 1982.

Brusco, Sebastiano and Righi, Ezio, 'Local Government, Industrial Policy and Social Consensus: the Case of Modena (Italy), *Economy and Society*, 18(4), pp. 405–23, 1989.

Cappellin, Riccardo, 'The European Internal Market and the Internationalization of Small and Medium-sized Enterprises', *Built Environment*, 16(1), pp. 69–84, 1990.

Commission of the European Communities (CEC), 'First Periodic Report on the Social and Economic Situation of the Regions of the Community', Luxembourg, Office for Official Publications of the European Communities, 1981.

——— 'Second Periodic Report on the Social and Economic Situation of the Regions of the Community', Luxembourg, Office for Official Publications of the European Communities, 1984.

——— 'Third Periodic Report on the Social and Economic Situation of the Regions of the Community', Luxembourg, Office for Official Publications of the European Communities, 1987.

——— 'Fourth Periodic Report on the Social and Economic Situation of the Regions of

the Community', Luxembourg, Office for Official Publications of the European
Communities, 1991.

Dei Ottati, Gabi, 'The Economic Bases of Diffuse Industrialization', *International Studies of
Management and Organization*, 20(1), pp. 53–74, 1991.

EUROSTAT, *REGIO codebook and data bank*, Luxembourg, EUROSTAT, various years.

EUROSTAT, 'Regional Statistical Yearbook', Luxembourg, EUROSTAT, various
years.

Garmise, Shari, 'Convergence or Divergence? The Empirical Evidence', paper prepared
for the second annual conference on The European Community, George Mason
University, Fairfax, VA, 22–24 May 1991.

Garmise, Shari O. and Grote, R.J., 'Economic Performance and Social Embeddedness:
Emilia-Romagna in an Interregional Perspective', pp. 59–78 in Leonardi and Nanetti,
1990.

Granovetter, Mark, 'Economic Action and Social Structure: The Problem of
Embededdness', *American Journal of Sociology*, 91(3), pp. 481–510, 1985.

Leonardi, Robert, 'The Implications of Economic and Social Cohesion on the
Community's Institutional Architecture after the creation of the Single Market', paper
presented at the Biennial Conference of the European Community Studies Association,
George Mason University, Fairfax, VA, 22–24 May 1991.

—— 'Cohesion in the European Community: Illusion or Reality', *West European Politics*,
October, pp. 492–517, 1993.

Leonardi, Robert and Nanetti, Raffaella Y. (eds.), *The Regions and European Integration:
The Case of Emilia-Romagna*, London, Pinter, 1990.

Nanetti, Raffaella Y., *Growth and Territorial Policies: The Italian Model of Social Capitalism*,
London and New York, Pinter, 1988.

Piore, Michael J. and Sabel, Charles F., *The Second Industrial Divide*, New York, Basic
Books, 1984.

Pridham, Geoffrey, *The Nature of the Italian Party System: A Regional Case Study*, London,
Croom Helm, 1981.

Putnam, Robert, Leonardi, Robert and Nanetti, Raffaella, *La pianta e le radici*, Bologna,
Il Mulino, 1985.

—— *Making Democracy Work: Civic Traditions in Modern Italy*, Princeton, Princeton
University Press, 1993.

Trigilia, Carlo, *Grandi partiti e piccole imprese*, Bologna, Il Mulino, 1986.

—— 'Small-firm Development and Political Subculture in Italy', pp. 174–97 in
Goodman, Edward and Bamford, Julia with Saynor, Peter (eds.), *Small Firms and
Industrial Districts in Italy*, London and New York, Routledge, 1989.

3   Regional policy-making in the European context

Raffaella Y. Nanetti

3.1 Introduction

When the Single European Act was signed by all Community member states and became operative in July 1987, only a few insiders, politicos and economic powerhouses could grasp the significance of the occasion. The European public and their regional political representatives were hardly made aware by the media of the momentous changes implicit in the implementation of the five-year programme to create a Single European Market by 1 January 1993. Yet, no other single policy decision made by any member state had ever changed the context – as well as the modus operandi – of regional governments as profoundly as the Single Market Programme was about to do.

Within a few years regions and localities were going to be thrust into an economic field whose geographical boundaries would expand from the Atlantic to the North Sea and south to the Mediterranean, and whose institutional players would include the European Community (EC) in a very central position, together with 156 regional governments. Inevitable changes in the rules of the decision-making game were about to occur from this restructuring, and force individual regions to deal with the issue of how adequately prepared they were in facing up to the challenge of becoming or remaining European-level players.

Tuscany represents a good case to investigate. A region with a developed and outward looking economy, strong civic and cultural traditions, and which is centrally located in Italy and along the Mediterranean flank of the EC, Tuscany embodies the essence of normality; a functional region with a chance to succeed within the new and expanded European context. While it does not have the advantages of size, wealth, and high-tech development of Lombardy in the North, Tuscany is not inhibited by the economic dependency, the law and order problems, or the relative isolation which plague Sicily in the south. Tuscany was studied in 1989–90 midway through the implementation of the Single Market programme, when the debate on this process and its projected impact had begun to take hold in the region and general expressions of support and criticism were being articulated into more specific arguments.

The study of Tuscany's preparedness for the Single Market of 1993 and beyond was constructed on the premise of the functionality (or lack of it) of its regional institutions. At a time when this phase in European integration was creating a new institutional architecture for decision-making and implementation based on a three-tier system – Community, states, regions – the investigation of the prospects of Tuscany's economy had to begin with the analysis of the region's own institutions and their performance. Three samples of respondents were surveyed: regional councillors and assessors, representatives of interest groups, and the public at large. The focus of the inquiry is on the effectiveness of the legislative function of the council and on the efficiency of the implementation function of the giunta.

The study then moves on to investigate the very purpose and content of Tuscany's regional development policies. Of interest is the extent to which they showed continuity with the past versus breaking new ground and identifying new issues and programmatic approaches; how localities and interest groups participated in the formulation of policies; the ways in which the region was involved in development projects and political networking with other Italian and European regions; and what was changing in the relationship with national ministries and the central government in light of the partnership role demanded of the regions by the EC.

Finally, the study addresses the question of how Tuscany looked at Europe and at the movement toward integration. Survey data from the three samples are again brought to bear on the assessment of the readiness of Tuscany's economy and social organizations to operate on a trans-national level. The prospective expansion of the EC's institutions is also probed, together with the opportunities for European regions to create new political and economic alliances within the increased scope of the Community's regional development policies.

3.2 Regional institutions in Tuscany

Notwithstanding the fact that the 1970 regional reform in Italy formally had created the same regional institutions in all fifteen ordinary regions, in time the societal humus in which they had taken root proved to be productive of distinctly different styles of governance and policy outcomes (Putnam, Leonardi and Nanetti, 1985; 1993). Tuscany, in the views of its councillors and informed citizens ('observers'), is found (Table 3.1) to be a region with very stable political institutions, in fact with a level of stability even above the norm for northern regions and much above the norm for southern regions. Tuscany ranked with northern regions in terms of the respectable degree of autonomy which in time it had acquired vis-à-vis the national government, a trait which is also reflected in the relatively high scores for modernity and programmatic style of government attributed to Tuscany by the respondents.

On the other hand, Tuscany also displayed other traits which make its

Table 3.1 Evaluation of the nature of regional political life in Tuscany (percentage of regional councillors and observers responding 'yes' or 'somewhat' to the first element of each pair of descriptors)

Elements of evaluation	Councillors			Observers		
	Tuscany 1989	North 1988	South 1988	Tuscany 1989	North 1988	South 1988
Modern/backward	53	65	19	45	46	17
Authoritarian/democratic	20	20	24	n.a.	n.a.	n.a.
Conflictual/consensual	25	20	16	29	22	40
Honest/corrupt	33	38	11	55	57	22
Unstable/stable	10	22	27	12	17	38
Programmatic/clientelistic	38	40	14	43	35	17
Productive/unproductive	20	39	15	35	39	21
Provincial/unitary	48	32	52	33	35	36
Ideological/pragmatic	33	14	9	n.a.	n.a.	n.a.
Autonomous/subordinate	35	38	16	43	44	21

political profile all its own, somewhat divergent from the norm in the northern regions. So, Tuscany's political institutions were viewed by its own councillors ultimately as less productive, the nature of its political debate somewhat more ideological and conflictual, and the degree of regional cohesion less pronounced in Tuscany than was the case in northern regions. There appears to be a tone of heightened localism and argumentativeness which is peculiar to Tuscany's political life. Nonetheless, Tuscany's unique institutional profile maintained this region very close to those in the north and quite distant indeed from the cluster of southern regions.

The operational capacity of Tuscany's institutions was found by the observers to be above that of the two clusters of regions in the North and South with which Tuscany is compared (Table 3.2), while a somewhat more critical view on the same capacity was displayed by the councillors. In particular, Tuscany's outreach to local authorities was most valued, followed by the acknowledgement of the region's relative strength in planning and its ability to follow that up with financial commitments. Indeed, the strength of contacts across the full spectrum of Tuscany's political and economic life was well documented (Tables 3.3 and 3.4). Regional councillors' outreach to local and national representatives and civil servants was the highest registered for all regions and so was the degree of interaction between the observers and regional and local elected officials and civil servants.

Clearly, such contacts are a good indicator of significant actions by the region aimed at social and economic organizations. The impact of regional government policies on the organizations of the observers (Table 3.5) was indeed quite profound: up to two-thirds of them acknowledged it and four out of five assessed it as positive. Again, this evaluation is more positive

Table 3.2 Principal regional functions as assessed by regional councillors and observers (percentage responding 'very' or 'somewhat' satisfied)

	Councillors			Observers		
Functions	Tuscany 1989	North 1989	South 1989	Tuscany 1989	North 1989	South 1989
Coordination						
Coordination with local authorities	29	16	6	21	23	16
Availability toward local authorities	70	73	56	67	60	51
Use of external research facilities	40	38	18	30	23	19
Planning						
Overall policy direction	25	38	35	42	46	28
Planning capacity	32	38	26	29	27	22
Implementation time	6	7	2	18	3	2
Implementation						
Feasibility of projects	19	17	15	22	23	15
Commitment of public officials	33	49	28	45	40	24
Allocation of financial resources	35	24	10	35	36	14

Table 3.3 Regular contacts of regional councillors with political, administrative, and interest group representatives (percentage of councillors responding one or more times a week or regularly)

Representatives	Tuscany 1989	North 1989	South 1989
President of the regional giunta	75	61	80
Regional assessors	80	88	90
Regional civil servants	85	78	84
Local civil servants	58	57	68
National representatives of groups and sectors	15	20	14
Regional representatives of groups and sectors	69	48	63
Local representatives of groups and sectors	80	58	71

than the average assessment expressed by observers in the northern regions. The reasons which explain this substantial level of satisfaction by Tuscany's observers with the functionality of regional institutions are numerous. They include (Table 3.6) a widespread view that the regional administration in Tuscany did not share the traits of marked inefficiency found in other regions, but rather that the administration showed political commitment in

Table 3.4 Regular contacts of observers with regional politicians and civil servants (percentage of observers responding one or more times a week or regularly)

Politicians and civil servants	Tuscany 1989	North 1989	South 1989
President of the regional giunta	35	28	25
Regional assessors	60	55	45
Regional councillors	55	51	58
Regional civil servants	59	47	69
Local government civil servants	60	55	69

Table 3.5 Impact of regional government on the organizations of the observers (percentage of observers)

Impact	Tuscany 1989	North 1989	South 1989
*Degree**			
Very strong	15	13	16
Quite strong	53	46	38
Not very strong	24	38	34
None	8	4	12
*Direction***			
Positive	80	74	53
Negative	20	26	47

* 'How significant has the impact of regional government been on the interests of your organization or company?'
** 'All in all, has this impact been positive or negative?'

addition to professional qualities. The council was also perceived as a rather well-functioning institution and one where, political debate aside, great convergence of views was found on major problems.

The other side of the coin is that Tuscany's functioning institutions nonetheless had the tendency to keep decision-making centralized and not to delegate enough responsibility to local authorities. The perception was that the region's institutions in time risked losing efficiency due to administrative bottlenecks, while they appropriately advocated for themselves greater financial autonomy from the central government in order to be able to make farther-reaching development decisions.

Overall, when the views of the public at large were also accounted for (Table 3.7) one found a marked degree of satisfaction with regional institutions in Tuscany – two-thirds of the respondents – which is a level higher than that measured in the cluster of northern regions and which is more than double that measured in the southern regions. Less embracing is the overall assessment of Tuscany's institutions made by the observers, although when the functionality of the region was compared with that of the state and of the observers' own municipalities, the region of Tuscany

Table 3.6 Observers' view of the functionality and limitations of regional institutions in Tuscany (percentage responding 'I agree completely' or 'I more or less agree')

Functionality and limitations	Tuscany 1989	North 1989	South 1989
In this region the administration is decidedly inefficient	33	43	90
In this region the administrative staff show great commitment and professional preparation	58	49	25
This region has delegated sufficient functions to the local authorities	32	33	42
The decision-making powers of the municipalities and provinces should be strengthened with respect to the decision-making powers of the region	68	65	73
The region should have a higher level of financial autonomy vis-à-vis the state	90	92	71
At the regional level there are no great differences of opinion on the major problems	25	34	33
All in all, the council in the region has functioned in a satisfactory way	75	68	36
Realistically speaking, it is difficult to foresee concrete achievements being made by the regional institution	46	54	79
The regional reform was a mistake	10	15	19

received the highest overall approval of any of the three levels of government.

It is therefore not surprising to see that in Tuscany there was strong support in favour of extending the policy areas in which the region should legislate and operate further, beyond the boundaries which were determined by the reform decree of 1976–8 and had been somewhat eroded, and at time expanded, by subsequent legislation (Table 3.8). In particular, support for the region's opportunity to break new ground was shown by both councillors and observers relative to industrial development, employment, taxation and the conditions of urban areas. Actually, the call to expand the functional scope of regional government through devolution from the state was widespread and reached into both northern and southern regions, notwithstanding the sharp criticism which regional institutions had been subjected to in many of the latter cases. This contradiction points to an even stronger indictment against the state and the unsatisfactory performance of its institutions in the south.

The strength of Tuscany's regional institutions was further underlined by

Table 3.7 Observers' and members of the general public's views of municipality, region, and state (by percentage)*

Authority	Observers			General public		
	Tuscany 1989	North 1989	South 1989	Tuscany 1988	North 1988	South 1988
Own municipality						
Very satisfied	12	9	2	8	6	5
Satisfied	25	28	21	50	53	26
Not very satisfied	48	50	39	32	29	40
Dissatisfied	15	13	38	10	12	29
Own region						
Very satisfied	5	0	1	11	3	2
Satisfied	39	38	15	56	51	27
Not very satisfied	50	57	50	18	35	45
Dissatisfied	6	5	34	15	10	26
State						
Very satisfied	4	2	1	–	1	2
Satisfied	13	17	23	12	28	24
Not very satisfied	55	57	51	53	44	42
Dissatisfied	28	24	25	25	27	32

* 'How satisfied are you regarding the way in which your municipality, your region and the state are governed?'

Table 3.8 Desire of regional councillors and observers to expand the sectorial powers of the regions (by percentage)*

Sector	Councillors			Observers		
	Tuscany 1989	North 1989	South 1989	Tuscany 1989	North 1989	South 1989
Health	82	90	74	71	74	65
Agriculture	93	92	91	85	82	92
Police	7	17	11	16	17	17
Environment	83	88	81	79	80	74
Primary & secondary education	39	59	45	40	47	45
Higher education	27	49	33	48	53	36
Industrial development	60	68	73	66	69	78
Foreign trade	35	42	29	37	33	40
Artisan sector & small industry	96	98	98	97	92	94
Banking & credit	52	49	57	49	42	61
Scientific research	20	29	34	52	47	31
Taxation	60	65	44	54	44	37
Transport	90	83	82	73	78	73
Employment	78	82	83	69	70	69
Public works	89	91	79	82	80	79
Cultural affairs	90	85	86	91	87	73
Urban areas	70	78	85	84	79	72

* 'In each of the following policy areas, please indicate if it is preferable that central government or the region has more power (irrespective of what each has now).'

Table 3.9 Interaction of regional councillors with state authorities (percentage of regional councillors)

Interaction	Tuscany 1989	North 1989	South 1989
Weekly or regular contacts with:			
Ministers or undersecretaries	14	19	28
MPs from own party	60	67	80
MPs from other parties	7	9	21
National civil servants	24	12	18
*Influence of central authorities**			
Great or considerable	40	46	58
Some	18	25	26
Little or none	42	29	16
Policy-initiating activity vis-à-vis the state			
Very satisfied	5	6	2
Quite satisfied	48	32	16
Rather dissatisfied	30	37	35
Very dissatisfied	17	25	47

* 'With respect to contacts between the regional institution and the central authorities, what degree of influence do the latter have on the choices and activities of this region?'

the councillors' relatively limited contacts with state authorities (Table 3.9). The influence of state political institutions on Tuscany's political life appeared to be more contained than in other regions. Notably, Tuscany's councillors had fewer contacts with high-level cabinet members and the degree of influence of the central authorities on the choices of the region was assessed to be considerably lower than the average for both northern and southern regions. In line with such a display of autonomy, Tuscany adopted a more proactive stance than others vis-à-vis the state, by taking initiatives on policies which ranged from developing options, to devising experimental programmes and accelerating programme-implementation schedules.

Tuscany's observers confirmed the councillors' views (Table 3.10). A greater proportion of observers in Tuscany than in other regions saw the region rather than the state as the key player in terms of the pertinent policy initiatives launched in sectors where they operated. In fact, the region often, though not in the majority of cases, was assessed to have moved against positions taken by the state, in a relationship which was not routinely cooperative. Thus, by 1990 in Tuscany not only the impact of regional decision-making appeared to prevail over that of the state in the majority of the cases involving the observers' areas of interest and work, but as was seen above (Table 3.8) the sentiment was strong in favour of relegating the central authorities to playing an indirect role in many policy sectors. Midway through the five-year preparation for the implementation of the Single Market, Tuscany had secured a respectable level of societal support for the working of its regional institutions.

Table 3.10   Assessment of the ability of the region to deal with the state in sectors of interest for observers (percentage of observers)

Region vs state	Tuscany 1989	North 1989	South 1989
In your sector of interest, where are the most important planning policy initiatives taken?			
Central level	52	67	56
Regional level	48	33	44
In your sector of interest, what are the relations between the regions and the central authorities characterized by?			
Conflict	46	48	46
Collaboration	54	52	54
In your sector of interest, what decision-making autonomy has this region vs the central authorities?			
A lot	13	7	10
Quite a lot	42	41	30
Not very much	37	48	51
None	8	4	9

3.3   The nature and scope of regional policies

Two questions of interest are: what produced this consensus behind Tuscany's regional institutions and to what extent was such support justified? In light of the onslaught of regulatory changes being mandated by the EC and of their impact on regional and local markets, in particular when many observers and citizens perceived their economic and social interest to be promoted by the region's action rather than by the state's, which policies were Tuscany residents making reference to and how were such policies formulated and implemented?

Tuscany had moved in 1983 to create the Bureau of Community Policies (Servizio Politiche Comunitarie) within the regional president's office, with a mandate of managing the relations of the giunta with the EC and relevant national ministries. Soon the strong mandate of the Bureau appeared to be politically unworkable and it was changed to that of facilitating the direct involvement of the sectors of the regional administration in EC sectorial policies, while maintaining for the Bureau the coordinating function relative to large-scale and multi-purpose development projects. Examples of this fallback position are the planning and construction of the underwater aqueduct for the Isle of Elba, in part funded by the ERDF (European Regional Development Fund) of the EC and the improvements to the port of Piombino, the access point to the island.

Planning for multi-purpose projects was the approach taken for the formulation of an ambitious ERDF supported investment programme for the Tuscan archipelago, which focused on five interrelated objectives: the solution of the problem of water supply to the three main islands, including facing the consumption peaks during the summer; the implementation of environmental protection projects, from water treatment plants to the safeguarding of costal areas against erosion; increasing the access to the islands by improving sea and air connections; the lengthening of the tourist season over the whole year and the decrease of tourist concentration in the summer through promotional projects; and the preparation of economic development and conservation projects targeting key environmental and historical heritage resources, including the creation of mineralogical and archaeological parks, and the restructuring of Roman villas, Napoleonic forts, and Renaissance castles. To complement the overall investment programme was a plan for vocational education to be supported by the European Social Fund and aimed at tuning professionals and entrepreneurs to the implementation of the multi-purpose projects.

Because Tuscany's level of development was above 75 per cent of the Community's average, the 1987–8 reform of the structural funds did not incorporate any of its territory, including the islands, into the Objective 1 category, which defines the Community's areas of underdevelopment. Rather, three parts of Tuscany – Lunigiana, Monte Amiata, and the Grosseto area – were classified as undeveloped rural areas (Objective 5B areas). Two areas with an economic base of struggling and large manufacturing plants – Massa Carrara and Piombino – and the industrial textile district of Prato, embattled by foreign competition and in need of investments and restructuring measures, were classified as Objective 2 areas, or declining industrial regions. For these five areas, Tuscany formulated multi-purpose and integrated development projects and implementation 'measures'[1] were formulated as Tuscany's contribution to the preparation of the Community Support Framework plan proposal which Italy negotiated and signed with the EC in 1989 (Nanetti, 1994).

The new concept of development policies adopted by Tuscany's regional institutions in the 1980s indicates a high degree of congruence with the mandate for regional development planning promoted by the EC. Tuscany's concept of regional development policies had broken new ground in terms of both the approach taken as well as the very content of the policies. Tuscany's new approach builds on seven principles:

- interconnection between regional economic programming and physical territorial planning;
- identification of the geographical wide area (*area vasta*) upon which to plan;
- recognition of the key resources (*leve*) peculiar to each area;
- continuous integration of planning action (*measures*) across sectors;
- inclusion of a variety of partners in the formulation of policies and projects;

- definition of legally binding agreements to implement the policies; and
- interregional cooperation to incrementally expand the geographical base of and the opportunities for compatible development.

The first principle recognizes that regional economic programming and physical planning ought to intersect to promote development. For example, while policies of promotion and use of natural and cultural resources can produce growth in the short and medium term, their inherently limited or perishable nature mandates the inclusion of policies of environmental protection to ensure long-term growth. Conversely, planning for the location of physical infrastructure and for the territorial distribution of land uses should not be independent of the determination of the economic impacts produced, nor of the projections of investment resources needed and available to achieve the objectives of territorial planning over time. Rather, under the new approach to regional development the physical aspects of the plan and the economic programming of the use of all area resources are to be jointly tested against the specific social and economic development objectives which have been politically determined. The general and guiding instrument is the multi-purpose Regional Development Plan.

The second principle of planning at the level of the 'wide area' operationalizes the first principle articulated above by marrying the exigencies of territorial planning and economic programming within a relatively homogeneous territory. The balance between the conflicting objectives of the use of resources and the conservation of resources is sought through policies which bear on specific wide areas identified within Tuscany. In each of these areas, macroeconomic changes have produced a unique combination of both development problems and new opportunities. At the area-wide level, it is possible to create new conditions for growth by making an inventory of the present economic and territorial resources, investigating the potentials and limitations of new and unused resources, and determining the preconditions necessary and the modes to activate them. For example, in the case of the area Florence–Prato–Pistoia overcoming the severe transportation infrastructure deficit which restricts access to the area by road, rail and air is a precondition for considering the new development options, such as technological and scientific parks and a system of exhibition and convention halls. In a similar vein, the solution of the hydrogeological problems of the Arno Basin – including reliable water supply, pollution control and prevention of coastal erosion – is a precondition for new development.

The third principle is, therefore, a corollary which asserts the adoption of the development strategy of identifying key resources which are unique to any wide area and which represent the best lever to stimulate growth. In this perspective, an area such as that of Grosseto which traditionally has been considered marginal because of its relative underdevelopment and geographical isolation from the Florentine core has instead the chance to adopt a new model of growth which may avoid severe problems of urban congestion and better preserve the natural resources of its coastline and its hinterland.

The fourth principle mandates the coordination of the various regional sectoral plans which are prepared by Tuscany's regional departments and their integration with the sectoral plans of Tuscany's municipalities. It is the responsibility of the regional Department for Territorial Planning (Dipartimento di Urbanistica) and of the Department for Economic Programming (Dipartimento Programmazione) to promote intersectoral projects and to validate the compatibility between municipal and regional sectoral plans over time. The Department of Territorial Planning and the Department of Economic Programming determine the congruence of the two sets of plans in terms of, respectively, the planned use of territorial, natural, infrastructural and human resources and of budgetary resources. The principal means to accomplish this purpose has been the legal power of the Department of Territorial Planning to review the comprehensive and sectorial plans of the communes for compliance with Tuscany's urban planning law and with the Regional Development Plan, and to also monitor the continuous updating of all local plans. In turn, the municipality maintains total discretion over implementation proposals such as site plans. By the early 1980s, all of Tuscany's municipalities, large and small, had approved the appropriate local plans and had in place the procedures to update them in line with the mandate of the regional law.

The fifth principle of partnership in planning and development has been implemented through such devices as intercommunal associations and area development conferences. The associations are voluntary groupings of communes which have been promoted by the region's government and which have been most active in the rural areas where mutual aid among municipalities and technical assistance from the region are more needed and welcome. Planning partnerships between metropolitan municipalities and the regional government have been slower to evolve. They finally took off with the cycle of area development conferences which began in the late 1980s. The format of the conferences is very eclectic. They are well publicized political and planning meetings, which produce a Regional Development Scheme for the wide area in question, for example, that of Massa Carrara and Livorno. The broad-based participation of the private sector ranges from cultural institutions and environmental groups to trade unions and business interests. During the conference decisions are also made about specific joint-venture development projects to implement the scheme, such as land acquisition and development of regional parks or crop conversion and quality product marketing *measures* in agriculture.

The sixth principle of legally binding provisions speaks to the absolute importance of mandatory provisions to implement development plans. Tuscany's new regional urban law makes this possible for the area-wide development schemes formulated through the conferences. In fact, the municipalities within the area have to modify the land use provisions of pre-existing plans to bring them into line with both the scheme and the specific development projects. Reliance on land-use controls as implementation tools proves particularly effective because such controls are legally and administratively binding in relation to municipalities as well as private citizens. Other means to achieve the objective of compliance in plan implementation include legally binding agreements with municipalities and the private sector to finance projects co-funded by the European Community; joint ventures involving the regional government, municipalities and private business; and partnership projects in service provision which bring together the regional government, municipalities and the not-for-profit and volunteer sector.

The seventh and final principle of interregional cooperation which Tuscany endorsed has seen limited application until now. However, the completion of the Single Market has brought it to the forefront of the region's development agenda. One of the objectives of interregional cooperation is to maintain the economic position of those enterprises which already operate at a level higher than the local. Building regional and intra-European alliances allows them to compete more effectively outside Europe. Another objective of interregional cooperation is to multiply the opportunities for the coordination of sectoral projects which in the past have been scarcer. In border areas three sectors in particular are candidates for promoting interregional cooperation: large infrastructure projects, development and management of parks and protected environmentally sensitive areas, and river basin and water resources planning. A third objective of interregional cooperation is advanced by the European Community's regional development policy as it impacts its southern flank. It is the rediscovery of the importance of the Mediterranean as the largest maritime economic region in the Community, endowed with strong historical and cultural ties as well as other resources upon which to build for economic growth. In this perspective, the position of the Mediterranean basin becomes once again that of a 'core' area as it had been in the pre-Renaissance past, and not a 'peripheral' one (see Chapter 11).

3.4   How Tuscany looks at Europe

By 1990, as the movement towards the Single Market was picking up steam, how confident were Tuscany's policy-makers, informed citizens and the public at large about the strength of their regional economy to withstand and even benefit from this general change? After all, Tuscany's model of economic development, based on the small and medium-sized enterprises and on its intricate connections with the associational, employment, and entrepreneurial traditions of local communities, certainly had diverged from the canons of classical development models. In the past, Tuscany's model had confused many economists into thinking of it as a model producing a residual and closed economic system. Even when due recognition was finally accorded to Tuscany's development model (Becattini, 1975, Chapter 5), the question of its liability had to be raised in light of the enlarged economic and institutional frame of reference imposed by the Single Market.

Tuscany's system of small and medium-sized enterprises was producing a certain degree of concern in 1989 (Table 3.11). According to our respondents, while observers and citizens were more optimistic about the system's potential to thrive within a Single Market, just half of the councillors shared that view, far fewer than the number of councillors in northern regions. Great concern was expressed with regard to Tuscany's agricultural enterprises, with an overwhelming majority of opinion perceiving them as not structurally ready to face further competition. Yet, the assessment of Tuscany's system of enterprises also acknowledged its positive features, including the availability of a skilled labour force, a high level of technological innovation, and a very respectable degree of industrial restructuring. On the other hand, the weakest point of Tuscany's economy was found in its infrastructure deficit.

Though such deficits appear to be common to other regions, Tuscany's transportation networks were singled out as particularly deficient, with the relative exception of its port system. Indeed, in terms of the region's road and air transport, the assessments were as negative in Tuscany as those expressed by respondents in southern regions. As a consequence, the functionality of Tuscany's urban areas was determined to be quite low, as was generally true in all other regions. But when compared with the northern regions, Tuscany appears to also have a social service deficit, though not as severe as that regarding infrastructure. The exception was its university system, which received a strong endorsement by the respondents for its quality and competitiveness. Finally, Tuscany's economy was viewed as being better at utilizing its cultural and natural resources than other regions in the north and the south. At the same time, Tuscany was far from realizing the full potential of such resources within the expanded market.

If Tuscany's economy was only partially ready for the advent of the Single Market, which specific impacts were projected to occur on key elements of the region's economy and government (Table 3.12)? The change to a Single Market would first of all impact Tuscany's industries by forcing them to compete under different rules and, thus, to increase their pace of technological innovation to survive. But another expected outcome was a certain concentration of Tuscany's industry, though the scale of this projection remained uncertain. Tuscany's industrial system was expected to make definite gains in terms of its accessibility to new markets and to new sources to finance investments. Only a minority of respondents projected cost of production increases and increases in unemployment to occur as a result of the change to the Single Market.

Major changes were expected to accrue in the region's commercial distribution system, forcing an overall change which will greatly simplify the structure of wholesale distributors and increase the average size of retail facilities. A substantial impact was also expected to affect Tuscany's agricultural sector. Competition within the larger market would stimulate the conversion of agricultural output from traditional and generic products

Table 3.11 Tuscany's economy and the European Unified Market according to regional councillors, observers, and general public (percentage responding 'adequate' and 'quite adequate')

Structural elements	Councillors Tuscany 1989	North 1989	South 1989	Observers Tuscany 1989	North 1989	South 1989	General public Tuscany 1988	North 1988	South 1988
Structure of small and medium-sized industry	52	79	35	62	65	43	61	73	51
Port system	53	35	20	51	40	16	n.a.	n.a.	n.a.
Air transport	32	39	32	32	40	33	59	62	55
Road network	40	33	66	40	46	79	57	72	62
Railway network	24	20	24	39	31	27	67	62	54
Structure of agricultural enterprises	28	56	25	31	35	42	48	62	54
Network of social services	46	60	15	40	42	11	35	43	30
Health services	38	64	11	43	46	13	n.a.	n.a.	n.a.
University system	62	67	56	70	67	65	69	62	55
Level of associationism	59	77	47	62	71	46	n.a.	n.a.	n.a.
Skill level of workforce	58	73	40	75	73	37	68	68	51
Technological innovation in industry	75	81	40	80	81	45	70	79	52
Industrial restructuring	63	78	31	71	75	45	n.a.	n.a.	n.a.
Functionality of urban areas	9	12	7	12	13	10	n.a.	n.a.	n.a.
Utilization of historical–environmental resources	40	33	18	42	38	29	69	67	50
Structure of commercial network	51	55	35	53	56	48	75	77	56

Table 3.12 Impact of the Single European Market on Tuscany in the opinion of regional councillors, observers, and general public (percentage responding 'will have an impact')*

Structural elements	Councillors			Observers			General public		
	Tuscany 1989	North 1989	South 1989	Tuscany 1989	North 1989	South 1989	Tuscany 1988	North 1988	South 1988
Access new markets	86	86	80	75	81	80	83	83	78
Stimulate technological innovation	100	96	81	100	100	88	84	82	79
Increase competition	100	97	96	92	94	95	92	91	82
Provide access to new financial resources	75	83	86	79	85	83	n.a.	n.a.	n.a.
Increase the cost of production	31	21	36	22	32	34	53	50	54
Concentrate industry	100	86	78	81	83	71	n.a.	n.a.	n.a.
Increase unemployment	40	25	46	34	27	45	n.a.	n.a.	n.a.
Restructure commercial distribution networks	95	94	88	86	88	90	80	76	72
Stimulate reconversion of agricultural production	77	79	78	76	77	79	66	64	65
Worsen situation in underdeveloped areas	62	56	77	71	66	74	64	56	52
Improve public services	65	56	36	49	53	42	57	57	60
Raise standards in social services	62	49	63	67	73	64	n.a.	n.a.	n.a.
Stimulate adoption of new environmental standards	90	89	84	89	90	76	67	64	66
Stimulate institutional renewal	95	84	81	80	83	76	n.a.	n.a.	n.a.
Modernize regional administration	57	50	53	59	56	56	70	64	66
Confusion of functions	47	45	57	49	39	46	n.a.	n.a.	n.a.
Slow-down decision-making process	36	40	44	48	40	47	n.a.	n.a.	n.a.
Lose regional identity	10	8	20	12	9	18	27	27	36

* 'For each of the following areas, do you believe that the Single Market will have or will not have on impact on your region?'

to new and selected ones. Yet, in this general process of change, the region's underdeveloped areas were perceived by the majority of the respondents to lose out ultimately to the stronger areas.

A very noticeable impact of the Single Market was predicted to occur in the area of planning and production of standards for public goods produced by the public or private sector. Councillors, observers and public opinion in Tuscany expected the Single Market to bring Tuscany up to the higher European standards in its overall offer of public services. The area of social services which had raised concerns among all respondents was expected to receive a qualitative and quantitative uplift from its associations with the Single Market and to become a support sector to a technologically restructured economy as well as a growth area in its own right. But the most impact was predicted to occur on the region's environmental policies, where almost all councillors and observers saw the likely adoption of tougher environmental standards in the near future. All these expectations were higher than the averages measured in both northern and southern regions. Certainly, Tuscan residents and leaders had substantial confidence in the stimulus function of a better integrated European economy with regard to their own system of support services.

What explains these expectations? It is first of all the almost unanimous perception that more intimate integration with the rest of Europe will not be confined to Tuscany's economy but will expand to affect its regional institutions as well and stimulate the process of Tuscany's institutional renewal. Better institutions make for a stronger economy, thus this 'virtuous cycle' of mutually reinforcing impacts is set into motion by greater integration with Europe. In fact, the projections that respondents make are for the Single Market to also have a modernizing effect on the regional administration itself which will be called upon more often to respond directly to Brussels and fulfil Brussels' various mandates regarding the implementation of the Single Market.

A second explanation for the high expectations of betterment of Tuscany's economic system within the new European context is the widespread confidence that such integration will not cause the loss of regional identity, including the main characteristics of Tuscany's economic model. In other words, the Single Market is not seen as a force, least of all a deterministic force, which will bring about 'homogenization' of Europe's economies according to a few prevailing or imported models. Rather, and the written comments by many respondents explain this point forcefully, the view is that the Single Market largely remains a 'political' process of incremental integration where there is room for regional economies to carve out and assert their identities in cooperation with other regions. In essence, midway through the implementation of the Single Market, Tuscany's respondents not only did not believe in the 'Moloch theory' but overwhelmingly rejected it. Conversely, they endorsed the theory of 'new opportunities' for this regional economy within the larger and changing European context.

Tuscany's respondents also showed a healthy degree of realism when in substantial numbers they underlined that, particularly in the short run, there will be a confusion of functions brought about by the increase in both the vertical linkages with EC institutions and the horizontal linkages with germane and complementary EC regional economies. Relatedly, there is also the recognition, keener among the observers (almost half) than among the councillors (about one-third), that the implementation of the Single Market will slow down the decision-making process of regional institutions as they adjust to and go through a period of major changes.[2]

Tuscany's respondents undoubtedly recognized that as a key intervening change in the life of the EC occurred in the form of the Single Market, the Community's functional thrust (Table 3.13) and consequently its institutional architecture (Table 3.14) would not and should not remain as they were in 1987 at the beginning of the process of the creation of the Market. In short, the understanding was clear that changes and impacts in one direction – the increase in the Community's policy functions – had to go hand in hand with changes in the other – the increase in the number of Community institutions – and that the success (that is, the realization of positive impacts on Tuscany of the Single Market) was predicated on both.

The reciprocal of the impacts of the Single Market on the regions of the Community is first of all the question of what kinds of changes the Single Market should produce on the EC and, specifically, on the scope of the Community's functions (Table 3.13). A strong mandate for strengthening EC functions comes from Tuscany in regard to the Community's regional development policies. Uppermost, what is promoted is the greater role of the EC in its underdeveloped areas, a role which carries with it the responsibility for greater expenditures of resources for investment projects which should be designed in partnership with regions and states. The mandate also includes a more visible profile of the EC in the evaluation of such projects and the search for greater effectiveness and accountability.[3]

Related to a stronger EC role in regional development is the call for increased EC power to enforce environmental and planning standards across its regions. Respondents in Tuscany identified EC-wide development policies as a second area where EC functions should be strengthened. Included are policies regarding scientific research which is in need of a more specific European focus, technological innovation in the industrial and service sectors with efforts aimed at a pervasive promotion strategy which incorporates continuous training of the labour force, and support functions of monitoring financial and labour markets at the Community level. Finally, Tuscany's respondents wanted EC functions to expand vis-à-vis the Community's relations with the rest of the world. In 1989 when the issue of immigration from non-EC countries had not reached the critical proportions it has today, respondents in Tuscany and in all other Italian regions were decidedly convinced that this was a Community-wide problem and that more had to be done at that level. But, while consensus was almost total in support of Community policies to integrate into mainstream society immigrants currently living in the Community, the consensus dropped (although it remained a majority) relative to the question of

Table 3.13 Suggested functional changes in the European Community after the implementation of the Single Market (percentage of regional councillors and observers responding 'increase')*

	Councillors			Observers		
Functions	Tuscany 1989	North 1989	South 1989	Tuscany 1989	North 1989	South 1989
Control of the enforcement of environmental and urban planning standards	91	74	89	97	87	87
Evaluation of regional investment projects	81	64	75	58	66	76
Financing projects for underdeveloped areas	92	89	95	92	87	91
Monitoring financial markets	87	79	85	85	89	81
European perspective for scientific research	95	89	93	96	94	89
Financing European defence policies	28	33	34	16	26	28
Promotion of technological innovation	100	94	96	100	98	90
Formulating guidelines for professional education	89	79	90	88	90	84
Monitoring the labour market	88	79	91	94	83	85
Control of immigration from non-EC countries	58	54	64	52	62	53
Promotion of integration of immigrants	90	87	91	89	89	80
Coordination of foreign trade	97	91	91	96	92	88

* 'After the implementation of the Unified Market, how in your opinion should the role of the Community change? For each of the following functions please indicate your preference: increase, stay the same, decrease.'

control over the new immigration flows. This signalled an ambiguity towards the matter of immigration which events in subsequent years have proven to persist.[4]

In contrast, in Tuscany there was essentially unanimous support for strengthening EC functions in matters of foreign trade, recognizing increasingly the logic not of a 'fortress Europe' – as trans-Atlantic critics posited at the time – but that of a 'united market' as a source of strength for its component states and regions in dealing with the rest of the world. But the strong consensus regarding the expansion of EC functions stopped at the door of a European defence policy. Between 14 and 25 per cent of Tuscany's respondents suggested in 1989 that such a matter should be elevated to a Community profile.[5]

The strong support in Tuscany for changes in the scope of EC functions in light of the creation of the Single Market, produced even stronger

Table 3.14 Institutions necessary for the Community upon the implementation of the Single Market (percentage of regional councillors and observers responding 'indispensable' or 'necessary')*

Institutions	Councillors			Observers		
	Tuscany 1989	North 1989	South 1989	Tuscany 1989	North 1989	South 1989
Federal European bank	100	97	100	100	96	98
European environmental agency	100	99	100	100	98	100
EC europrogrammes for sectorial intervention	100	100	99	96	98	94
Interregional euroconsortia for the planning of services and public infrastructure	90	89	86	72	72	91
Euro-agencies for interregional cooperation for management of services and infrastructure	85	81	87	73	72	87
University postgraduate eurodiplomas in sciences	90	83	94	78	78	89
European administrative court	93	88	88	83	86	83
European agency to monitor labour market	100	99	100	92	94	96
European securities and exchange commission	100	95	99	96	92	85
European conference for regional presidents	90	91	93	65	74	77
European-level representation of regional councils	90	90	91	56	61	73
Regional offices in Brussels	75	83	92	71	65	72
European telecommunication agency	95	98	99	84	87	96

* 'After the implementation of the Unified Market, in your opinion what operative instruments should the Community create in order to meet the challenges of the post-1992 period? Please express your opinion of whether the Community needs to or does not need to create each of the following policy instruments.'

support for many components of a new institutional architecture for the Community (Table 3.14). The strength of consensus was often almost unanimous in Tuscany and in the other regions, with only minor differences between northern and southern regions. Ranking at the top of both councillors' and observers' views about the need for new EC institutions are the Community counterparts of visible national regulatory and policy-making agencies. They include a federal bank, an environmental agency, an observatory for monitoring labour market changes, a securities and exchange commission, an administrative court and a telecommunication agency in recognition of the importance of such policy areas in the EC and of their being directly impacted by the Single Market.

Next, what was being promoted in 1989 were interregional agencies for the formulation and implementation of the development policies of the EC.

Table 3.15   Transregional cooperation upon the implementation of the Single
Market (percentage of regional councillors and observers responding 'indispensable'
or 'opportune')*

	Councillors			Observers		
Common initiatives	Tuscany 1989	North 1988	South 1988	Tuscany 1989	North 1988	South 1988
Lobby the European Commission	33	48	61	39	40	52
Formulate development programmes	100	99	98	88	91	97
Cultural/touristic exchange programmes	100	98	100	92	96	100
Plans for applied research	100	100	98	100	98	99
Policy to protect the environment	100	100	99	96	98	97
Activity to promote products/services	95	93	96	96	96	97
Strengthen regional airline service	89	84	90	96	96	93
Preparation of administrative personnel	99	97	99	95	98	92
Promotion of joint-ventures between enterprises	95	88	93	92	94	95
Integrated programmes for contiguous border regions	100	97	96	92	94	93

* 'After the implementation of the Unified Market in your opinion what are the common
initiatives that should be created among regions located in different European countries? For
each of the following possibilities please express your opinion: indispensable, opportune, not
necessary.'

The range of options included consortia and joint ventures to finance
service and physical infrastructure projects. Moreover, the respondents
supported the creation of specific new institutions to increase representation
and presence of regional governments in Brussels, such as the Conference of
Regional Presidents, a representative body for regional legislatures and the
opening of regional government offices in Brussels.

Finally, in the views of our respondents, the changes to be brought about
by the Single Market were to impact upon the way in which regional
governments looked not just at the EC institutions but also at other regions.
As regions saw themselves thrust into a wide-open market, other regional
institutions and economies were becoming the object of closer scrutiny and
of new joint opportunities. Modes of transregional cooperation and areas in
which to experiment with them found strong support everywhere (Table
3.15), in Tuscany and in other regions. The range of options considered
covered more general cooperation on, for example, development programs
and development targeted to border regions, as well as sector-based
cooperation, such as the strengthening of the regional airline service and
the joint promotion of products, services and cultural and tourist

exchanges. Faith was also expressed in the beneficial effect of transregional efforts to upgrade and modernize the skills and the professional profile of regional administrators. The almost unanimous support for transregional cooperation initiatives found one important exception among the respondents in Tuscany and in the northern regions – but not in southern regions – namely, the reluctance to lobby jointly the Commission in Brussels. The position is reflective of the fact that the concept and practice of institutionalized lobbying is foreign to the Italian political system – where it assumes negative connotations – while it is a common and accepted trait in others.

3.5 Conclusions

In 1989–90, on the eve of the implementation of the Single Market, how were regional institutions and regional economies in Europe expected to be impacted by the changes in the Community's institutional architecture for decision-making and implementation? Focusing on the case of Tuscany, this chapter reports on the findings of a study of this region's institutions, the nature and scope of its development and social policies, and of the outlook of regional elected officials, interest groups, and the public at large relative to the convergence and integration of policies and planning.

Tuscany, a region centrally located on the southern flank of the Community, characterized by a solid economy based on small and medium-sized enterprises and endowed with strong civic and cultural traditions was found to be quite confident of the abilities of its economy and regional institutions to partake of and amplify the growth opportunities induced by the Single Market. Tuscany had adopted regional development policies in tune with principles promoted by the EC and which stressed, among others, intergovernmental partnership and transregional cooperation. Finally, Tuscany's economy was found to be noticeably but not wholly prepared to operate on a transnational level, pointing out shortcomings affecting its agricultural enterprises as well as a serious infrastructure deficit.

Notes

1. In the terminology used by the European Community, 'measure' refers to specific actions, the sum total of which comprise and operationalize a development project. The measures are the instruments by which the project is implemented in detail in reference to schedule, available financial resources and personnel.
2. In 1993 after the implementation of the Single Market one is compelled to point out how the results of three of the referenda of 18 April, which eliminated the Ministries of Agriculture, Tourism and State Participations, are indeed reconfiguring the vertical relations of Italian regional governments in these policy areas, that is away from Rome and toward Brussels.

3. The general evaluation of the first five-year Community Support Framework Plans indicates that there is a long way to go in fine-tuning and applying project evaluation methodologies on the part of the EC and the regions which are at the same time scientifically valid as well as institutionally workable and socially useful. This notwithstanding, the movement towards such a goal has large support and remains a key ingredient of the CSFs (Nanetti, 1992).

4. After the fall of the Berlin Wall, the magnitude of the immigration problem into the EC has grown exponentially, fed by influxes from the south of the world and the former eastern European bloc countries. The EC with difficulty is developing a common immigration policy. Meanwhile, in response to what some EC countries saw as a too timid response on the part of the Community, in the last two years and in 1993 in particular there have been moves by member states to tighten national immigration laws (e.g., France and Germany) or to maintain control over their entry points (e.g., UK and Denmark).

5. Interestingly, as with immigration, defence is a policy area where the events of the last few years have confirmed rather than overturned the views of our respondents. By extrapolation the events in the former Yugoslavia seem to indicate that the Community's public opinion is not yet in favour of major devolution of power to the EC in the defence area.

References and sources

Amministrazione provinciale di Firenze, *L'apparato produttivo deisistemi territoriali della provincia di Firenze*, Florence, IRPET, 1984.

Bianchi, Giuliano 'Maturità precoce: una modernizzazione a rischio', pp. 927–1002 in *Storia d'Italia. Le regioni dall' Unità ad oggi, La Toscana*, Turin, Einaudi, 1988.

Becattini, G. (ed.) *Lo sviluppo economico della Toscana con particolare riguaurdo all'industria leggera*, Florence, Guaraldi, 1975.

Comune di Firenze, *L'artigianato nel comprensario fiorentino*, Florence, Tipografia nazionale, 1980.

—— *Industria e sviluppo nell'area fiorentina*, Convegno, 19 January 1980, Florence, Nuova Grafica Fiorentina, 1980.

—— 'Le attività di formazione professionale dell'Amministrazione comunale', Florence, March, 1987.

—— *Studenti e mondo del lavoro*, Florence, Tip. Giutina, 1983.

Comune di Firenze and IRPET, *Lineamenti del programma pluriennale*, Florence, 1982).

—— *Progetto sullo sviluppo metropolitano dell'area Firenze–Prato*, Florence, 1982.

Comune di Firenze, Ufficio Sviluppo Economico, 'Il censimento deiconsumi energetici nelle strutture del Comune di Firenze', Florence, April 1985.

Conferenza per il coordinamento degli interventi di pianificazione territoriale dell'area, *Processo di urbanizzazione nell'area Firenze–Prato–Pistoia*, Florence, La casa Usher, 1984.

Federazione Regionale Associazioni Industriali della Toscana, *Industria toscana anni settanta*, Florence, Duplioffset, 1983.

—— *Atti dell'incontro sul tema: I paradossi della piccola e media industria. Il caso toscano*, Florence, Duplioffset, 1986.

—— 'Osservazioni al Programma Regionale di Sviluppo 1986–1988 della Giunta Regionale Toscana', Florence, 5 March 1986.

—— 'Osservazioni al Programma Regionale di Sviluppo 1987–1989 della Giunta Regionale Toscana', Florence, 13 March 1987.

—— 'Osservazioni al Programma Regionale di Sviluppo 1988–1990 della Giunta Regionale Toscana', Florence, 17 March 1988.

Federindustria Toscana, *Atti del Convegno: Merchant Banking. Opportunità per l'industria italiana*, Florence, Duplioffset, 1986.
—— *Atti del Convegno: Il danno ambientale dopo la 349*, Florence, Duplioffset, 1987.
Garavini, Roberto, et al., *Il Parco dei minerali dell' isola d'Elba*, Padua, Marsilio, 1987.
Grassi, Mauro, 'La Toscana negli anni 80: una analisi macro-economica', *Studi e Informazioni*, 3, pp. 101–18, 1988.
IRPET *Il finanziamento pubblico dello sviluppo toscano: aspetti istituzionali e profili quantitativi*, Florence, IRPET, 1975.
—— *Caratteri e prospettive dello sviluppo toscano*, Florence Officine grafiche, 1976.
—— *Ricerca e programmazione nell'esperienza della politica turistica della regione toscana*, Florence, Eurografica, 1977.
—— *Il Buyer in Toscana*, Florence, Le Monnier, 1980.
—— *Le trading companies in Toscana*, Florence, IRPET, 1981.
—— *L'artigianato toscano: relazione di sintesi*, Florence, IRPET, 1982.
—— *Rapporto 1983 sulla situazione economica della Toscana*, Florence, Eurografica, 1983.
—— *Letture di analisi e programmazione dello sviluppo regionale*, Florence, Tipografia Giuntina, 1984.
—— *Rapporto 1984 sulla situazione economica della Toscana*, Florence, IRPET, 1984.
—— *Rapporto 1985*, Florence, IRPET, 1985.
—— *Rapporto 1986 sulla situazione economica della Toscana*, Florence, IRPET, 1986.
—— *Tour 1985: Turisti italiani e stranieri in Toscana*, Florence, IRPET, 1986.
—— *Rapporto 1987*, Florence, IRPET, 1987.
—— *Rapporto sul lavoro 1990*, Florence, Guintina, 1991.
Nanetti, R.Y., *Rise of the Periphery*, London, Frank Cass, 1994.
PCI Comitato Comprensoriale, *Oltre le periferie*, Florence, Press, 1982.
Putnam, R.D., Leonardi, R. and Nanetti, R.Y., *La pianta e le radici: Il radicamento delle regioni nel sistema politico italiano*, Bologna, Il Mulino, 1985.
—— *Making Democracy Work: Civic Traditions in Modern Italy*, Princeton, Princeton University Press, 1993.
Regione Toscana, *Programma Regionale di Sviluppo 1979–1981*, Florence, Bollettino Ufficiale della Regione Toscana, 43, 20 August 1979.
—— 'Relazione sulla situazione economica e sociale', Florence, November 1980.
—— *Programma Regionale di Sviluppo 1982–1984*, Florence, Bollettino Ufficiale della Regione Toscana, 37, 29 June 1982.
—— *Programma Regionale di Sviluppo 1983–1985*, Florence, Bollettino Ufficiale della Regione Toscana, 27, 1 June 1983.
—— *Piano Sanitario Regionale 1984–1986 e Piano Regionale dei Servizi Sociali 1984–1986*, Florence, Bollettino Ufficiale della Regione Toscana, 61, 12 December 1984.
—— *Programma delle iniziative promozionali per l'anno 1988 in favore delle risorse dell'agricoltura, dell'artigianato e dell'industria toscana*, Florence, Bollettino ufficiale della Regione Toscana, 61, 16 December 1987.
—— *Programma nazionale di interesse comunitario perl'arcipelago toscano (PNIC–FEDER) 1987–1991. Parte 1*, Florence, Luglio, 1987.
—— *Programma nazionale di interesse comunitario perl'arcipelago toscano (PNIC–FEDER) 1987–1991. Parte 2, Il programma FESR*, Florence, Luglio, 1987.
Regione Toscana, Consiglio Regionale, 'Legge Regionale sulle Aree Protette', Florence, Centro Stampa, 1982.
Regione Toscana, Dipartimento Programmazione, 'Rapporto sulla produzione e sull'impiego dell'energia in Toscana, 1983', Florence, September 1984.
Regione Toscana, Giunta Regionale, *Arno-Per attuare il progetto pilota*, Florence, Tipolito, 1980.
—— 'Relazione sullo stato di attuazione del programma regionale di sviluppo – verifiche e aggiornamenti per il triennio 1981–83', Florence, Ufficio stampa, 1980.
—— *Toscana – Le Aree Verdi*, Florence, La Girandola, 1985.

—— *Piano regionale di risanamento delle acque*, Florence, Centro stampa, 1986.
—— *Cambiamo aria con la benzina pulita*, Florence, Litografia della Giunta Regionale, 1987.
—— *Piano Regionale Integrato dei Trasporti*, Florence, 1987.
—— *Programma regionale di sviluppo 1987–1989: Le strategie di governo e i resultati programmati per l'anno 1987*, Florence, Litografia della Giunta Regionale, 1987.
—— *Programma regionale di sviluppo 1987–1989: Relazione economica e sociale*, Florence, Litografiadella Giunta Regionale, 1987.
—— *Programma regionale di sviluppo 1988–1990*, Florence, Tipografia Giuntina, 1988.
—— 'Programma Speciale ai sensi del Regolamento CEE N. 219 del 18.1.1984 – Provincia di Arezzo', Florence, 1987.
—— *Raccolta della Normativa statale e regionale sulla distribuzione commerciale*, Florence, Litografia della Giunta Regionale, n.1/1987.
—— 'Conferenza di Programmazione della Provincia di Massa Carrara-Proposte', Massa, 26–27 February 1988.
—— *Programma Integrato Mediterraneo della Toscana*, Florence, March 1988.
—— 'Conferenza per il coordinamento degli interventi di pianificazione territoriale nell'area Firenze–Prato–Pistoia, Studi preparatori', Florence, April 1988.
—— 'Trasformazioni e governo del territorio 1971–87 – Prima Parte', Florence, 1988.
Regione Toscana and Università di Firenze, *L'organizzazione sanitaria in Toscana*, Florence, March 1987.
Rogari, Sandro, 'Eurosportello per le imprese. Già apre a Firenze', *Industria Toscana*, 16 October 1987.

Part II

The Tuscan economy and its industrial structure

4 The development of light industry in Tuscany: an interpretation

Giacomo Becattini

4.1 A note on the historical origins of postwar events in Tuscany

The characteristics and potential of a development process can only be understood through an analysis of how it arose because most of the preconditions for development in terms of its pace and modes were created at an earlier stage. We know that development is the antithesis of socio-economic stagnation, stagnation being a stage in which all the economic, social and cultural variables interact to produce a generalized lack of faith in the prospect of change, an overestimation of the risks of any innovation and a widespread dislike of innovators of all kinds. Any analysis of a development process must therefore take as its starting-point this – fortunately not entirely stable – equilibrium of stagnation and identify within it the embryonic developmental features and potential.

The role of 'social culture' (defined by Bertolino (1961, p. 181) as 'knowledge and faith welded together in a basic doctrine which is present in all the various activities of every individual, whatever his or her place in society') in preserving this 'equilibrium' has been well put by Bertolino (ibid.): 'This culture is inhibitory, and is reflected in the structure of the economy and of society, that is the whole system of institutions in which are embodied, whether in legal or customary form, the principles informing the behaviour of the population, and also in the moral and political philosophy, at various levels of elaboration but always fitting the respective social classes, which is used to justify and defend that structure.'

This is, of course, not the appropriate place, nor is the writer the appropriate person, to carry out even a quick historical survey of what occurred in Tuscany between the achievement of Italian national unification and the Second World War. A task of this type must be left to the experts in the field; nevertheless I shall have to devote a few lines, for which I must apologize to my readers, to a brief review of certain limited aspects of the region's history which form an essential background for the situation which we can term the 'starting-point' of development in Tuscany since the last war.

The question which looms largest in this part of my account, a question which is really rather rhetorical, is whether Tuscany had a 'vocation' for light industrial development. Although these days it is the case that there is so little faith in analyses of so-called 'area vocations' that the question might well be ignored, I think it is both valid and relevant to ask whether Tuscany might have been able to accommodate a classic type of industrialization in the postwar period, i.e. with more heavy industry and more intensive urbanization.

In any case, the scholar cannot ignore this question, if he wishes his research to be of use to men of flesh and blood, since it serves to distinguish, if not to divide, the different analyses of development in the region and to some extent has implications for the choice of practical policies to be applied to it.[1] In fact, because of its considerable mineral resources, its remarkable financial structure and its long history as a centre of trade, Tuscany appeared to be, as early as the first half of the nineteenth century, a suitable site for a process of industrialization as intensive, all things considered, as that which occurred subsequently in areas such as Piedmont, Lombardy and Liguria. Yet this potential was not fulfilled. Tuscany – despite certain considerable strides towards the building up of a modern industrial structure – failed to develop, up to the Second World War, the classic sectors of industrialization (the cotton industry first, and then engineering) and this was due to factors which, in Tuscan terms, can be defined as 'exogenous' as well as to influences stemming from Tuscany society itself, from its structure and cultural outlook.

'Exogenous' and 'endogenous' factors

Among factors which can be regarded as 'exogenous' at a regional level one can certainly include the way in which Italian unification was achieved and the consequences which this had in terms both of power- and role-sharing agreements among the ruling groups of the pre-unification states, and the territorial organization set up in the country. While I must refer readers to the works of specialists in relation to the first of these factors,[2] since it would require an account outside the scope of this chapter, as regards the organization of the territory of Italy after unification I would stress the relative isolation for many decades of the interior of Tuscany in terms of the provision of roads and railways. The mountain barrier of the Apennines and political and military considerations combined to tip the balance in favour of the railway policy which bypassed Tuscany and hinged rather on a central axis running directly from the Po valley down the Adriatic coastline to the heel of Italy.[3]

Further exogenous factors, in the sense employed here, appear to have been the change of Italy's capital first to Florence and then to Rome,[4] the tariff policies of the Kingdom of Italy and the differential effect on the different regions of the two world wars taken together with the periods of preparation, reconversion and reconstruction which preceded and followed them. Each of these events – and doubtless others besides – had important effects in terms of the intranational (interregional) division of labour of which, however, no more than a mention can be made here.

Among the 'endogenous' factors, in my view, first place must go to the 'grand design' which was lucidly formulated and energetically carried out, first in the Tuscany of the grand-dukes and later in the Kingdom of Italy, by that section of the Tuscan ruling group known as the 'Tuscan moderates' (*moderati toscani*).[5] This was actually a very heterogeneous group, in which traditionalists and romantics combined with forward-looking individuals who anticipated subsequent developments but which, taken as a whole, sticks to a maintenance of a status quo assuring ample economic rewards to the small (though not tiny) number of landowners or to the partly overlapping group of coupon-clippers, and even greater social and moral rewards in terms of the enjoyment of a cultural hegemony, in addition to political dominance, over the 'plebeian' mass, as it was then called, in the region.

This policy, which can be summed up as anti-industrial, aimed to spare the streets and squares in Tuscany the social stirrings which were then shaking Europe and its drawing-rooms; the vulgarity of artisans grown rich, plays an important role in holding back the formulation in the region of an 'industrial base' while encouraging it, through investment, elsewhere. It should not, of course, be thought that this 'grand design' was so simple and staightforward as may appear from such a brief survey, nor that it prevented all industrial development in Tuscany, where indeed important and significant episodes occurred, especially around the turn of the century, on which ample light has been shed by historians.[6] If this were not so, it would be hard to explain both the political importance and the strong cultural influence of this region in the decades between unification and the First World War, and in some respects also during the fascist period.

The 'moderate' strategy in fact gives general tone to what happened in Tuscany but left untouched many important economic and sociocultural developments,[7] related to the highly differentiated make-up of society in the region, which in turn were the result of a very complex history.

Controlled development and the light-industrial specialization of the Tuscan economy

It was by the interaction between the exogenous and endogenous factors mentioned above that the relative development of the region was shaped. A few data will suffice to give a fairly clear idea of what happened in relative terms. The strengths of the Tuscan economy at the time of its absorption into the Kingdom of Italy were its financial credit structures and its famous agriculture. One need only point out that in 1865 52.3 per cent of capital in limited companies operating in the credit sector in Italy was from Tuscany and that in 1861 the livestock population of Tuscany was 200kg. per hectare as compared with 154kg per hectare in the green meadows of Cattaneo's Lombardy.

On a much more modest scale, though far from negligible, was the position of manufacturing in the region. Measured in terms of the number of persons employed, the 1881 census shows that in Tuscany about 7 per cent of the population was engaged in manufacturing industry, a figure below that of the region's share of the country's total population (7.4 per cent). In terms of its share of the capital of limited companies operating in the industrial sector the figures for Tuscany were (in 1865) still lower (5.2 per cent), illustrating the small number of large and modern units.

This situation of widespread craft-industry and small factories had already been given theoretical expression in the work of Raffaello Busacca, one of the main economists of the 'moderate' group. 'The special characteristic of its manufactures lies in its exquisite taste . . . if Tuscany is to become a genuinely manufacturing country it will be when manufactures of this sort grow large enough to satisfy most of the foreign market . . .'

Busacca and his friends believed, indeed, that Tuscany's hopes 'should not rest in manufactures', however artistic, but in the agriculture 'which will always form the main basis of its economy' and above all 'in its rich and diverse mines'. And, in fact, Tuscan mining in the period following Busacca's 'memorandum' (1855) was the object of considerable attentions on the part of capitalists from inside and outside of the region.

If we compare these data with those of the years around the First World War we find (a) that Tuscan agriculture in 1908 is still more or less at the level of 1861 (200kg/ha), while in regions like Lombardy capitalization had raised to the order of 366kh/ha of livestock; (b) capital in Tuscan limited companies in the credit sector had fallen by 1916 to 25.3 per cent of the national total; (c) large-scale industry had lost ground in relation to the national average as is shown by the unchanged share (5.2 per cent) it had of the capital of industrial limited companies (1916) and by its falling share of employees in the heavy-industrial sectors (engineering, metals and chemicals): from 7.5 per cent in 1881 to 6.7 per cent of the national total in 1921.

The interwar period is complex and contradictory from the viewpoint which concerns us here. Some public support for heavy industry produces a halt in the falling trend of the previous period and even a modest improvement. Tuscany's share of the national total of those employed in these sectors (engineering, metals and chemicals) rises by 1936 to 7.4 per cent. But there is a much greater rise in the numbers employed in the same sectors in the industrial triangle (from 48.8 to 54.4 per cent of the national total) while there is a fall in Tuscany in the number of personnel in industrial enterprises with more than 500 employees (from 7.6 in 1927 to 6.3 per cent in 1937–50). If one adds to this the proliferation of productive units in light-industrial sectors, especially after the Great Depression, it is clear that fascism does not halt the trend towards regional specialization which had already started in previous decades.[8]

To conclude this rapid outline of the evolution of industry in Tuscany between unification and the Second World War, I believe one can say that the nature of development there was led rather than leading and that, apart from some important developments in mining, steel and chemicals (due mostly to investment and entrepreneurs from outside Tuscany) it affects sectors which most easily 'fit in with' the social environment of the region. Symbolic of this gradual fading away of the prospect of Tuscany becoming one of the driving forces in Italy's industrial development during this period is what happened to the iron-ore resources on Elba which for many decades were mined and exported and where it was decided to make use of them only when they were virtually exhausted.[9]

Thus the answer I would give to the question raised earlier – whether development in Tuscany since the war might have taken a different course – is that, as early as the beginning of the Second World War, the process of the interregional division of labour had already gone a very long way towards cutting Tuscany off from the 'heavy' sectors of industry. Clearly, this does not mean that the trend could not have been reversed, but simply that such a shift (had it been clearly conceived and really desired at both regional and national levels – which was not the case, for reasons which do not allow one to pin the blame squarely on any one political party) would inevitably have conflicted with trends already well established both within and outside the region.

4.2 Formation of the prerequisites for industrial take-off

The long series of events between unification and the Second World War had the effect of producing at one and the same time, as we have seen, a relative decline in industrial activity (manufacturing) in Tuscany as compared with the regions of the industrial triangle and a growing relative specialization in the 'light' and 'traditional' sectors of industry. This 'controlled development' was, however, accompanied by a gradual modernization of Tuscan society and a growing diversification of its productive apparatus.

We shall examine, first, the infrastructural aspects, especially those with the greatest influence on the development of industry. From the standpoint of communications the period was marked by steady extension and improvement of both the road system in Tuscany and the region's links with the outside world (the Apennine passes); there was, indeed, little improvement in the railway system between the 1870s and 1934 when the main Florence–Bologna line was opened, overcoming central Tuscany's winter isolation from the Po Valley. The importance of this road and rail network for a region without navigable rivers and canals needs to be stressed.

As regards the distribution network (commerce), Tuscany achieved the same figure per head of population as the 'industrial triangle' did twenty years earlier. In 1936 Tuscany had 366 persons employed in this sector per 10,000 inhabitants, while as early as 1911 the figure was 307 per 10,000 in Piedmont, 443 in Liguria and 352 in Lombardy.

Turning to the educational system and illiteracy levels we find a similar picture of backwardness compared with the regions of the industrial triangle. The number of those employed in teaching (both private and public) in Tuscany was 32 per 10,000 inhabitants in 1911 compared with

37/38 in the 'triangle' as early as 1881. By 1936 the situation was much better (58 per 10,000) but still clearly lagging behind the triangle and, indeed, below the national average. Tuscany was some 30 years behind the 'triangle' with respect to literacy rates. Only in 1931 did the region achieve a literacy rate of 81.8 per cent; the rate in Piedmont was higher as far back as 1901, a level also achieved in Liguria and Lombardy later in the same decade.

A similar backwardness in relation to the 'triangle' is found in Tuscany with respect to the number of those employed in health services: 24 per 10,000 in 1936, which is little better than 21/22 per 10,000 which the 'triangle' regions had achieved in 1881. One hardly needs to point out that Tuscany's backwardness in comparison to the 'triangle' was matched by all the other regions of the centre and south (except for Latium).

All in all, it can be said that Tuscany's infrastructure at the end of the last war (ignoring war-damage) was on the same scale as the 'triangle's' at the end of the First World War. From the standpoint of infrastructural prerequisites Tuscany was thus ready for a process of rapid industrialization by about 1949–51. Of course, this means merely that industrial development was a possibility, not that any direct stimulus for it existed.

From the strictly industrial point of view, the situation in Tuscany at the end of the last war looks highly differentiated. A vast agricultural area virtually without manufacturing industry, though with some important units in mining, accounted for the south of the region. Along the coast stretches a chain, broken in places, of large and medium-sized industrial establishments operating in engineering (e.g. the Livorno shipyards), metals (the Ilva and Magona ironworks in Piombino), chemicals (the Solvay sodaworks at Rosignano, etc.), and glass (the St Gobain glassworks in Pisa).

In the central valleys, to complete the list, there was a more or less unbroken string of towns and villages with some industry, with considerable industrial concentration and population density especially in the Prato area and in the lower Arno Valley (from Empoli to Cascina). The population of manufacturing firms in this area was made up of a very small number of significant large industrial units, a number of medium-sized firms, and a multitude of small and very small enterprises, these last being connected by a sort of umbilical cord to the independent craftsmen and the world of wage and agricultural labourers. Thus we have a very broad productive base in which the unchanged craft-character of the organization of production was mixed up with an attitude to the domestic and foreign market which was no longer just that of the independent craftsman; a market whose demand moreover was met and to some extent stimulated (often through the direct or indirect activity of middlemen) by the production of short-run products, probably differing only in details such as colour, material, trim and so on.

If we deepen the analysis we find that in each of the subsectors comprising this system there coexisted different types of productive activities and that almost always the same was true of enterprise differing considerably in size.[10] It is worth pointing out that this gave rise to a social environment in which wage-labourers, particularly skilled ones, lived side by side with independent skilled craftsmen, producing an extremely interesting sociological blend. The world of the non-agricultural labourer (often an ex-agricultural labourer) thus reveals a unique structure which is penetrated by demands for social emancipation stemming from a constructive ideology of the social role of labour. It was from this matrix, which is at once economic and sociocultural, that flowed the form of development typical to the region, with the results that we shall see.

To employ a concept much used by Alfred Marshall, the course of Tuscan history leads to a form, still incomplete but already clear in outline, of 'industrial district' (which I understand as meaning 'an integrated industrial area') which produces economies external to the single firm and even to the industrial sector defined by technology, but internal to the 'sectorial–social–territorial' network.

Tensions and tendencies in Tuscan society

From the standpoint of the search for the forces which may have led Tuscany astray from the path of 'controlled development', the accumulation of civic infrastructures or industrial plants (the physical growth of the basis of production) is less important than the build-up of tensions and the ripening of tendencies favouring a form of development based on economic self-assertion by individuals. The problem is a particularly knotty one and here I can only offer the bare bones of the very tentative results of reflections which really need much more thorough and painstaking comparison and checking.

From what I have been able to grasp of this complex matter, there are three main sociocultural premises specific to development in Tuscany. First of all, there is a peasant protest, particularly by women and youth, not so much against the country itself as against the rigidity of the pecking-order in the family and against their close economic dependence on its older male members. The share-cropping system (*mezzadria*) in particular, with its considerable economic adaptability and its unchanging social patterns, is crucial to any analysis of Tuscan society: it can be said that, for centuries, the tensions within a social structure so obviously unfair in its distribution of duties and rights had been absorbed or even socially channelled by an appropriate ideology which contrasted, often in a subtle and sophisticated manner, the combined virtues of family hierarchy and solidarity, of the certainty of survival that farming activity provided and the wholesome properties of country air and food, with the unbridled self-seeking, the uncertainty of life, the pollution and stress of factory work and urban system of living.

This ideological superstructure, only a few of whose features we have touched upon (perhaps the most striking ones as opposed to the most important ones) was still in place at the outbreak of the Second World

War, as a coherent pattern of political and economic conditions which undermined any strong and determined aspiration for change.

A second premise for development was, I believe, intimately linked to the first, namely the work ethic which is thrown up by an environment such as the one I have described. As I understand it, this work ethic is made up of three fundamental aspects: first, an arbitrary but categorical dividing-line between those 'willing to work' (as it was crudely expressed, meaning those who are prepared to seek their fortune or at least their survival within the existing framework of institutions) and the 'workshy'.

This distinction is made, in my view, right across the social and political spectrum: even the gospel of socialism is taken to mean that labour is then a source of legitimation for all wealth and material prosperity as opposed to the non-labour of both the bosses and of parasites and idlers. The notions of 'alienated' labour and of 'the right to leisure' of a part of the Marxist and semi-Marxist tradition would have seemed to the great mass of Tuscan workers as no more than the twittering of intellectuals.

Second, a high esteem for work well performed, a 'mastery of the craft', provided social discriminators of great importance. Third, an acceptance of the risk of industrial accidents as a normal physical feature of work activity.

This work ethic is the result of a social formula and historical process in which low average wage-rates are associated – for a number of reasons both historical and natural (the mild climate and the ideological conditioning of most Tuscans), but also because of restraint in pursuing tendencies to harsher exploitation implicit in the original 'grand design' – with living conditions which as a whole were not abysmal, so that work as such was not felt to be purely negative in its characteristics.

It is hard even to guess at the role played in the creation of this work ethic by the Catholicism with which the Tuscan people's worldview was so deeply imbued. I shall merely point out that Catholicism is more in line with the principle of work well done than with that of unremitting toil.

It may be of interest to quote the words of an official of the British Embassy in Florence in November 1870: 'As former physician to a hospital in London, relieving from 30,000 to 40,000 yearly, I often met with diseases resulting from overwork, either too prolonged or too severe. For many years I attended the Florence Hospital, but I do not think I ever met with a case of illness from a similar cause.'[11]

A third premise of development was what may be called the cultural-touristic open-mindedness of the region – an open-mindedness obviously assisted by the wealth of its traditional artistic resources and by the fact that the national language came to correspond with the speech of Tuscany, but which might not have exerted much influence had it not been nourished and supported by a well established tradition of foreign links and of warm and efficient 'hospitality'.[12]

Trading in relation to a continuing, though declining, rich export trade, should be added to the still important regional traffic in imports and exports, and to the commerce of ideas in relation to the whole great coming and going of foreigners, tourists and merchants, artists and scientists who flocked to Tuscany. The long tradition of business, cultural and tourist contacts with foreigners, often merging together, embodied in highly specialized intermediary structures (e.g., international banks, travel agencies, buyers, hotels, etc.), constituted privileged channels, indeed almost pipelines, for economic relations with the outside world. On the other hand they were instrumental in training Tuscan town-dwellers for the trauma-free absorption of the 'modern' way of life.

The 'priming-mechanism' of development

I should now like to refer to certain aspects of the situation during and immediately after the last war which acted in a way, as a 'priming mechanism' for the developmental process in Tuscany. The first of these is the war-damage and the subsequent intensive rebuilding which occurred in the region. Tuscany and Emilia-Romagna are recognized as being the two regions which suffered most from the campaign in Italy: bridges, tunnels, road and railway junctions, factories and houses were all largely destroyed as the battle raged. By a paradox now generally accepted by researchers and embodied in the literature, this higher rate of destruction caused a higher rate of public expenditure, an exceptional renewal of industrial and civic structures and a greater effort at reconstruction. In a climate of common determination, looms come out of their hiding-places, warehouses are repaired, houses, roads, bridge and railways rebuilt. Real incomes rise rapidly if inflation spreads unequally, expenditure is accelerated and both official and 'black' markets pass on the stimulus to industry itself.

A second element is represented by the different impact of the process of reorganization of national and international markets following the disruption of the Second World War. The economic rebirth of Tuscany did not get much help from the Allied Military Government at first, or from the central government later. Large-scale light industry got started on its own: Prato with the odds and ends of clothes, the furniture industry with local timber, the footwear factories with any raw and semi-finished materials at hand. Against this prompt recovery of light industry we find in the central and southern regions of Italy an enormous delayed demand for consumption goods of all kinds, mainly durables and semi-durables. Even abroad the situation is favourable for anyone capable of producing anything.

The reconstruction period is thus marked by an outstanding boom in textiles from Prato, reinforced and spurred on by the currency exchange measures adopted by the government to encourage exports. But the boom is not confined to Prato: several light sectors and several geographical areas quickly get off the mark.

A third element, whose relevance may be open to argument, but which I do not believe can be ignored without losing sight of an essential and singular aspect of this development process, is the effects of the difference between the balance of social and political forces in Tuscany and that prevailing elsewhere in Italy. Numerous symptoms can be found of an overall plan of disengagement on the part of the major industrial groups in respect of regions such as Tuscany where the parties of the left and the CGIL (General Confederation of Labour) are much stronger than else- where. The effects of this plan merit a more thorough investigation than I have been able to carry out and I will do no more than refer to an aspect which cannot fail to be intriguing because it represents a unique feature in Tuscan regional development, a feature with very serious consequences. Much of the political and trade-union leadership after 1948 found it difficult or impossible to remain inside the large factories in the region and so set up their own small firms, often with an alacrity on a par with their feelings of anger and political frustration, and contributed to the economic development of the region.

More generally, the dissipation in 1947–8 of the cultural atmosphere of the postwar period – an atmosphere full of uncertainties but also rich with hope – channelled energies into economic self-assertion which might have been directed, and would have preferred to be directed, to political activity in the broad sense (trade unions, running public concerns, etc.).

4.3   The 'mechanism' of development

The flight from the land

The logical and historical starting-point for the mechanism of development in Tuscany must be sought, in my view, in what is termed the labour market. A labour market which, in this case, at the start of the period we are concerned with, possessed a singular feature which has already partly been touched upon: behind what is usually defined as the primary labour supply, and behind a secondary supply which, as is usual, comprised the very young, the elderly, women and those workers willing to take on two jobs, there was in Tuscany a potential supply of farmworkers, both male and female, mainly young people, anxious to escape the living and working conditions associated with the 'family farm' and hopeful of finding elsewhere an environment less redolent of poverty and stagnation and above all less inimical to individual initiative and personality. This group comprised a huge pool of underemployed who had been affected by the breakdown of age-old psychological barriers as a result of war, resistance, foreign invasion and the recovery of civil liberties.

It was a mass of farm labourers who rejected the paternalism and subordination of yesterday's world but not its faith in the providential connection between effort and reward, between commitment to a job and social success. Just how this came about, by virtue of precisely what sociological and economic processes, in response to what political promptings, is still semi-virgin soil which needs to be approached with both rigour and open-mindedness: it points, in my view, to a good many of the reasons for that sociocultural process whereby the Tuscany of yesterday, to all appearances still imprisoned within a hegemony of 'moderatism', has been transformed into the Tuscany of today, in which, despite factors of continuity (whose significance and role are currently the subject of lively debate in the region), the characteristics of the region's culture seem to foreshadow new social relationships.

The INAIL data on worker's earnings and accidents at work, for all their well-known limitations, do seem to fit this hypothesis of exogenous pressure by the peasant masses in Tuscany on the region's labour market: they show indeed, for the fifties, a slower rate of growth in wages in Tuscany than in the country as a whole and a rise in the number of accidents at work greater than the national average. These figures, and the others used to test the hypothesis of the existence of a surplus of pressure on the labour market stemming from a local potential labour supply, are not of course unambiguous: nevertheless they seem on the whole to allow us to regard it not merely as plausible, but as highly likely. (See Becattini (1975), pp. 95–6.)

The expansion of world trade

Of course, this pressure by the peasants on the local labour market, despite its new intensity and new characteristics in the postwar period, had also existed beforehand and might have been relieved in the form of emigration as it was elsewhere (e.g., in share-cropper regions such as Marche and Umbria). That this did not occur is apparently due to the influence of special features, one peculiar to the postwar period and the other to Tuscany as it then was. The first is the exceptional expansion in world trade, and, from the standpoint of the Tuscan region in trade with other regions of Italy, Tuscany found itself operating for some twenty years in a very rapidly expanding 'external' market, both national and international. This expansion, I must stress, was due to factors outside the control of Tuscan manufacturers.

Without this exogenous extension of the external market, the development of the region, given the social and economic structures which had been consolidated there in earlier decades, would simply not have taken place. This obviously does not mean that the tension would have found no outlet, merely that the outlet would have been different, probably in the form of emigration to other parts of Italy or abroad. I consider that this would have occurred even had there been a radical reform of agriculture, since the latter would in any case have had to reduce the size of the rural population which even in 1951 was still over 40 per cent of the total.

The interaction of economic and sociocultural factors

Even the condition just mentioned would not, however, have sufficed to ensure expansion as can be seen from the fact that the external market was enlarged for all the regions of Italy: for Lombardy which did develop as for Lucania which did not; the factor which differentiates some of them and brings others into line is, in my view, the existence in Tuscany of that 'sectorial–territorial–social' network of industrial activity and infra-structures already described. Although not yet, at the start of the period, a genuine 'integrated industrial area', it was certainly rather more than just the embryonic form of one: it represented a set of activities which still had large gaps, both sectorial and territorial, but was already arranged in a non-random way across the region and was easily capable of filling the gaps once the process of expansion was underway. It was from this continually growing network of industrial activities and concentrations of manpower that there arose a simultaneous and linked occurrence (by a process of proliferation whose analogies may be sought more in the realm of biology than in that of mechanics) on the one hand of the catalyzing factor of entrepreneurship and on the other of the ceaseless flow of external and internal economies which gave Tuscan goods a decisive competitive edge compared with those of firms which, despite having manpower available willing to accept even lower wage rates, were not working within such a rich and diversified socioeconomic network.

It should be noted that the bulk of Tuscan industrialists in the postwar period was not coterminous with the prewar industrial bourgeoisie but was made up of a mixture of entrepreneurial types with a preponderance of very small-scale industrialists, most of whom began as craftsmen, workers and peasants and grew in step with the environment, both entering and leaving the field of industry, but which even when throwing its hand in left behind its deposit of know-how, wealth produced and aspirations baulked but not abandoned.

All the same, it would be very odd and almost incomprehensible for a capitalistic industrial development to be brought about by 'new men' alone, without the involvement of the social classes which previously controlled the process of capital accumulation.

And in fact when we move from the numerical and quantitative plane to the 'qualitative' one, we have to recognize that the role of certain sections of the industrial bourgeoisie and especially of the mercantile and financial bourgeoisie of the region was far from being a minor one. One example will suffice: the brokers (buyers acting for foreign firms who were already installed in Florence before the war, international banks, etc.) played a considerable part both in channelling international demand towards Tuscany and in inducing Tuscan manufacturers to adopt the price–quality combinations enabling them to compete in the mass markets of the industrialized countries.

Another important aspect was played, right from the start, by the 'unified budgeting' of the Tuscan family, in both financial terms and allocation of time, which acted as an invisible transmission belt between the sectors of production in which different members of the family were working. A fall in the income of one member tended to produce a fall in the supply-price of the services of the other members; a change in the hours one member had available for leisure produced a corresponding overall redistribution of the tasks assigned within the family. The consequence of this is a linking-up, outside the workplace, of the production costs in the different sectors of industry, and this made it increasingly unsatisfactory to deal with the problem of industrial competition in terms of industrial sectors defined by their technology alone. The production cost of any given product in Tuscany thus became an extremely complex function of all the technical, economic, social and cultural factors which interacted within the 'sectorial–social–territorial' network.

Industrial development without vertical integration

A necessary step in this formula for development, as in all others, is its comparative capacity for absorbing technological progress: this is even more important and urgent after a period of partial isolation such as occurs in wartime. In a period of intensive innovation, such as that which in fact took place after the war, the sectors of production typical of Tuscany also had to face the challenge of the technological progress which had gone on elsewhere. To cope with this necessity there exist two general strategies: the first aims for a gradual development of the firm as a whole so as to maximize within it the advantages of line organization of production and of the advanced specialization of labour which the former permits and promotes. This naturally requires an enlargement of both technical and economic units in accordance with fairly precise economic and technical laws. Any innovation which increases the economic minimum unit size (flow per unit of time) requires a complex reorganization of the whole process which in turn leads to enlargement or rearrangements of the organizational and managerial structure and, after a certain point, a move towards a legal status which will ensure an ample supply of capital.

This is the classical strategy of capitalistic industrial development, but it is not the only strategy, and not even necessarily the most rational from the microeconomic viewpoint in cases where the following two conditions apply at the same time: where the process of production comprises stages which can be technically separated from each other, and where demand is diversified and varies over time. In such cases a second strategy is possible which brings about the same advantages of line organization (overcoming the problems of the elimination of idle time, of what Georgescu-Roegen (1971) calls the 'fund-factors') without the need for any substantial enlargement of premises and management.

The strategy concerned is not one of integration, but is just as intensively specialized, and the shrewdest economists from Adam Smith onwards have always been aware that it represents a viable alternative to the obvious model of capitalistic centralization and vertical integration. All the same it would be quite misleading, in my view, to say purely and simply that this strategy was chosen by industry in Tuscany: there certainly was an element of choice but it was by no means a free one: it was clearly conditioned by external circumstances and choices made elsewhere, and invisibly but no less effectively by sociocultural traditions prevailing in the region. The work ethic and the rejection of share-cropping were not the reasons for choosing a particular type of firm: they did no more than enable the choice to be made, but the strong identification with the firm of a first-generation population of entrepreneurs was what prevented any shift towards types of firms based on the association of anonymous sources of capital. This cultural bottleneck, which might have had a negative effect on a form of development moving towards mass-production on a large scale, proved to be harmless as part of a model of development whose main direction, in line with that followed in previous decades, was towards typical products.

There thus occured a development by proliferation of industrial units which were predominantly diversified and specialized within those sectors allowing such a strategy of growth: textiles, clothing manufacture, furs, leather, furniture and others. Among these 'others', it should be noted, there were significant subsectors belonging to quite untypical statistical categories such as papermaking and packaging, plastics, secondary process-ing of non-metal minerals and even engineering. This was the process of 'non-integration' (rather than 'disintegration') which characterized the 'classical' stage of development in Tuscany.

This diversification and specialization did not stop at industries produc-ing finished goods such as those just mentioned but reached into the huge and decisive area of industrial services. The extension of the overall size of the process actually allowed an increasingly detailed specialization in the sectors of road transport, technical servicing, administrative and fiscal wholesales trade advisory service, brokerage services for trade, and banking and insurance services. An increasingly detailed and ramified specialization thus developed which was translated into a growing capacity to meet the specific needs of the sector directly concerned with production of goods in terms of both the quality and the speed with which services become available on (and were required by) the market.

The characteristics of the labour supply

Faced with this rapid multiplication of productive enterprises, but also largely as a result of it, there arose an extremely complex diversification of the labour supply: the most obvious aspects of this are those relating to primary supply, both original and induced, local or otherwise. This part of the development of the labour supply in Tuscany is the most visible one, although it is far from having been adequately explained, and indeed cannot be explained in isolation. But it is the other part of the labour supply, the so-called secondary supply, which is most interesting. It was a supply dependent on both objective and subjective conditions, a supply that could not or would not be fully integrated into the production process of the firm, which provided industry with a few hours per day or a few years in a life, which may have been of great value to industry (such was the case of the physically active and experienced retired worker) but those who supplied this labour had not made a firm and irrevocable decision to work for others and in particular to do a specific job which would be a continuing and not merely temporary feature of their existence. This supply of 'uncommitted' labour, which was often involved, because of the haphazardness of the labour legislation, in unregulated or illegal forms of work, naturally encountered and easily fitted in with a demand for labour which, by the very nature of the goods produced, fluctuated greatly over a period of time: production grew, incomes grew (though unevenly) and ever higher levels of expectation among the working population were produced and reproduced. To a certain extent the mechanism was self-sustaining: bits of an archetypal ideology of consumption, which was the expression of the way in which a population only just emerging from poverty sought to benefit by the expansion of capitalism, merge with bits of the work ethic previously mentioned to produce peaks of hectic and single-minded dedication to money-making (as, for example, at Prato in certain aspects) reminiscent of the heyday of early capitalism.

But the picture is even more complex than that investigated in the classics of the sociology of capitalism: the shortening of the working-day, improved transportation, the introduction of machines for doing housework, the changed standards socially acceptable in relation to the latter, all this leaves time and energy free, to capture which, in a somewhat bewildering and muddled way, employers and sociocultural structures frantically compete with each other and with the time objectively needed to use and maintain the ever-growing mass of privately owned consumer durables which clutter people's lives. The picture of the contradictions within the 'affluent society', even in an often cheap and wasteful version of such a society, is just as instructive as that of the contradictions within poverty.

Yet, the Tuscan industrial formula serves remarkably well, at least to a certain extent, to turn this supply of surplus hours in people's lives to productive purposes, as demonstrated also by the good response of the Tuscan economy to cyclical fluctuations (see Bianchi, 1976).

This process of development, in which I have tried to connect the strictly economic aspects with the sociocultural one, has given rise to the formation of a new socioeconomic entity: the industrial district of central Tuscany. The future prospects of Tuscany depend largely on the capacity of the decision-makers to understand the peculiarities and the contradictions of this industrial district and to develop its potential.

Notes

1. Against the approach originally formulated in the two overall interpretations put forward by IRPET (1969); Becattini (1975), one can contrast the essay by P. Cantelli and L. Paggi (1973), which has also inspired a number of papers on the Tuscan economy.

2. Besides the classic monography by A. Salvestrini (1965), I would draw attention to the shrewd lecture by G. Mori in Mori (1977), pp. 65–82.
3. See Mioni (1976), pp. 74–107.
4. For a good account of the social and political background to the drama of the transfer of the capital from Florence to Rome, see Ciuffoletti (1977).
5. The essential lines of this 'design' have been clarified by the specialized historical literature. Among the more important manifestations before Italian unification, see Carpi (1974). For the subsequent period see Mori (1977). On the 'reactionary' epilogue of this moderate plan, see Pinzani (1963).
6. On this point see G. Mori's ample treatment in Mori (1977).
7. Many examples of 'anomalous' developments have been revealed by historians of this period, to whom I refer the reader. I will merely mention, since its importance has only recently been given due weight and is therefore not widely known, the foundation even before the end of the Grand-Ducal period (1857) of a Tuscan Technical Institute which became the main prop of the attempts made by Tuscan craftsmen to industrialize themselves and market their goods. It is certainly an accident, but a highly significant one, that the first nucleus of the Galileo engineering works in Florence was born from the closure of the technological laboratory at the Technical Institute. For this episode and others relating to this rather anomalous initiative in the Tuscan context see the brief but informative introduction by Paolo Galluzzi (1977).
8. On this topic see G. Mori, 'Materiali, temi ed ipotesi per una storia dell'industria nella regione toscana durante il fascismo (1923–1939)' in Mori (1977).
9. On this point see Lungonelli (1978).
10. For a survey of what has been written on these subsectors I refer the reader to the Comprehensive Bibliography by V. Spini, in Becattini (1975), 185–241.
11. 'Further Reports from Her Majesty's diplomatic and consular abroad respecting the condition of the industrial classes and the purchase power of money on foreign countries', London, Harrison and Sons, 1871, p. 245.
12. 'On our arrival at Schneider's, a most excellent hotel (I know no better anywhere), we found a good dinner quite ready for us and every accommodation we could desire', wrote a truly exceptional traveller, David Ricardo, from Florence on 13 October 1822 (Ricardo 1951).

References

Becattini, G. (ed.), *Lo sviluppo economico della Toscana*, Florence, IRPET, 1975.

Bertolino, A. *Cooperazione internazionale e sviluppo economico*, Florence, La Nuova Italia, 1961.

Bianchi, G., 'Congiuntura e prospettive dell'economica toscana 1976: primi appunti', *Il Ponte*, pp. 189–97, 1976.

Cantelli, P. and Paggi, L., 'Strutture sociali e politica delle riforme in Toscana', *Critica Marxista*, 5, 1975.

Carpi, V. *Letteratura e società nella Toscana del Risorgimento: Gli intellettuali dell'Antologia*, Bari, De Donato, 1974.

Ciuffoletti, Z., 'I moderati toscani, la caduta della destra e la questione di Firenze (1870–1879)', pp. 23–56, 229–71 in *Rassegna Storica Toscana*, 1977.

Galluzzi, P., 'L'Instituto Tecnico Galilei nella cultura e nelle società toscane del secolo Ottocento', introduction in *Catalogo dell'esposizione di un Saggio delle collezioni scientifiche dell'Instituto Tecnico Gaetano Salvemini (già Galileo)*, Florence, 1977.

Georgeseu-Roeger, N. *The Entropy Law and the Economic Process*, Cambridge, MA, Harvard University Press, 1971.

IRPET, 'Lo sviluppo economico della Toscana: un'ipotesi de lavoro', *Il Ponte*, November 1969.

Lungonelli, M., 'Le miniere di ferro dell'isola d'Elba dall'Unità al 1987', *Rassegna Storica Toscana*, January–April, pp. 47–56, 1978.

Mioni, A., *Le trasformazioni territoriali in Italia nella prima età industriale*, Venice, Marsilio, 1976.

Mori, G., *Il capitalismo industriale in Italia*, Rome, Editori Riuniti, 1977.

Pinzani, C. *La cirisi politica di fine secolo in Toscana*, Florence, Barbera, 1963.

Ricardo, D., *The Works and Correspondence of D. Ricardo*, ed. P. Sraffa, Vol. 10, Cambridge, Cambridge University Press, 1951.

Salvestrini, A., *I moderati toscani e la classe dirigente italiana (1859–1876)*, Florence, L.S. Olschki, 1965.

5 The Tuscan model: an interpretation in light of recent trends

Fabio Sforzi

5.1 Introduction

This chapter analyses the most recent changes in the Tuscan model of development placing particular emphasis on its organization within the regional territory. Subsequent to the interpretation of the Tuscan model of development proposed by IRPET (1969, 1975) covering the period from the end of the Second World War to the end of the 1960s, there have been a number of attempts to analyse the tendencies and structural changes that have impacted on the territorial and socioeconomic configuration of the region (Mori, 1986; IRPET, 1989). Nevertheless, it is necessary to take up this issue once again and begin from the conclusions initially formulated by IRPET. It is necessary to validate the capacity of the model to interpret and explain the tendencies and changes that have intervened in the region during the last two decades. New elements have been introduced into the analysis of the region's development – such as, for example, the genesis of the metropolitan system in central Tuscany which has not been used to modify or update the interpretation of the Tuscan model of development (Regione Toscana, 1984). It has been argued that the explanatory capacity of the IRPET model has disappeared given the decline in the competitiveness of the Tuscan productive formula of flexible specialization. On this basis, the need to develop a 'new' interpretative model involves also the analysis of the ability of the Tuscan form of production to permit its local productive systems located in urbanized countryside – and in particular its industrial districts – in continuing to maintain their specific competitive advantages in a national and international socioeconomic context that has changed profoundly.

The chapter will discuss the role played in the region by the urbanized countryside, which since the beginning of the 1970s presents itself as the *most developed* and the *most differentiated* aspect of Tuscany from the other regions in the country, but which has changed profoundly during the last twenty years. Other local systems in Italy have also developed along the same urbanized countryside model of Tuscany by specializing in similar sectors of light industry and becoming competitors in allied product lines. A similar process has also surfaced among competitors in newly industrialized countries in the Far East while traditionally industrialized countries, which had in the past abandoned light industrial manufacturing and sectors judged too hastily to be on the decline, have resumed production in response to new forms of international competition.

The IRPET interpretative model is capable of explaining even the more recent transformations in the socioeconomic and territorial structure of Tuscany within the confines of the mechanisms that are described within it – i.e., the local systems of urbanized countryside and its industrial districts. However, the crisis of deindustrialization that has manifested itself in the region's tourist–industrial local systems – i.e., the manufacturing poles concentrated around heavy industry – cannot be explained by the IRPET model. This consideration also holds true for a part of Tuscany's urban systems because many of the mechanisms operating in them are of the same nature as those present in the urbanized countryside; the difference is that since current service activities are concentrated more on the treatment of information (i.e., *information-handling services*) than goods (*goods-handling services*) it has a greater influence on the process of change and the prospects for development. The recent publication of the 1991 census data, even if still provisional and incomplete in nature, helps us in the task of evaluating, at least at the macro level, the important changes in employment that have taken place in the 'different Tuscanies'.

5.2   The Tuscany development model

Industrialization through light industry

The development model that surfaced in Tuscany during the course of the two decades immediately following the Second World War brought to completion a process of industrialization whose characteristics were already evident in the form assumed by the territorial location of industry during the late 1920s. The distribution pattern saw the steel and chemical industry located along the coastline and industries producing consumer goods (above all textiles but also fashion, leather goods and furniture) concentrated in the Arno Valley, thereby significantly favouring the latter.

The reasons why Tuscany proceeded along the path of expansion of light industry have already been explained in Chapter 4. Here, we need to examine the Tuscan development model based on the conviction that it represents the foundation for understanding the reasons for the proliferation of light industry in the region.

Once the original nuclei of light industry have been localized they operate as an impulse for growth. In this manner, the initial infrastructure of industries functions as a vital growth mechanism in favouring the territorial concentration of industry through the creation of external economies by virtue of the fact that the firms all belong to the same industry and are located in the same place.

The reasons why an industry once established in a place decides to remain and consolidates itself are to be sought in the advantages it derives from the skills which are developed locally and shared due to territorial proximity, and in becoming an attribute of the physical space. The increase in technical skills tied to a progressive increase in the professional skills of the population stimulates innovation which is reflected in both the quality and variety of goods produced and in the improvement of the machines used in the production process. It is also the basis for the creation of new firms in the principal industry dominating the local economy and in the auxiliary industries that provide supporting instruments and raw materials as well as commercializing the products. The sum total of these activities provides an advantage in costs derived locally for the local firm system.

The social division of labour found in local systems provides the basis for the formation of efficient firms with relative modest dimensions specializing in phases, products and parts of products given their location within a specific industrial organization. Connected to this mechanism of firm proliferation is the increasing differentiation of functions that involves the production, planning and commercialization of the goods produced. The very nature of industrialization through the growth of light industry activates the development of support service activities.

These services – in addition to those tied directly to the production process – involve important activities that meet the exigency of connecting single local producers to the final markets, maintaining stable direct relations with clients, and undertaking the search for new buyers and even new producers.

A locally concentrated industry offering a constant market for specialized labour generates new entrepreneurial initiatives internally and is able to attract them from the outside. As a consequence, it stimulates the influx of workers and their respective families, and it creates the basis for further penetration into the community and the expansion of the productive base. In fact, to the complementarities in economic activities created by a locally concentrated industry (i.e., increase in the variety of production) must be added the complementarity that gradually penetrates into the immediately contiguous areas through the growth of the labour market (i.e., increase in the variety of employment) as well as in the creation of employment opportunities for female workers.

Complementary to the variety of production is the variety of employment which results from the increased density of connecting networks between economic activities and different localities where people live and work, thereby increasing the earning power of families and attributing a specific local identity to productive systems.

The 'four Tuscanies'

In Tuscany the process of light industrialization created an articulated spatial configuration in which four distinct socioeconomic contexts corresponding to individual mechanisms of local development can be identified: the urbanized countryside, the touristic–industrial areas, the urban areas and the countryside, as illustrated in Figure 5.1.

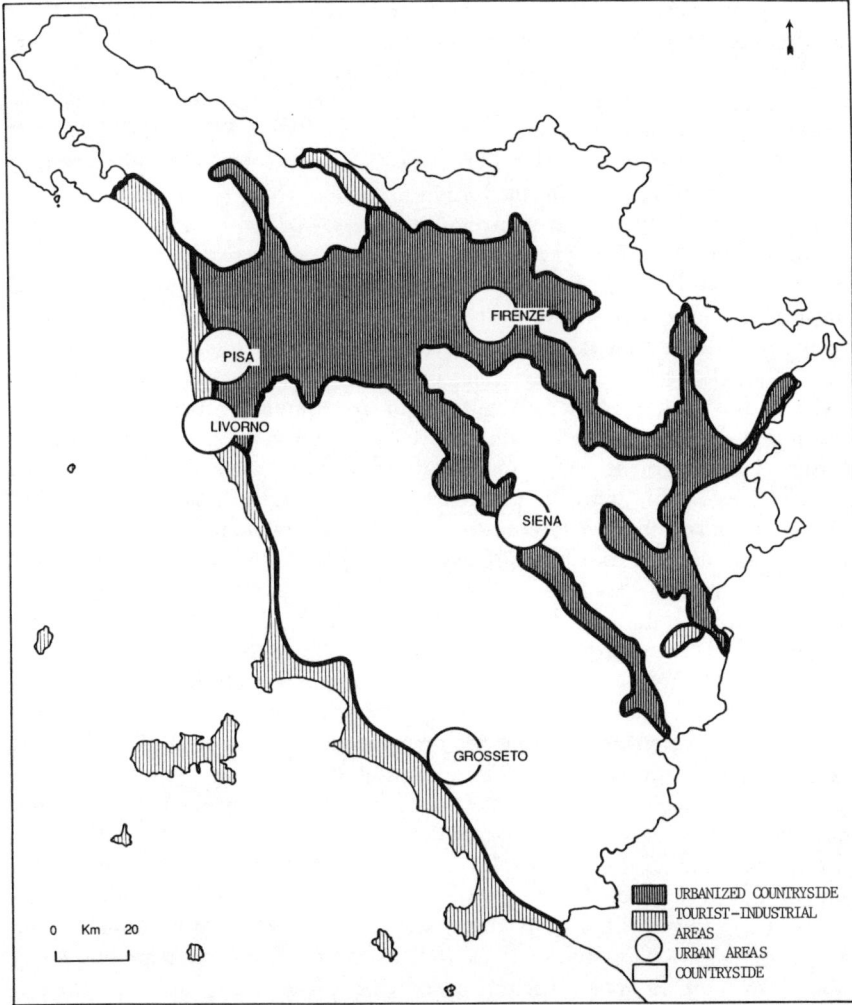

Figure 5.1 'The four Tuscanies', 1971

The urbanized countryside represents a composite of the local systems of light industry. Its dominant characteristic is constituted by the phenomena directly connected with the development of nuclei of specialized small firms in typical Tuscan light industry (textiles, clothing, shoes, leather goods and furniture) in addition to other significant concentrations of firms operating in the production of utensils, machines and other equipment for light industry. In the urbanized countryside we find complementary and auxiliary firms whose birth is directly correlated with the growth of light industry; the simultaneous presence of primary product and auxiliary firms in the same territory creates an intense and complex network of inter-industry relations and local commercial exchanges. The fact that the development of the industrial sector took place primarily through the proliferation of small manufacturing firms has favoured the expansion of autonomous productive units in the service sector to carry out admini-strative, consulting and intermediation functions. In general, the productive units in light industry are particularly endowed with flexibility in the combination of the factors and organization of production permitting them a rapid level of response to market requests and an equally rapid adjustment in employment patterns. The extended family guarantees a supply of labour that is compensated by the offer of social services on the part of local government – at times integrating the supply from the private market and other times substituting for it – and favours the extended participation in the production workforce through a variety of different forms of employment. A typical example is piece work subcontracted to females staying at home to take care of their children. But the extended family ties also function to create a sense of familial identity with the firm owner and the transmission of skills and vocational training from one generation to another or between different components of the family.

The touristic–industrial areas (Piombino, Isola d'Elba) prevalently coincide with the coastline and islands and cover only a few other limited areas in the interior of the region. These areas are characterized by the presence of important manufacturing poles specialized in heavy industry which were located here during the first phases of industrialization initiated at the turn of the century. These coastal cities, along with their local productive systems, offer a demand for labour proportional to the considerable dimensions of the productive structures. The large vertically integrated firms in the manufacturing poles are flanked by the presence of a tourist industry whose characteristics are those of a typical form of mass tourism (artistic sites and 'sun–sea–sand' beach attractions). The progressive growth of national as well as international tourism has come about through a combination of service production oriented toward individual needs by highlighting the use of human capital in addition to the wide diffusion of both house and apartment lettings and forms of family and seasonal management of many hotels and commercial enterprises. The parallel presence on the territory of large industry is reflected in the exasperated competition between different land uses, especially for residential-touristic and industrial needs. A similar competition arose in the property market between accommodation for tourists vis-à-vis that for the resident population.

The urban areas are identified as the principal cities of the regions in which are found the important decision-making centres in the public and private sectors and the headquarters and affiliates of the major industrial and commercial firms. Here are principally concentrated the supply of administrative, financial and commercial services and in these localities we find the universities, important social and health service structures, and cultural and recreation services whose location is also stimulated by the presence of substantial tourism flows. In northern Tuscany (e.g., Florence) the urban areas are the location of important centres of the mechanical industry endowed with a substantial level of technology along with light industry and traditional artisan pursuits. Small artisan shops can be found in the historical centres while the larger concerns are located in the suburban areas and in specifically designated industrial areas in the immediate vicinity. The potential separation of economic activities and social classes concentrated in urban areas is attenuated by the relative dependence of some of these activities – e.g., the export firms and, in general, the firms concerned with commercial and financial services – on manufacturing which is usually more prevalent in the urbanized countryside.

The countryside includes the areas in Tuscany which have been negatively impacted by the effects of the industrialization process. It has provided to light industry a high number of its residents in the form of salaried workers and piecework at home in addition to a significant amount of human capital in the form of non-salaried and small entrepreneurs. As Chapter 9 will discuss, the cultivation of agricultural products has been limited to typical regional produce – such as grapes and olives. The raising of livestock, a typical Tuscan agricultural occupation in the past, has declined considerably, though it still plays an important role especially in the food-processing industry. Even if in the production of wages the local systems remain of primary importance for the resident population, the countryside is heavily dependent on other parts of Tuscany in satisfying its demand for consumer goods. As a consequence, the recurrent changes in population flows toward the 'other Tuscanies' – motivated mostly by educational and employment reasons – continue along with the occasional, temporary shift of people spurred by the used of social–health services, more specialized distribution services, or recreation and cultural activities offered elsewhere.

Organizational dependence on the 'other Tuscanies' does not only involve the countryside. It is also manifested in the exchanges that take place between the urbanized countryside and a few of the urban areas, especially that of Florence, due to the presence of numerous administrative and commercial activities indispensable for the functioning of the light industry operating in the urbanized countryside. The relationship between the urbanized countryside and major urban areas reflects elements of complementarity and conflict that are capable, through time, of modifying the spatial configuration of the region's development pattern to the extent that service activities are concentrated in the urban areas and labour flows to them from the urbanized countryside.

In summary, if the urbanized countryside is the part of Tuscany where we find the highest concentrations of employment in manufacturing, the urban areas represent the Tuscany of services; the tourist–industrial areas manifest their duality in the territorial concentration of industrial and commercial employment, even if the latter often arrives at levels above the

Table 5.1   Location and share of employment in the 'four Tuscanies', 1971

Four Tuscanies	Location quotient			Percentage share		
	Industries	Commerce	Services	Industries	Commerce	Services
Urbanized countryside	1.16	0.81	0.66	49.11	34.45	27.96
Touristic–industrial areas	0.96	1.15	0.89	14.42	17.27	13.37
Urban areas	0.84	1.13	1.45	31.00	41.69	53.74
Countryside	0.96	1.16	0.87	5.47	6.59	4.93

Source: Calculated by the author from ISTAT data.

Note: The location quotient (LQ) is LQ $= (e/E)/(n/N)$, where e and n are local and regional employment levels in individual economic activities; E and N are local and regional total employment levels in all economic activities. The percentage share is related to Tuscany.

Table 5.2   Location and share of manufacturing and other industrial employment in the 'four Tuscanies', 1971

Four Tuscanies	Manufacturing		Other industries	
	Location quotient	Percentage share	Location quotient	Percentage share
Urbanized countryside	1.26	53.31	0.77	32.67
Touristic–industrial areas	0.85	12.77	1.39	20.84
Urban areas	0.83	30.76	0.86	31.95
Countryside	0.55	3.16	2.56	14.54

Source: As Table 5.1.

Note: As Table 5.1.

regional average; finally, the countryside is defined in the last analysis by the commercial activities located there as is illustrated by the data in Tables 5.1 and 5.2.

Contradictions and limitations of the Tuscan model

The advantages in terms of social and economic development produced in Tuscany by the formula of flexible specialization has been amply documented, but it is necessary to recall that the quality of this development is inexorably linked with the urban polycentrism of the urbanized countryside. The geographical distribution of industry and population according to a tight network of small and medium-sized semi-urbanized centres connected by differentiated relationships of employment and residence is confronted by the challenge posed by the formation of large urban agglomerations and by the relative peripheralization of industrial areas that is typical of the process of industrialization based on large, vertically integrated industrial establishments. The latter is visible in the manufacturing poles even if the presence of a single or a few large enterprises limits the demographic dimensions of the residential centres, but it certainly does not eliminate the polarization of residential or social patterns.

The model of socioeconomic territorial development that has affirmed itself in Tuscany is not without its contradictions and limitations. These depend, above all, on the method in which the localized industry reproduces itself and the professional profiles which find employment within the territory in response to the mechanism of industrial expansion and the levels of socioeconomic well-being that the model generates.

With regard to the economic activities, it should be remembered that the services to industry required by the formula of flexible specialization are not entirely produced locally. In fact, there are some that are excluded or seriously ignored by this 'automatic' mechanism of generation, and they are the ones – as, for example, scientific research and initial technical training – that the enterprise system does not succeed in expressing or which one single firm is not able to realize on its own because the major part of the utility produced remains only for a short time as its exclusive property. With the local system there is a great propensity for know-how to escape and be distributed – even with a certain speed – among other firms.

These advanced services, given that they are necessary for the functioning of the localized industries and the maintenance of the level of competitiveness, develop outside of the local systems, and there is a tendency on the part of these advanced services to concentrate their production in the large urban areas. To the extent that they manifest themselves locally, one observes the paradox that a decentralized and rural industrial model leads to a centralized and urban services model. One needs to add that the spontaneous nature of the tendency is also supported and accelerated by the action of public authorities because various regional and local administrations have identified in these service functions the *ubi consistam* in the development of the regional capital or of the corresponding metropolitan area and have elaborated programmes to make them the capitals of 'higher service' activities (Fuà and Zacchia, 1983).

Such an approach represents a typical example of the underutilization of the overall benefits produced by the model of light industrialization discussed above. Focusing on the role of large urban areas as the capitals of service activities runs the risk of seriously compromising the continued viability of the Tuscan model of development which has seen the affirmation of light industry.

What has just been said for services can also be said for the 'new' occupations created in the countryside – even if they remain in small numbers – following the high levels of well-being created by the development of localized industry. Given that the needs to which they respond tend to expand in correspondence with the increase in the level of well-being, one would expect that they would absorb an increasing percentage of the active local labour force. It is towards these jobs that the sons of the workers and small entrepreneurs who pursue higher-level education (upper secondary diplomas or university degrees) point to instead of substituting their parents in productive endeavours. Accordingly, we bear witness to the second paradox involving the valorization of human resources within the productive formula of flexible specialization that operates against the interests of reproducing through generation change the prevalent industrial structure.

Social mobility assumes two basic forms. The first is characterized by various paths of mobility that permit, with a certain ease, the passage of workers across different forms of employment: from salaried work to self-employment and all the way to entrepreneurial activity based on a continual change in location that makes available and accessible new jobs. The second is tied to the provision of higher levels of education on the part of the new generations as a mark of the higher social status achieved by the family. This change in educational base can determine the creation of a workforce whose specialized skills do not find an adequate demand in the local enterprise system; in addition, they are not adequate for the skills and qualities necessary to become the head of a family enterprise. In this manner the increase in the level of education might block, rather than ease, the substitution of parents in productive roles and provide the stimulus to search for alternative forms of employment different from those focused on industry that are normally found outside of the urbanized countryside and in particular in the urban areas.

Nevertheless, the process of generational change in the entrepreneurial class seems to be strongly limited if it depends exclusively on changes within the family group. In reality, things are different, at least in part, because continuity in entrepreneurial roles in localized industries is assured by the salaried workers who become self-employed given that they have the necessary technical skills, managerial capacity and access to sufficient capital to initiate production assisted by commercialization firms which find them their customers.

What we have discussed here calls attention to the exigencies that the industrialization model based on flexible specialization and localized small enterprise systems requires in terms of local public policies, that is, locally differentiated industrial and social policies formulated and managed on a territorial basis and oriented toward the support of diverse types of external economies. If the access to external economies was decisive in the initial phase of development of light industry and found support in the long-term plans of the local authorities who often directly contributed to their development or favoured the private initiative that stimulated their growth, these types of public inputs are even more important during the phase of consolidation. It becomes vitally important if among the objectives of the local authorities there is the goal of blocking the phenomenon of polarization towards urban areas and peripheralization of industry in the urbanized countryside.

In the final analysis, what is necessary is the recognition of the principal lesson to be drawn from the model of light industrialization: the genesis of production does not reside within the enterprises, considered in their individual form or separately within the context of their location, but rather in the local territorial system that the firms constitute together with the working population. A consolidation of the development model that wants to block the dismantling and removal of the obstacles to social reproduction requires the formulation of policies that have as their objective the intervention into the local system in its entirety and oriented not towards the single firm but towards the entire productive system as well as towards the local community.

5.3 The major changes during the 1970s

The consolidation of light industry

The dynamism of light industry, which in the IRPET model sustains the process of industrialization in Tuscany and represents the motor of regional development, moves during the following decade along the lines already experimented and discussed above. If we consider the region according to the division into the 'four Tuscanies', we find that between 1971 and 1981 it is the urbanized countryside which registers the largest amount of growth in jobs in manufacturing followed by the touristic–industrial and urban areas. The effect of this growth is that the urbanized countryside again increases its regional quota of manufacturing jobs and contributes to a further territorial concentration. In contrast, the other areas (such as the countryside) register a decline or at most a stable state in industrial employment (Table 5.3).

In the touristic–industrial areas we find the largest employment growth in commerce, a sign of the expansion of tourist activity that becomes predominant over industrial employment. More generally, the decade consolidates the respective occupational profiles of the 'four Tuscanies' in a manner that the urbanized countryside becomes more than before the Tuscany of industry; the urban areas represent the Tuscany of services and the touristic–industrial areas constitute the Tuscany of commerce; the countryside remains characterized by levels of sectoral employment located around the regional means (Table 5.4).

The consolidation of industrial manufacturing in the urbanized country-side was made possible through the growth of inter-industry relations between firms in typical light industry, firms engaged in the production of capital goods (e.g., the machine industry) and auxiliary industries supplying materials and components in the production process, including specialized services. This phenomenon multiplied the territorial interactions between productive and residential areas rather than sifting it out. The process was also sustained by a local redistribution of population that took place according to the mechanism of gradual adjustment which tended to

Table 5.3 Location and growth of manufacturing employment in the 'four Tuscanies', 1971–81

Four Tuscanies	Location quotient 1981	Employment (percentage share) 1981	1971	Share of job growth 1971–81
Urbanized countryside	1.31	56.65	53.31	32.77
Touristic–industrial areas	0.82	11.78	12.77	9.49
Urban areas	0.77	28.66	30.76	8.87
Countryside	0.56	2.91	3.16	7.53

Source: As Table 5.1.

Note: The location quotient is described at Table 5.1. The share of job growth (SG) is SG = $[(e/81) - (e/71)]/[(E/81) - (E/71)] \times 100$, where e is local employment level in individual economic activity and E is local total employment level in all economic activities; 81 and 71 are the initial and terminal observations, respectively. The percentage share is related to Tuscany.

Table 5.4 Location and growth of employment in the 'four Tuscanies', 1971–81

Four Tuscanies	Location quotient 1981	Employment (percentage share) 1981	1971	Share of job growth 1971–81
Industry				
Urbanized countryside	1.23	53.10	49.11	38.94
Touristic–industrial areas	0.90	12.94	14.42	7.19
Urban areas	0.78	29.19	31.00	11.08
Countryside	0.91	4.77	5.47	3.10
Commerce				
Urbanized countryside	0.82	35.52	34.45	8.92
Touristic–industrial areas	1.30	18.69	17.27	19.87
Urban areas	1.07	39.81	41.69	7.09
Countryside	1.15	5.98	6.59	5.01
Services				
Urbanized countryside	0.75	32.42	27.96	52.13
Touristic–industrial areas	0.96	13.89	13.37	72.93
Urban areas	1.30	48.28	53.74	81.84
Countryside	1.04	5.41	4.93	91.89

Source: As Table 5.1.

Note: As Table 5.3.

bring together within a daily temporal-spatial dimension places of residence and production. The outcome of the transformation was the formation of localized networks of socioeconomic interaction which took place in territorial contexts relatively self-contained where residence and place of work operated to create a sense of self-identity. This explains also the persistence of the industrial geography of the region and the fact that outside of the urbanized countryside new local systems of light industry were not created. There was, instead, the formation of an increasingly precise productive identity on the part of those that already existed, a few among which we can now recognize as having the outlines of 'true and proper' industrial districts.

The industrial districts

The industrial districts are local systems characterized by the active co-participation between a community of persons and small firms specialized in different parts of the production process. Co-participation consists of the process in which the community of persons exercises an autonomous function on the organization of production based on the contents of a common social culture. The system of values and normative orientations is dominated by the spirit of initiative widely shared by the general public as is the case in relation to attitudes toward the principal aspects of life such as employment, consumption, savings and economic uncertainty. Such a widely shared base of common values serves to create a cultural context favourable to economic enterprise; it influences industrial relations and the activities of the local government and administration. The high capacity and availability of individuals and their families to engage in non-salaried activity in its various forms (such as piecework at home, artisanry, small business, self-employment) favours the formation and diffusion of managerial capacity, creativity, pragmatism and ability to act individually and collectively.

On the other hand, the organization of production that is realized through independent small and medium-sized enterprises – more or less coinciding with the single phased production units – and connected by networks of specialized transactions and coordinated by forms of cooperation more or less explicit is made possible by the technical ability to subdivide the productive process, take advantage of the external location economies, and build on internal scale economies. Such a division of labour between firms is the product of an expansion in demand for non-standarized products rather than by the high level of fragmentation in quality and temporal differences. The former permits industry located in the district to manifest a dynamic of adaptability that satisfies needs of elasticity (i.e., *quantitative variation in demand*) and of flexibility (i.e., *qualitative variation in production*) derived from the diffused functional capacity present among the workforce and the specificity of the productive formula.

The organizational ability, capacity to experiment and act practically, creative talent, artisan and technical skills and drive to innovate confer an overall dynamism to the district that represents its strength in international competition. The principal industry in the district − along with the auxiliary industries and the multiplicity of services connected to it − pervades the local environment and provides jobs for virtually all strata in the population: youth, adults and elderly, men and women. The result is a local community dominated by the social figure of the small entrepreneur and non-salaried worker, but it also leaves room in the social hierarchy for the skilled salaried employee. The industry provides a high level of participation for young people and married women while the prevalent family structure is that of the extended family. It is easy to understand why there is a localistic identification on the part of the local community in the district instead of the 'company' as happens in the industrial poles dominated by large industry. Tuscany's industrial districts are found in urbanized countryside along the lower Arno Valley and its tributaries in that part of the region comprising the urban systems of Florence, Pisa and Siena, while only one district is found in the south-east part of Tuscany (Figure 5.2).

These districts register a percentage of regional employment (20.2 per cent) higher than their quota of population (17.2 per cent), and an even greater quota of manufacturing employment (29.5 per cent), which is the equivalent of a coefficient of territorial concentration that is greater than the percentage of manufacturing employment in the region (Table 5.5).

The principal industries in Tuscany's industrial districts are those in fashion (textiles, clothing, tanning, leather goods, shoes) and in furniture (wood furniture) accompanied by secondary industries specialized in the transformation of non-metal minerals, in particular glassware. Other manufacturing, such as the mechanical industries, machines and related items, even though present does not possess a sufficient territorial concentration (Table 5.6) to constitute an industrial district. Nevertheless, its location is reflected in the form of different levels of specialization in a manner similar to what is reflected in the industrial district (Table 5.7).

The transformation of the metropolis

The process of residential and occupational suburbanization manifested in the Florence area has reversed the tendencies of urbanization which were manifest until the end of the 1960s. Movement of manufacturing units and population into the surrounding urbanized countryside has contributed, together with the change in the flows of daily travel for work reasons, to the completion of an interactive network of relations and dualistic flow of traffic between the city and its surrounding territory.

What is involved here is a dynamic common to a large number of urban systems in Italy. In Florence this dynamic is less developed than it is in other urban systems of the north, in particular in the urban systems in the

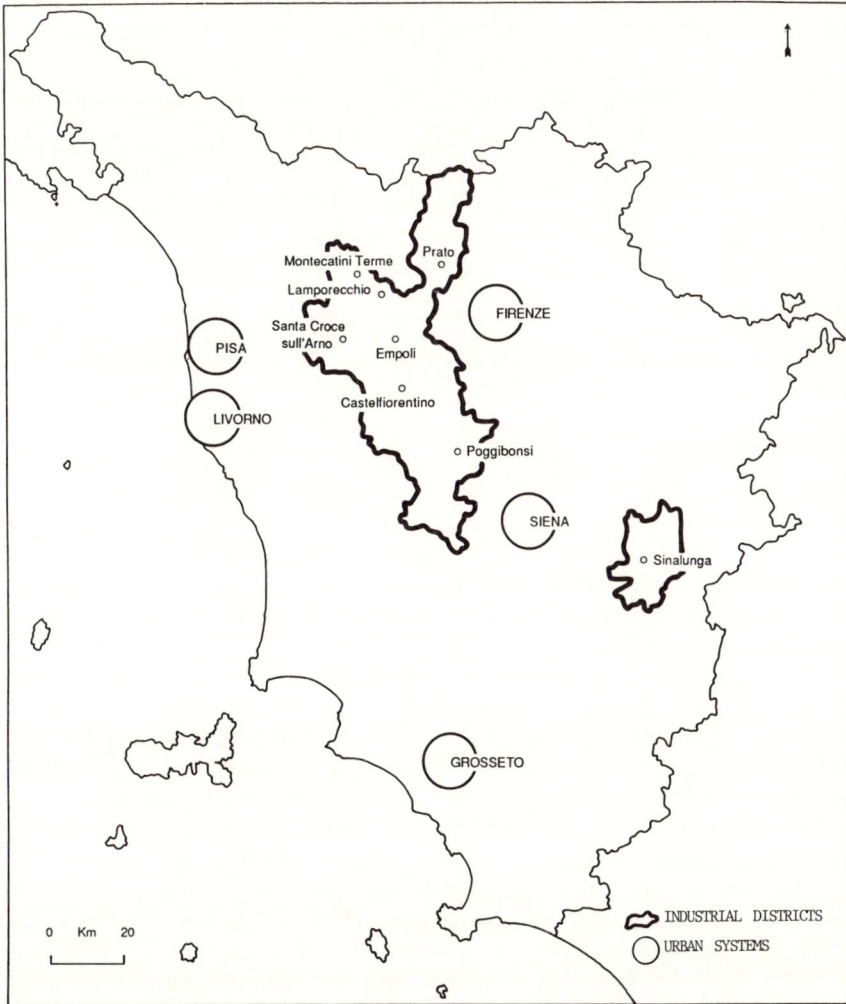

Figure 5.2   The industrial districts, 1981

industrial triangle (Milan, Turin and Genoa). The phenomenon is also characteristic of Bologna's urban system which, in the decade between 1971–1981, passed through a phase of deurbanization. Both population and employment declined in the Bolognese urban system as a whole (Table 5.8).

What has just been highlighted suggests that the Florence area may be transforming itself into a metropolitan area covering the urban system of Florence and the other local systems in central Tuscany. Such a

Table 5.5 Location and growth of employment in the industrial districts, 1981

	Location quotient 1981	Percentage share 1981	Retrospect analysis		
			Location quotient 1971	Percentage share 1971	Share of job growth 1971–81
Industry	1.33	27.00	1.22	24.76	45.44
Commerce	0.77	15.60	0.72	14.66	10.08
Services	0.63	12.69	0.57	11.54	44.49
Manufacturing	1.46	29.52	1.37	27.72	38.32
Employment	–	20.25	–	20.29	–
Population	–	17.20	–	16.32	–

Source: As Table 5.1.

Note: As Table 5.3.

metropolitan area would go from the local system of the upper Valdarno, concentrated on Montevarchi, all the way over to the local system centered on Pistoia (Figure 5.3).

This hypothesis is based on the observation that in localities of light industrialization the metropolitan area tends to transform itself into a 'network of local systems' connected by complex mechanisms of interdependence rather than according to relationships of hierarchical dependence on the part of the various local systems to one principal centre. This phenomenon derives from the fact that each single local system remains strongly marked by its own economic-territorial identity in addition to a sociocultural one, and it is this identity that confers on the metropolitan system a multicentre nature (IRPET, 1986).

The nature of the metropolitan system of central Tuscany superimposes itself but has not succeeded in substituting itself for the structure of local systems which continue to possess a primary identity and role in the explanation of socioeconomic change in the region. In order to understand the relevance of the above, it is necessary to recall the fact that in the metropolitan system of central Tuscany we also find the industrial district of Prato, which certainly does not represent an industrialized periphery; nor is its industry dependent on the services located in the urban system of Florence. On the other hand, it is not surprising that this so-called 'system of local systems' existing around Florence represents a remarkable percentage of the region's entire employment and population (respectively, 38.6 and 35.5 per cent).

If we can no longer reasonably argue that the metropolitan economy dominates each individual local system incorporated into the metropolitan system of central Tuscany and that it has succeeded in suppressing their individual identities, it is possible to draw the implication that such a

Table 5.6 Location and level of employment in the industrial districts, 1981

Industrial districts	Non-metallic mineral products	Chemicals, rubber and plastics	Food products, beverages and tobacco	Textiles	Tanning, leather goods and footwear	Wearing apparel	Furniture and wood products	Paper, printing and publishing	Other manufacturing industries
Location quotient									
Lamporecchio	a	1.06	a	1.04	9.01	a	2.46	1.06	a
Montecatini-Terme	a	a	1.03	a	10.73	1.21	a	1.29	a
Castelfiorentino	1.46	a	a	a	6.36	2.42	1.91	a	a
Empoli	3.55	a	a	a	2.55	4.78	a	a	a
Prato	a	a	a	10.01	a	a	a	a	a
Santa Croce sull'Arno	a	a	a	a	16.83	a	a	a	a
Poggibonsi	3.17	a	a	a	a	a	3.84	a	a
Sinalunga	2.93	a	a	1.43	1.15	1.41	3.83	a	1.45
Employment level*									
Lamporecchio	b	8.94	b	8.91	43.82	b	19.29	5.19	b
Montecatini-Terme	b	b	7.45	b	52.18	9.54	b	6.32	b
Castelfiorentino	8.54	b	b	b	30.96	19.07	14.96	b	b
Empoli	20.81	b	b	b	12.41	37.64	b	b	b
Prato	b	b	b	85.72	b	b	b	b	b
Santa Croce sull'Arno	b	b	b	b	81.86	b	b	b	b
Poggibonsi	18.57	b	b	b	b	b	30.16	b	b
Sinalunga	17.15	b	b	12.27	5.61	11.14	30.10	b	2.47

Source: As Table 5.1.

Note: The location quotient (LQ) is $LQ = (e/E)/(n/N)$, where e and n are local and national employment levels in individual economic activities; E and N are local and national total employment levels in all economic activities.

* Percentage share of industrial employment.
a Location quotient less than 1.
b Employment level is ignored because Location quotient is less than 1.

Table 5.7 Location and specialization of manufacturing employment in the industrial districts, 1981

Industrial districts	Location quotient 1981	Specialization index 1981	District-dominant manufacturing industry 1981
Lamporecchio	1.85	50.27	Tanning, leather goods and footwear
Montecatini-Terme	1.23	55.24	Tanning, leather goods and footwear
Castelfiorentino	1.66	43.48	Tanning, leather goods and footwear
Empoli	1.62	46.43	Wearing apparel
Prato	1.75	85.97	Textiles
Santa Croce sull'Arno	1.78	82.20	Tanning, leather goods and footwear
Poggibonsi	1.56	45.53	Furniture and wood products
Sinalunga	1.46	40.88	Furniture and wood products

Source: As Table 5.1.

Note: As Table 5.6. The specialization index of manufacturing (Sp) is Sp = $\sqrt{[P_1^2 + P_2^2 + P_3^2 + \ldots + P_n^2]}$, where P is the percentage of local total manufacturing employment of each local industry in turn.

transformation is not desirable, and its realization should not become part of public policies.

The structure of the 'metropolitan scheme' of analysis can be usefully used to understand developments relative to the specific relations between economic and social spheres in this part of the region. In a similar manner, it is useful for the formulation of public policies oriented towards the location of infrastructure and activities for the development of the service sector in the prospect of promoting further consolidation of the productive structure of each constituent local system, producing synergies among development activities, and having a generally positive impact on the development of the rest of the region.

5.4   The recent trends

An overall view

At the beginning of the 1990s, Tuscany visibly demonstrates in an accentuated manner the different processes of industrialization that have characterized its spatial mode of development. We still do not have sufficient information to provide a comprehensive overview of the structural changes which have taken place between 1981 and 1991, but what emerges clearly from the initial data shows the break with the past. The long and practically uninterrupted trend of growing industrial employment has come to an end.

Table 5.8 Stages of development in urban areas of selected metropolitan systems, 1971–81

Metropolitan Systems	Employment*			Population*			Stage of development	
	Inner	Outer	Total	Inner	Outer	Total	Employment	Population
Florence	1.04	42.06	13.76	-2.07	16.70	4.54	II3	II4
Turin	-8.62	7.41	-4.30	-4.35	2.38	-2.55	III5	III5
Milan	-11.34	20.10	-4.57	-7.35	13.16	-1.53	III5	III5
Venice	1.49	38.19	9.15	-4.66	15.57	2.64	II3	II4
Bologna	0.59	48.89	16.25	-6.41	11.99	-0.35	II3	III5

Source: As Table 5.1.

Notes:
II3 Suburbanization with relative decentralization.
II4 Suburbanization with absolute decentralization.
III5 Deurbanization with absolute decentralization.
* Percentage share of change 1971–81.

Figure 5.3 The metropolitan system of central Tuscany, 1981

This is a phenomenon present in the entire country. On the basis of provisional data from the 1991 census, the clearest change in the Italian workforce is the one registered in the general decline in industrial jobs and the parallel increase of jobs in commerce and services. The fall in industrial employment does not hit all regions in an equal manner; it is clearly evident in the oldest industrialized areas and regions. It is most evident in the regions of the industrial triangle while the regions with light industry – the Third Italy – register a lower level of decline. Despite the drop in total

Table 5.9 Location and growth of employment in the 'three Italies', 1981–91

	Location quotient 1991	Employment (percentage share)		Share of job growth 1981–91	Location quotient 1981
		1991	1981		
Industries					
Industrial triangle	1.19	38.65	39.96	−171.19	1.16
Third Italy	1.12	39.00	37.85	−33.00	1.09
South	0.68	22.35	22.19	−16.95	0.72
Commerce					
Industrial triangle	0.93	30.22	30.84	52.98	0.89
Third Italy	1.00	34.69	34.82	25.45	1.00
South	1.07	35.09	34.34	21.19	1.12
Services					
Industrial triangle	0.87	28.24	29.79	218.21	0.86
Third Italy	0.90	31.19	30.55	107.55	0.88
South	1.24	40.57	39.66	95.76	1.29

Source: As Table 5.1.

Note: LQ and SG are calculated as noted in Tables 5.3 and 5.6. The percentage share is related to Italy.

Table 5.10 Location and growth of employment in Tuscany, 1981–91

Sector	Location quotient 1991	Employment (percentage share)		Share of job growth 1981–91	Location quotient 1981
		1991	1981		
Industry	1.04	37.20	47.70	−101.33	1.08
Commerce	1.04	24.10	22.01	51.66	0.97
Services	0.94	38.70	30.29	149.67	0.92

Source: As Table 5.1.

Note: As Table 5.9. The percentage share is related to Tuscany.

number of industrial jobs, the regions in the Third Italy increase their overall percentage of national industrial employment, even surpassing that of the industrial triangle (Table 5.9).

Tuscany's performance is in a position between those of the regions in the industrial triangle and the regions of the Third Italy given its dual industrial structure. The region is caught between the manufacturing poles of heavy industry in the touristic–industrial areas and the industrial districts of the urbanized countryside. This combination is unique among the regions with light industry (Table 5.10).

Table 5.11   Location and growth of employment in the 'four Tuscanies', 1981–91

	Location quotient 1991	Employment (percentage share)		Share of job growth 1981–91
		1991	1981	
Industry				
Urbanized countryside	1.29	54.87	53.71	−150.00
Touristic–industrial areas	0.86	11.76	13.21	−532.51
Urban areas	0.75	28.88	28.29	−43.13
Countryside	0.86	4.49	4.79	−142.62
Commerce				
Urbanized countryside	0.87	37.18	35.72	72.81
Touristic–industrial areas	1.30	17.73	18.25	193.79
Urban areas	1.02	39.14	39.84	30.61
Countryside	1.14	5.95	6.19	53.30
Services				
Urbanized countryside	0.80	34.20	32.74	177.19
Touristic–industrial areas	0.95	12.93	13.43	438.72
Urban areas	1.23	47.46	48.51	112.51
Countryside	1.04	5.41	5.32	189.32

Source: As Table 5.1.

Note: As Table 5.3.

The fall in industrial jobs in the decade between 1981 and 1991 takes place in each of the 'four Tuscanies', even if with different tendencies and, above all, with different results in each of the single economic structures (Table 5.11). The urbanized countryside experiences a fall in industrial employment much higher than that in the urban areas but small vis-à-vis the rural areas. The areas worst hit by the fall in industrial jobs are the touristic–industrial zones along the coast. The consequences of this pattern are that the quota of the industrial workforce present in the urbanized countryside and, to a lesser extent, present in the urban areas increases; it declines very little in the rural areas while it drops considerably in the touristic–industrial areas. The latter continue to register a relative decline that had already manifested itself in the previous decade, 1971–81, in the number and percentage of industrial jobs vis-à-vis the regional mean. Its coefficient of industrial workforce is now equivalent to that of the rural areas.

On the other hand, the touristic–industrial areas register the highest increase in employment in commerce and transform themselves into the areas with the highest percentage commercial employment in the region. Even in services, these areas register the highest concentration in the region, though the comparisons with other areas in Tuscany do not reflect large differences. Service employment also increases in a sustained manner in all of the other areas in Tuscany. The short-term impact on the trend in

Table 5.12 Location and growth of employment in the industrial districts, 1981–91

	Location quotient 1991	Employment (percentage share)		Share of job growth 1981–91
		1991	1981	
Industry	1.39	27.03	27.30	−436.71
Commerce	0.85	16.46	15.77	157.68
Services	0.72	14.06	13.00	379.03
Manufacturing	–	–	–	–
Employment	–	19.46	20.43	–
Population	–	17.90	17.20	–

Source: As Table 5.1.

Note: As Table 5.3.

industrial employment is the drastic reduction in the industrial component in employment in favour of the tertiary sector, and the traditional duality of coastal Tuscany – large industrial firms on one side and tourism on the other – has seen the rising supremacy of the latter. Large manufacturing poles in Tuscany and elsewhere in the country have undergone a strong process of deindustrialization.

The urbanized countryside has increased its overall concentration of industrial jobs in such a manner that, despite the shift to services, an important industrial occupational component has been maintained. Thus, in 1991 the areas of the urbanised countryside contained a concentration of both industrial and commerce/service jobs above the regional means.

The industrial districts demonstrate an accentuation of the phenomena already observed in the urbanized countryside as a whole. Both the negative growth in industry and positive growth in commerce and services demonstrate a greater dynamism, and what seems to have most characterized the decade is the process of shift to services. The percentage of industrial employment remains unchanged between 1981 and 1991, but it increases in relation to the regional mean while employment in commerce and services increases from every point of view (Table 5.12).

The phenomenon of diffused tertiarization, subject to different types of interpretations depending on where it takes place, explains the lack of evolution in the metropolitan system of central Tuscany. The urban areas reduce their own percentage of occupation in commerce and services while industrial employment remains unchanged, but the percentage decreases in relation to the regional mean in a manner that reduces its specific characteristic as the focus of service employment. This phenomenon is very evident among the local systems in the metropolitan system of central Tuscany if we compare what has taken place in the principal urban system (that of Florence) and the others. The increase in commercial and service

Table 5.13 Location and growth of employment in the metropolitan system of central Tuscany, 1981–91

	Location quotient 1991	Employment (percentage share)		Share of job growth 1981–91	Location quotient 1981
		1991	1981		
Metropolitan system					
Industry	1.03	40.77	39.33	−61.31	1.02
Commerce	0.93	36.89	36.01	41.07	0.93
Services	1.02	40.40	39.70	120.24	1.03
Urban area (Florence)					
Industry	0.84	20.24	18.97	−28.45	0.84
Commerce	1.00	24.05	23.63	31.04	1.05
Services	1.15	27.57	27.19	97.40	1.21
Other local systems					
Industry	1.31	20.53	20.36	−227.34	1.25
Commerce	0.82	12.84	12.38	91.72	0.76
Services	0.82	12.83	12.52	235.61	0.77

*Source:*As Table 5.1.

Note: As Table 5.3.

sector jobs has proceeded in a sustained manner, but even more so in the local systems that constitute the other parts of the metropolitan system (Table 5.13).

The changes in employment during the 1980s offer a number of points for discussion in the interpretation of the Tuscany development model. One of these is the evaluation of the capacity of the IRPET model to explain what has taken place in the industrial districts in the urbanized countryside – that is, in the shift to services that appears to be the 'fundamental element' in their recent evolution.

The shift to services taking place in Tuscany touches a fundamental aspect of development that is linked to the other changes: the so-called deindustrialization, the change in industrial employment in the urbanized countryside and touristic–industrial areas rather than in urban systems, the transformation of the industrial districts and urban systems. If we separate the process from the place, it is more difficult to understand both aspects – that is, the nature of the processes as well as in the transformation of the sites where development is present.

The shift to services in the industrial districts

The principal explanation of the shift to services in the industrial districts has to be sought in the mechanism of firm proliferation that is at the base of the productive formula of flexible specialization that distinguishes localized industry. The interpretive model of light industrialization is based on the idea that the increased demand for goods produced by typical Tuscan industry and the expansion of production do not take place through an increase in the size of industries or exploitation of internal economies of scale; it takes place, instead, through a proliferation of small and medium-sized productive units through a specialization in production by phases, products and parts of products internal to the sector – i.e., by taking advantage of external organizational economies.

The proliferation of firms is made possible by the characteristic of the 'fragmentary and variable' nature of demand for goods produced by localized industry found in the industrial districts and by the characteristics of the local labour market that permit the nucleus of specialized manufacturing industries a considerable level of the vertical and horizontal disintegration of the productive processes. Small firms are fundamental to the process in that productive phases and operations can be technically separated from the process of transformation and delegated to producers (small firms and non-salaried workers) external to the enterprise.

The evolution of productive phases, i.e., the location of firms specialized in productive phases, takes place under conditions of spatial proximity within a contiguous and relatively restricted territory. The spatial proximity of specialized phase firms is necessary for the recomposition of the productive process given that the determination of whether the phases can take place close or far away depends on the exigencies of production – i.e., if the nature of the product needs a constant supervision of the details – required by a product (e.g., if it requires a frequent variation of its characteristics) and by the rapidity with which the order has to be delivered to the client. The efficiency of the productive formula is the combined result of the methods of production, design, collection of orders and distribution of the final products. The commercialization network uses the input of commercial agents and independent intermediaries in addition to shippers who provide a specialized understanding of the market as well as additional capital.

In any case, both in the initial stage of the firm proliferation process as well as that of consolidation forces for territorial agglomeration predominate.[1] This depends on the fact that the productive system has to develop through the formation of a common base of skilled workers, the growth of auxiliary industries capable of responding to the specific needs of the dominant product line and development of habits that favour the exchange of ideas between producers which combine to form a common local conscience. Only when the process has proceeded sufficiently far is it reasonable for an inverse tendency to emerge moving functions outside of the district. De-agglomeration can assume the connotations of a relative dispersion in the territory of a few functions which are often the least important ones for the production process, are the most easily standardized, or require a particular ability not commonly present internal to the district. Internal restructuring through the expulsion of functions can take place in a manner in which the district expands by increasing its territorial allocation of productive units and employment to other local systems in the region, the country or the rest of the world. De-agglomeration also takes place when the district is still growing. In this version de-agglomeration represents a reaction to negative factors located within it.

The basic causes of externalization are to be found in the emergence through time of external diseconomies. Increased labour costs, high value of land, urban saturation and high levels of pollution represent some of these external diseconomies. As a consequence, phases of the productive process concerned with the physical transformation of the product more easily adapted to standardization or conducted elsewhere can be effectively transferred outside of the district. It is possible to affirm that these can be transferred elsewhere because they lose their local specificity, and there is no longer an advantage in being located in the district. As a consequence, the producing firm can seek cost advantages in the production of standardized products or process – i.e., where the crucial input is not the quality of the manual input – through the use of machines. The cost of transportation in bringing the manufactured goods to market is more than compensated by the cost of labour inside and outside of the district.

On the other hand, there are other phases given their increased importance – such as the design of the model and commercialization of the product – which might not find an adequate response within the district. Obstacles to their expansion can be traced to the sociocultural attitudes of the population as well as to the role of these phases in the production process. If this were the case, they would tend to emigrate from the district and relocate themselves in urban systems or be carried out by firms and individuals operating within them. These urban service firms are in a better position to produce services – such as the commercialization of products among retail and wholesale and specialized and generic firms – tied to the promotion of publicity than are their counterparts in the districts because the city is a larger place for the exchange of ideas and information. It is also more easily accessed from the outside by buyers as well as by general visitors.

If among the phases that tend to relocate on the outside of the industrial district there is a prevalence of design and commercialization rather than production, in the long run we would expect to see a progressive peripheralization of the district and, following certain lines of urban growth, even its metropolitanization. A large part of the shift to services in the industrial district, therefore, is generated by the same mechanism that is at the base of its growth and is explained by the model of light industrialization.

Analyses of the kinds of commercial and productive services which have been developed during the course of the 1980s are not possible with the statistics we have available at the present time. Nevertheless, the provisional results related to the Prato textile district indicate that there has been a doubling of services to firms in terms of the percentage of workforce employed (from 3.2 to 7.3 per cent), while commercial intermediation has also doubled (from 1.7 to 3.4 per cent). In the services-to-firms category, the major increases have been registered in management consultancies (from 0.7 to 11.2 for each 1,000 workers) and data processing services (from 2.8 to 10.7 per thousand). It is useful to remember that in 1981 commercial intermediaries operating in the sector of typical Tuscan products (textiles, including raw materials and semi-processed goods; clothes; shoes; and leather goods) represented a ratio of 9.5 workers per thousand employed in the Prato textile district which was more than half (4.4 per thousand) of those employed in the urban system of Florence. Similar situations are found in services provided to industry; the quantitative difference between industrial-district and urban systems is not sufficient to support the thesis of the supremacy of the city over the district. One can reasonably conclude that the increase in service functions has also been motivated by the relocation of some manufacturing phases outside the district.

The increase in employment in the service sector represents, therefore, a manifestation of the indirect and increasingly complex means by which production is undertaken. Manufacturing and the distribution of finished products take place between firms that employ productive relations extending outside of the district. This translates itself in a greater opening of the district to the outside world and bringing into the productive process other districts, regions, countries and continents and different economic sectors. The coordination of such a complex set of activities creates new demands for increasingly diversified and specialized services. A few of these services may even seem trivial, but their location inside the district rather than in single local systems increases the potential in creating external organizational economies.

However, there is another explanation of what underlies the shift to services of industrial districts in the urbanized countryside. It is tied to the increase in well-being of the population. The general increase in well-being of the local community gives support to economic activities that respond to 'new' needs, and the tendency is to increase the amount and variety of services in proportion to the wealth of the population. Given that these new service activities do not derive their immediate impulse from technological or organizational innovation and in many cases they represent labour-intensive processes, their increased presence on the local market is realized above all through increases in employment.

The shift to services of the industrial districts is in contrast to the hypothesis of metropolitan development formulated in Tuscany during the 1980s; in general, the idea was that the productive relations between the major urban systems and industrial districts in the urbanized countryside should have evolved in the direction of a territorial division of functions, thereby reserving service activities to the city and the manufacturing ones to the district. A closer look at this argument reflects a basic rejection of the Tuscan formula of flexible specialization because it establishes a 'ceiling of development' on districts due to the proposed inability of the districts to generate additional service functions capable of meeting the needs of the manufacturing firms, other than that of the commercialization of their products.

The deindustrialization of the manufacturing poles

In light of what has been stated above, the trend of deindustrialization does not function well in explaining the decline of manufacturing jobs in the local systems located in the urbanized countryside nor in the industrial districts which represent its productive focus and more dynamic element. We are not trying to affirm that all of the industrial districts find themselves in the same situation in terms of development. This can be categorically excluded. Many differences exist between the various districts given that they are characterized by different industries and lines of production, and the existence of different levels of industrial specialization reinforces the differentiation in response to external economic shocks such as a decline in consumer demand. The result is that the process of shift to services does not present itself within all industrial districts at the same level and intensity, even if it is implicit in their mechanism of internal regeneration.

Deindustrialization, interpreted as a progressive reduction in the guiding role of the principal industry in the development of the local economy through an extensive and systematic disinvestment in its productive capacity, is in a much better position to explain the fall of employment in the manufacturing poles in the touristic–industrial areas than elsewhere. Here, the collapse of primary industry – the vertically integrated large plants – has the effect of a progressive destruction of the local productive and social fabric. In these areas there is a lack of alternative forms of employment for a population of salaried workers with few technical skills – given the Fordist-Taylorist organization of the plant – and accustomed to moving between different jobs inside the factory and temporary unemployment (cassa integrazione) rather than finding jobs in different firms. Thus, even if disinvestment in the 'old' industry were motivated by a reallocation of capital toward 'new' industries located in the same local system, the workers who lose their jobs would rarely have the opportunity to find a new job in an alternative industry. What is more likely is that the manufacturing pole is abandoned and the capital reallocated elsewhere, usually in geographic areas that permit a new process of industrialization on the basis of lower salaries and a lower propensity toward unionization.

The social costs of deindustrialization through the closing of industrial factors and the transfer of capital elsewhere have a permanent impact on the workers and their families. Individual families as well as the local community undergo a significant loss of purchasing power. But there are also costs for the national economy. In addition to wasting human capital, the state is forced to collect less in taxes while at the same time being obliged to transfer more scarce resources to the local community in terms of unemployment compensation and other types of social support for the unemployed.

The shift to services undergone by Tuscany in its manufacturing poles cannot be interpreted as a sign of post-industrial vitality. If that were the case, we would be able to identify the new professional and technical skills and occupations using theoretical understanding and scientific know-how as the basis for innovation or how the provision of services has become dominant over manufacturing. Such an alternative is only possible if, after all, a post-industrial society really exists and is not merely a more complex form of a developed industrialized society.

Even when the phenomenon of deindustrialization relates to local systems that are poles of manufacturing development, it is legitimate to express doubt on whether the decline in industrial employment needs, by necessity, to imply the reduction in the size, productivity and competitiveness of local industry. In some industrial poles in Tuscany, as seems to be the case in the local system of Piombino and its steel industry, the loss of jobs reflects the impact of innovation aimed at the acquisition of efficiency through the reduction of employment. Such processes are part of industrial policies aimed at the modernization of production facilities, reorganization of the productive cycle, and the introduction of technological innovation to which are attributed the growing difference between growth of productivity and decline in employment.

The actions that can be carried out by the local government to block the process of deindustrialization of a manufacturing pole are minimal, in that it has a low level of input and, therefore, little sway over the local economic system. This is true even if the process of deindustrialization is relatively long and the signs of crisis clear enough to enable the government to develop alternative economic policies and productive investments capable of creating new economic capacity and employment before the local community finds itself in an irreversible and catastrophic situation. But when the process of deindustrialization reaches an advanced stage, generic appeals for a process of reindustrialization are not sufficient in facing the problem of a loss of jobs in industry and high levels of unemployment without investments in education through local programmes of vocational and higher education.

5.5 Conclusions

According to the interpretation that has been presented in this chapter, the changes that have taken place between 1981 and 1991 have accentuated the differences in development between the 'four Tuscanies'. On the outskirts of the touristic–industrial areas, there is a growing affirmation of the industrial districts of the urbanized countryside in relation to the other Tuscanies, including the urban systems and a marginalization of the countryside.

In a national overview, the general fall in industrial employment in Italy has created a more territorially concentrated industrialization than was the case ten years ago. In the local systems of light industry existing in Tuscany and the Third Italy, industry is more territorially concentrated in the urbanized countryside, in particular in the industrial districts. This involves a relative phenomenon that still has to attract the attention of analysts and public and private decision-makers. In a similar vein, the fall in industrial employment is not necessarily directly connected with the rise of service employment.

If it is true that these changes correspond to a development process contained in the interpretative model of light industrialization, it should also be said that the present conditions of national and international development are different from those of twenty years ago. Italy has a much higher level of public debt, and the economy has undergone a rapid opening and internationalization. The consequences are that the shift to services of the districts requires at the present time an active contribution from local industrial and social policies and not a renunciation to intervene. The districts have demonstrated their ability to fend for themselves in an era of global changes by creatively interpreting the tendencies of development, but nevertheless local changes have not been without negative ramifications. If the relocation of manufacturing activities outside the district are misinterpreted as a sign of 'modernization' and public policies insist on favouring the trend, public policies run the risk of destroying the skills and activities that characterize the district. All that would be achieved is a Pyrrhic victory.

What is necessary at this point is a thoughtful policy reflecting a combined goal of reinforcing productive capacity and the maintenance of local consumption levels through an efficient use of the human capital available locally. Local entrepreneurship has to be favoured rather than discouraged, and it should be able to make use of the local service networks, services to industry, vocational education, laboratories of scientific and technological research aimed at increasing the knowledge base of individuals and the community.

In Tuscany the urban systems remain 'the dark object of desire' of regional development. The hope is that they can become the motor of development, but on the whole the motor is still in mothballs. As we have seen, this role is still being carried out by the urbanized countryside and the industrial districts. Excluding Florence, the service sector is a local one, and in general it has very little global or metropolitan in its content. It should be recognized that the role of urban systems in relation to Tuscan development does not pass exclusively through local metropolitan relations based on a growing interdependence between local urban and manu- facturing systems; instead, it depends on the capacity of single urban systems to develop global, service metropolitan functions. These are such when they belong to a national and international network capable of directly accessing global exchange networks. Under this light, in Tuscany only the urban system of Florence presents itself in a similar manner on the basis of its cultural function. On this basis, it is possible to move on to the search for competitive advantages. The artistic and cultural patrimony and the scientific research and university centres – along with other activities such as publishing houses – which are present in the major urban centres in Tuscany (Florence, Siena and Pisa) need to be considered assets to be used as an economic resources in competition with other urban systems in

Italy and the world through the stimulation of local entrepreneurial initiatives or attracting them from abroad.[2] In fact, it is not a matter of taking advantage through the development of local services of the past and the tradition of diffused light industry but to become competitive at the international level. Individual economic-territorial entities endowed with their own development capacity can face the competition from other urban systems whose activity is characterized by the processing of information and promoting the exchange and diffusion of know-how.

The objectives of regional and local planning should no longer be the goal of integrating on a socioeconomic and territorial basis the four 'different Tuscanies' but rather to contribute to a better development of the characteristics that each enjoys in the cases of both local development systems as well as those concerning local systems in decline. This can only be done through the formulation and implementation of public policies designed to safeguard the interests of the individual local communities and by making maximum use of the available human capital.

Notes

1. As we have already affirmed above, for Tuscany this stage of development manifested itself during the 1970s.
2. See the chapter by Floridia on the economic potential of the region's artistic-cultural patrimony.

Bibliography

Fuà, G. and Zacchia, C. (eds.), *Industrializzazione senza fratture*, Bologna, Il Mulino, 1983.

IRES-Toscana, *Toscana che cambia. Economia e società nella Toscana degli anni '80*, Milan, Angeli, 1988.

IRPET, *Lo sviluppo economico della Toscana: un'ipotesi di lavoro*, Florence, Il Ponte, 1969.

—— *Lo sviluppo economico della Toscana con particolare riguardo all'industrializzazione leggera*, ed. G. Becattini, Florence, Guaraldi, 1975.

—— *Mutamento economico e trasformazioni urbane nei sistemi metropolitani medi in Europa*, International seminar, Florence, 18–19 December 1986.

—— *Materiali per un'interpretazione dello sviluppo economico della Toscana*, eds. A. Falorni and F. Sforzi, Florence, 1989.

ISTAT, *5° Censimento generale dell'industria e del commercio*, Rome, 25 October 1971.

—— *6° Censimento generale dell'industria, del commercio, dei servizi e dell'artigianato*, Rome, 26 October 1981.

—— *6° Censimento generale dell'industria, del commercio, dei servizi e dell'artigianato*, Provisional results, Rome, 26 October 1981.

—— *7° Censimento generale dell'industria e dei servizi*, Provisional results, Rome, 21 October 1991.

—— *11° Censimento generale delle popolazione*, Rome, 24 October 1971.

—— *12° Censimento generale delle popolazione*, Rome, 25 October 1981.

—— *13° Censimento generale delle popolazione e delle abitazioni*, 20 October 1991.

Mori, G. (ed.), *La Toscana, Storia d'Italia-Le regioni dall'Unità a oggi*, Torino, Einaudi, 1986.

Regione Toscana, *Processo di urbanizzazione nell'area Firenze–Prato–Pistoia*, Florence, La casa Usher, 1984.

6 Case study I: Prato and its evolution in a European context

Gabi Dei Ottati

6.1 Prato before the war

Before the Second World War Prato was already an important manufacturing centre. It was well known in Italy and abroad as the 'city of rags'.[1] The buying and selling of rags was an important activity. Prato was also specialized in the transformation of rags into regenerated wool for the production of textiles. Thus, the commerce in rags and their transformation into a raw material for textile produce represented an important basis of Prato's economy and, more in general, of its society. It is sufficient to note that by the end of the 1930s 90 per cent of the rags collected in Italy (estimated to be between 120,000 and 130,000 tons) and of those imported from abroad in great quantities – especially by Prato raw materials dealers and woollen mills – were concentrated in Prato.

Rags were first sorted and classified – that is, subdivided by quality and colour by particularly skilled workers – and then transformed through various processes (carbonizing bath, battened, washed and combed) into regenerated fibres. A good part of these fibres were then exported, while the rest were utilized in the local textile industry (Tamburini, 1945, pp. 26–7).

The textile industry, which in Prato had a long and illustrious history going back to the Middle Ages,[2] was the other typical local industry; from the mid-1800s Prato's textile manufacturing was tied to the transformation of the rags utilized as the principal raw material for the production of woollen fabrics.[3]

Prato was not only characterized by a diffused presence of the buying, selling and transformation of rags and by the textile industry proper (different from the point of view of both the technology and of the skills involved) but tied together by a symbiotic relationship. It also had a sort of 'double circuit' productive structure (Mori, 1988, p. 1471). The first circuit was represented by a few complete cycle woollen mills and the second consisted of a large number of small enterprises specialized by phases and functions.

Before the war there were about thirty complete-cycle woollen factories which integrated internally all of the production phases (the wool underwent all of the phases of manufacturing from sorting and cleaning to spinning and finishing) in addition to the functions of buying the raw materials, designing and selling the final product (Tamburini, 1945, p. 25). Inside these factories were concentrated the major part of the textile workforce in addition to the carding and combing spindles and mechanical looms present in the Prato area. Moreover, the products of these factories (tartan rugs, shawls and blankets made of woollen, cotton and mixed fibres and ordinary cloth in grey and khaki wool flannel) were standardized and mostly exported to India, China and South Africa (Tamburini, 1945, pp. 27–8), countries in which these products were well received and where the competition came from other mills in Prato. To understand the importance of these exports, one should consider that at the end of the 1930s, the export from Prato's factories (derived mostly from complete-cycle wool mills) accounted for over 30 per cent of the total value of Italian wool exports or 100 out of the 321 million lire worth of wool products exported from the country (Tamburini, 1945, p. 28).

Next to and around the complete cycle wool factories were located hundreds of small enterprises specialized in the trading, classification and other phases of the rag transformation process producing regenerated raw materials as well as a few medium and a lot of small (and even very small) enterprises specialized in phases of production (finishing, dyeing, spinning, warping and weaving) working as subcontractors for the incomplete-cycle woollen factories and above all for the *impannatori*. The *impannatore* is a typical figure of Prato's local industry. He is a sort of pure entrepreneur who buys the raw material for textiles; he has the material transformed by specialized local firms through the various phases of manufacturing based on his own design; and he sells the final product on the open market or in response to orders from buyers (Marchi, 1962, p. 156). These small firms (specialized in production and marketing) were tied by a relation of complementarity and made mostly coloured fabrics destined for the female garment industry which, for the most part, were sold on the Italian market (Tamburini, 1945, p. 25).

Even though the number varied over time, the large number of specialized small firms were distinguished from vertically integrated mills not only by a different organizational structure, but also from the point of view of the goods produced and the markets supplied. However, despite the persistence of the population of small specialized firms, the technological, commercial and (above all) cultural importance of the model of the 'modern', vertically integrated enterprise made the system of small, independent firms and self-employed *impannatori* appear to be residual in nature or at least subordinate to the complete-cycle woollen factories.

6.2 During the war

During the second half of the 1930s Prato's industrial base grew in a consistent manner to the point of becoming one of the three principal wool centres in Italy along with Biella in Piedmont and Vicenza in Veneto. In

1935 there were about 4,300 mechanical looms in Prato compared to 7,150 in Biella and 3,100 in Vicenza (Tamburini, 1945, p. 23). Up until 1938 the woollen factories exported to their traditional overseas markets. With the advent of the war, these external markets were substituted by internal, military orders. Even the small firms and *impannatori* increased in number due to the effects of the autarkic policy which reduced the importation of raw materials as well as the ability to evade the 'corporate' controls imposed by the fascist regime (Balestri, 1990).

The expansion of the Prato textile industry did not cease even when the country went to war. The new situation clearly favoured the larger factories which could negiotiate directly with the central authorities for military contracts and the supply of raw materials. Nevertheless, in order to allow part of the small enterprises and independent *impannatori* system to survive, an alternative system was created comprising so-called 'affiliated contracts' permitting groups of firms/*impannatori* to participate in the supply of products for the War Ministry (Marchi, 1962, p. 169). This state of affairs continued until the autumn of 1943 when the Germans occupying Prato announced the closure of 227 textile firms employing approximately 6,000 workers. The Germans decided to concentrate production in the remaining factories (for the most part the larger ones incorporating complete production cycles) in order to facilitate production (Palla, 1990). The German decision represented a threat to local industry and Prato's way of life. This decision – along with the initiation of Allied bombings and the disappearance of raw materials – served to slow down production significantly and finally brought it to a halt. The general strike of March 1944 elicited a fierce German response which concentrated on the indiscriminate rounding-up of residents and their deportation to Germany. Thereafter until liberation took place in September, the principal objective of the population (both workers as well as the owners of small and large firms) was to survive. In these circumstance, survival meant hiding all the machines and raw materials that could possibly be moved. Saving these resources along with the skills tied to the textile industry guaranteed the possibility of resuming production and traditional economic pursuits after the war. The major damage inflicted by the war on the local economy and society took place during the period of the German occupation, from the autumn of 1943 until the Allies reached Prato in September 1944.

Despite the brevity of the period, the damage inflicted on Prato and its industry by the war were substantial, especially in comparison to what happened to the textile plants in northern Italy. In fact, Allied bombing and German sabotage made inoperative a large part of the communications infrastructure: a part of the railway line to Bologna and the highway to the sea were destroyed; all of the bridges on the highway to the sea and those on the Bisenzio river were also rendered impassable. Even the aqueduct and the electricity distribution system were severely compromised (Tinacci Mossello 1990). In addition, about 30 per cent of residential property and a significant part of industrial property was damaged and contemporary estimates were that one-third of the industrial machinery installed in the

Prato area was equally damaged during the war and its aftermath (Tamburini, 1945, p. 36; Giovannelli, 1983, pp. 72–3).

6.3   From reconstruction to the 'making of millions'

Despite, or maybe even because of, the extent of wartime damage, as soon as the Germans left the people of Prato set out frenetically to take their machines, raw materials, and finished products out of hiding; to repair damaged equipment; to reconstruct the buildings and bridges damaged by the war; and to reopen the roads and means of communication. In the textile industry the first to start up were the *impannatori* and the specialized small firms which found it easier during the war to hide their raw materials and machines. For the small firms it was also easier to evade, in turn, the administrative controls imposed by the Allies on the trade of both textile products and raw materials. Even the large woollen mills – despite the fact that twenty-nine of these were used to house Allied troops (Giovannelli, 1983, p. 98) – immediately started to prepare their return to production. Where possible, and with the help of the workers, the damage was repaired; new machines were installed, a part of which were purchased locally in the textile machine manufacturing industries.[4] Above all, commercial and administrative ties were re-established for the sale of finished products and the buying of raw materials. Thus, by the end of 1945, a year after the arrival of the Allies, the overall production capacity of the Prato textile industry had returned to more or less what it had been before the war (Giovannelli, 1983, pp. 102 and 104). This initial impulse in the postwar period did not exhaust itself after 1945; instead, the external conditions in the structure of demand for Prato's products improved.

The first opportunity to expand industrial activities in Prato was provided by an enormous demand for textiles which could not be satisfied by either national or even international productive capacity. To the demand from the internal market where the local population needed to replace clothes worn-out and never renewed during the war years was added the fact that for eight months Prato remained the only wool manufacturing centre in liberated Italy. In addition, even after the liberation of the entire country, the shortage of virgin wool gave the Prato area an advantage. It had the capacity to produce from rags the raw materials and the fabrics that were valid substitutes for wool.

The possibility of exporting finished goods was also significant when taking into consideration that the war had destroyed a good part of Europe's textile industry. Beginning in 1945, the Prato woollen factories started to export again to South Africa using the clearing system – that is, exchanging finished goods for raw wool and rags.[5]

The second external condition that permitted Prato's large mill owners to make significant profits was the decision taken by the Italian government in 1946 to permit entrepreneurs to use at their discretion 50 per cent of their export earnings. This disposition made both possible and very profitable the trade in raw materials which were difficult to obtain locally and, above all, were traded in foreign currencies. In fact, the official exchange rate was significantly lower than the rates available in the open market. In the case of the US dollar, for instance, the market rate was at times as much as 50 per cent higher than the official rate (De Cecco, 1974).

A third opportunity for development put to use by the Prato entrepreneurs was the Allied foreign aid programme: UNRRA (United Nations Relief and Rehabilitation Administration) which was set up to promote economic recovery in Europe. Under the programme Italy was allowed to import raw materials under favourable conditions which Italian firms could then transform into finished products. The Prato woollen manufacturers were successful in obtaining important UNRRA orders in the textile field, thereby guaranteeing the supply of cheap wool and rags and the sale of their products in the period between the end of 1946 and the beginning of 1949 (UNRRA, 1947; UIP, 1948–9, p. 14). Thus, within about two years, the woollen industry in Prato was able to double its workforce and stock of machinery (see Tables 6.1 and 6.2). Numbers employed in the textile industry went from about 10,000 in 1945 to almost 22,000 in 1948 (Giovannelli, 1983, pp. 104 and 124; Marchi, 1962, pp. 173–4).

More than the overall dimensions of the development, what is of concern here is its impact on the local productive structure which, as we have already seen, before the war was characterized by two distinct organizational models. The limited number of complete-cycle firms – even though they could not resume production until some months after liberation due to the war damage and the need to house Allied troops – were quickly able to return to a dominant position in the Prato economy in relation to the machinery and workforce employed, at least according to the available data.[6] The resumption of exports, the government's foreign exchange policy and the UNRRA orders had, in fact, prevalently if not exclusively gone in favour of the complete-cycle larger mills.

The high level of internal demand for textiles combined with the involvement of the large factories in production for the export market and UNRRA served to leave space for the *impannatori* and the small enterprises specialized in the various production phases. In fact, the number of small operators began to increase. Even if the statistical data on micro enterprises are understandably scarce and fragmentary, a scrutiny of various sources from that period (proceedings of City Council meetings, registration of firms with the local Chamber of Commerce, local press reports, licences issued by the local government for setting up equipment) makes it possible to affirm that their increase was indeed exceptional. The demand for cloth was so strong that whoever was able to produce it, or even to supply it, could make money. Thus, many started a new business either as an *impannatore* or as a phase subcontractor,[7] thereby giving rise to a general ability 'to make millions' (*L'Impannatore*, 11 May 1947). In addition, due to the scarcity of wool already mentioned above, the firms specialized in various activities concerning the transformation of rags into regenerated fibres multiplied. From before the war this activity was conducted by

Table 6.1 Territorial distribution of wool spinning machines in Italy (numbers of Carding spindles, 1938–63)

Year	Piedmont/ Liguria	%	Lombardy/ Emilia	%	Three Veneto	%
1938[1]	–		–		–	
1945[1]	–		–		–	
1949[2]	357,179	45	56,846	7	89,636	11
1953[3]	388,588	44	55,165	6	82,733	10
1957[4]	347,910	41	45,260	5	81,866	10
1963[4]	293,374	32	38,671	4	60,209	7

Year	Tuscany*	%	Other Regions	%	Total	%
1938[1]	118,500	19	–		630,000	100
1945[1]	114,685	16	–		700,000	100
1949[2]	243,789	30	52,550	7	800,000	100
1953[3]	290,000	33	59,200	7	875,686	100
1957[4]	320,000	37	60,127	7	855,166	100
1963[4]	470,567	51	52,592	6	915,413	100

Sources: [1]UIP, 1955, p. 15; [2]UIP, 1953, p. 10; [3]Barbieri, 1957, p. 38; [4]UIP, 1967, p. II.

Note: * Almost all in the Prato district.

Table 6.2 Territorial distribution of wool spinning machines in Italy (number of combing spindles, 1938–63)

Year	Piedmont/ Liguria	%	Lombardy/ Emilia	%	Three Veneto	%
1938[1]	–		–		–	
1949[2]	465,454	62	77,226	10	183,280	24
1953[3]	476,547	62	84,274	11	173,508	22
1957[4]	373,034	55	75,882	11	167,944	25
1963[5]	434,077	57	69,112	9	146,370	19

Year	Tuscany**	%	Other Regions	%	Total	%
1938[1]	4,000*	0.6	–		650,000	100
1949[2]	23,620	3	6,100	1	755,680	100
1953[3]	33,212	4	1,354	1	768,895	100
1957[4]	36,816	6	22,178	3	675,854	100
1963[5]	79,252	11	28,252	4	757,063	100

Sources: [1]UIP, 1955, p. 15 – 1945: 9,900 spindles corresponding to 1.5% of the total; [2]Barbieri, 1957, p. 38; [3]UIP, 1953, p. 10; [4]UIP, 1967, p. II; [5]UIP, 1967, p. II.

Notes: * The source indicates Prato and not Tuscany but the figure indicated must be the one estimated by the Italian Wool Association for Tuscany.
** Almost all in the Prato area.

Table 6.3   Population shifts and resident population in Prato from 1945 to 1963

Year	Cumulative population increase	Residents on 31 December
1945	215	75,189
1946	292	76,023
1947	725	77,267
1948	873	78,506
1949	693	72,999*
1950	600	73,786
1951	960	77,730**
1952	2,163	80,147
1953	1,520	81,931
1954	1,447	83,711
1955	2,106	86,096
1956	2,844	89,129
1957	3,578	93,046
1958	4,872	98,326
1959	3,437	102,323
1960	4,042	107,005
1961	4,167	111,634**
1962	3,769	116,079
1963	3,373	120,359

Source: Comune di Prato, *Annuario Statistico*, 1979, p. 39.

Notes: * The decrease in the population is due to the creation of the autonomous Commune of Vaiano.
** Data revised on the basis of the population census.

specialized small firms given the importance of certain phases such as the sorting and the classification of the rags which required highly skilled workers.

The number of micro firms grew such that there was a qualitative change. A sign of this was represented by the request on the part of the *impannatori* no longer to consider themselves as having a subordinate role in the context of the local economy and civil society.[8] A more visible sign of the change brought about in the immediate postwar period by the economic boom was the demographic growth. At the end of 1947, the city of Prato had over 77,000 official inhabitants which represented an increase of 6,000 inhabitants in relation to 1940 despite the deaths during the war (ACP, Atti del Consiglio, 10 December 1947 and Table 6.3).

The demographic increase was due mostly to the influx from Prato's hinterland and other parts of Tuscany (Table 6.4). The area around Prato had a mostly share-cropping agricultural economy (see Cianferoni, Chapter 9 in this volume); agricultural households had already experimented with non-agricultural labour, usually in the manufacturing sector in the form of work in a textile factory or in piecework at home (Pazzagli, 1988). A good number of these immigrants were among the first who took advantage of the favourable conditions emerging in the 1946–7 period (Cioni, 1990). Many of them already had the required skills, but they were also prepared,

Table 6.4   Immigrants to Prato based on geographic origin from 1945 to 1964 (by percentage)

Year	North	Tuscany	Centre (excl. Tuscany)	South & islands	Abroad
1945–47	19.2*	60.2**	8.3	8.6	3.7
1948–51	17.1*	66.0**	4.6	10.5	1.8
1951–56	7.5	67.6	12.9	10.0	2.0
1957–60	6.2	62.9	11.4	18.5	1.0
1961–64	4.5	54.5	11.8	27.2	2.0

Source: Santini and Martelli, 1994 data refer to the period 1945–51; Ricasoli 1984, data refer to the period 1951–64.

Notes: North: Piedmont, Valle D'Aosta, Liguria, Lombardy, Trentino, Veneto, Friuli-Venezia Giulia.
Centre: Emilia-Romagna, Umbria, Marches, Lazio.
South & islands: Abruzzi, Molise, Campania, Puglia, Basilicata, Calabria, Sicily and Sardenia.
* Also contains Emilia-Romagna.
** Of which 27.9% in 1945–47 and 35.5% in 1948–57 in the Prato area-wide district.

due to their work experience of managing a farm to (1) work hard and in a relatively autonomous and self-disciplined manner, (2) accept an uncertain return, and (3) practise reciprocal cooperation, for instance, giving and receiving help to and from family members and, at times, even neighbours (Becattini, Chapter 4 in this volume; Bagnasco, 1988, pp. 88–95). During the two-year economic boom there was not only a quantitative growth in industrial activity and population in Prato, but there was also an expansion of the social and cultural basis which facilitated a qualitative change in the structure of the local economy.

The birth of numerous micro enterprises and the example of their success placed into motion an imitative mechanism which fostered the diffusion of the necessary skills (commercial and technical abilities) in almost all classes in the population. In addition, this dynamic contributed to the diffusion of an attitude that was already present in the local culture but which during the 'making of millions' became a generalized phenomenon: the ambition to try one's luck in becoming self-employed.

The expansion of specialized small firms also brought about an increase in number and depth of interfirm and interpersonal relations between individuals and firms who were formally independent but who structurally were highly interdependent. This process was enhanced by the relative cultural homogeneity of the population. The stability of the resident population also contributed to the diffusion of implicit norms of behaviour to ever wider sectors of the population. These norms of reciprocity extended to the economic arena and prescribed a correct business code of behaviour, mutual adaptation and cooperative interaction so that an almost automatic coordination of the different specialized activities was possible (Richardson, 1972; Jones, 1983).

6.4   From the first signs of change to the 'dismantling' of the large factories

Beginning in 1947 the first signs of an inversion of the external conditions, which had favoured the extraordinary growth in the postwar period, began to manifest themselves. Some of the traditional export markets of Prato's large mills suddenly shut down. Among the first to register a negative sign was the South African market where the government in 1947 threatened to embargo all goods coming from Prato based on regenerated wool on the pretext of being hazardous to the health of the local population. In fact, the real reason for the embargo was the protection of the country's infant textile industry (Silvestri, 1954, p. 54). For a while, the large woollen factories were able to compensate for the reduction in exports on the basis of the UNRRA orders.

1947 also brought a drastic reduction in internal demand for textile products which had an immediate impact on the small firms specialized in particular phases of the production process and on the *impannatori* who did not have alternative markets for their products. Demand for Prato's textile products declined due to the coming together of a number of factors. Some of these had to do with more general monetary policies, such as the anti-inflationary measures adopted in September 1947 by the Minister of the Budget, Luigi Einaudi. Einaudi decided to freeze bank deposits at the Treasury and the Bank of Italy. As a result, not only did inflation stop rising, but domestic demand and output fell sharply (De Cecco, 1974). Other circumstances, on the other hand, were more specific, such as, for example, the distribution of UNRRA textile products on the Italian market at cut-price rates (*Il Nuovo Corriere*, 2 June 1948 and 18 July 1948); this turn of events reduced even further the middle to lower part of the market serviced by cloth produced to a great extent by the *impannatori* and small firms of Prato.

The difficulties run into by the system of small enterprises immediately produced a ripple effect of financial problems. Given that the small enterprises operated to a large extent on the basis of the granting of mutual credit between those placing orders and the subcontractors and between the suppliers of raw materials and the *impannatori*, the potential for a major financial crisis was great. However, in order to limit the possibility of setting off a chain reaction which might force a number of firms into bankruptcy, the reaction of those operating within the system was a cooperative one. As was written in a newspaper of the time, everyone tried 'to save himself by helping others save themselves' (*Toscana Nuova*, 28 November 1947). Credit was extended and ways were found to pay off debts.[10] During the first half of 1948, many *impannatori* who had some production phase in-house closed it down. The machinery was rented or given to the workers by discounting it from the payment for future orders which the *impannatori* promised to subcontract to them.

The workers accepted these terms because the immediate alternative was either unemployment or emigration. However, these conditions were also acceptable because the workers had already considered going off on their own and becoming self-employed. Past personal ties with the *impannatore* gave them the confidence that the commitment received was credible and, sooner or later, the debt would be repaid.

The *impannatori*, on the other hand, tried to innovate, diversify and improve the quality of their products in order to remain in business (*Il Nuovo Corriere*, 18 July 1948). They tried to get their products exported (*Il Nuovo Corriere*, 10 and 22 April 1951). This became possible once the purchase and sale of textile goods was liberalized among the European countries in 1950 (*Laniera*, 1951, 3, p. 169) as part of the opening-of-markets strategy implemented by the OEEC. Thus, during the boom of the 1945–7 period, the system of small firms and self-employed *impannatori* grew in number; paradoxically, this was also the case during the subsequent period of recession. The impact of the recession took its toll on the whole Prato textile industry, but the firms that suffered the most were the large ones.

After the difficulties with South Africa, the large woollen mills re-established their contacts with the Indian market from which they received large orders thanks also to the appreciation of the pound (UIP, 21 July 1949, p. 7). However, when in September 1949 the pound was devalued by more than 30 per cent in relation to the US dollar, the Prato woollen mills were significantly affected. Devaluation cut into Prato's exports by about two billion Italian lire (UIP, 16 October 1951, p. 14). Soon thereafter, Prato's factories were dealt another blow by the loss of one more important foreign market through the adoption of protectionist measures by India.[10]

By this time, the UNRRA orders were being phased out, and the internal market could no longer absorb even the production of Prato's small firms. The financial blow dealt by the devaluation of the pound came on top of a significant contraction of foreign markets. The 1949 crisis had the impact of forcing the lay-off of thousands of workers.[11] The latter, predominantly organized by the CGIL (communist trade union), initially reacted with strikes and demonstrations to try to stem the dismissals. Even if the owners of the larger factories seemed already determined to reduce the scale of their operations, for the moment the objective was carried out only in a partial manner. Many of the workers placed on temporary lay-off were, in fact, quickly returned to their jobs in the summer of 1950 because of an upsurge in the internal and external demand for textiles. New orders were generated by the war in Korea.[12] During the following spring with the stabilization of the front along the 38th parallel, the demand for textiles declined and the price of wool and rags underwent a significant drop (Figure 6.1).

Once again, within the space of less than two years, for many woollen mills in Prato the reduction in the demand in the export market was combined with a financial crisis. A number of firms, especially the larger ones, had hoarded great quantities of raw materials despite the fact that prices had increased significantly (Provincial Council of Florence, 1953, p.

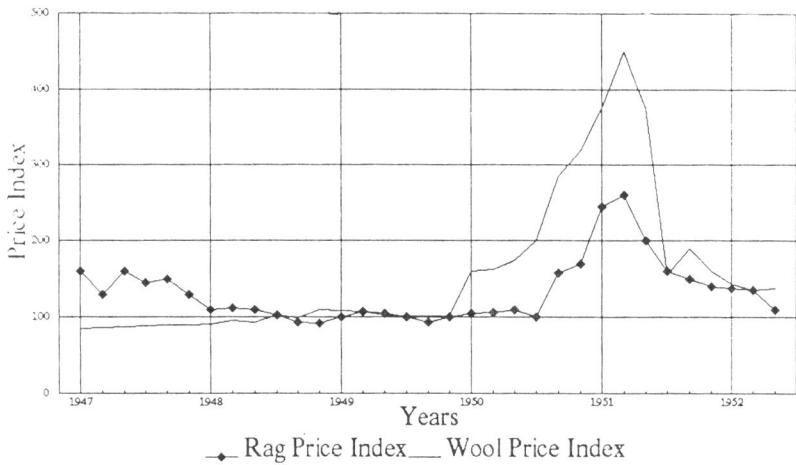

Figure 6.1 Evolution of average prices of wool and rags in Italy

Source: Laniera, 1952, 10, p. 827.

32; Avigdor, 1961, p. 47). Thousands of workers were once again laid-off or suspended from their jobs.[13] In particular, some of the phases of production, such as the weaving and the darning raw fabric, were 'dismantled', i.e., transferred outside the factory. This process of externalization of production phases, as had already taken place in the smaller firms and the *impannatori*, was implemented through the same transformation of the former workers into self-employed operators by offering them the looms or other machinery in rent or by instalments. In this manner, the number of single-phase firms, artisans and piecework increased considerably.[14] Already by the end of 1951, on the heels of the two waves of mass lay-offs during the most acute crisis period for the large woollen factories, the structure of Prato's industry was transformed. The local economy saw the emergence of specialized small firms as the dominant industrial system, even though this was not perceived at the time as a viable economic outcome.[15]

Before considering a few endogenous factors which allowed a new industrial structure to emerge and grow in the Prato area, it is useful to cite briefly the external circumstances which induced the owners of the large, complete cycle mills to externalize whole sections of their factories to outside firms. We have already seen that within a few years it became 'almost impossible' for these firms to export their output (UIP, 26 June 1953, p. 1) given the closing of former markets and the blocking of commercial ties with China and the countries in Eastern Europe which before the war had provided markets for a part of the Prato export trade. In addition, even the large military orders before and during the war and

Table 6.5 Top five countries importing woollen products from Italy, 1939–51

1939	%	1946	%
France	40.0	South Africa	51.9
United Kingdom	13.3	Pakistan/India	11.9
South Africa	12.0	Protuguese Africa	10.9
Portuguese Africa	10.8	Hong Kong	6.6
Albania	4.2	Syria/Lebanon	2.5

1947	%	1948	%
South Africa	31.8	Pakistan/India	57.0
Hong Kong	14.0	South Africa	8.0
Pakistan/India	11.1	Hong Kong	7.8
Ireland	11.1	Palestine	6.0
West Germany	5.5	British Malaysia	4.1

1949	%	1950	%
Pakistan/India	66.0	British Equ. Africa	21.5
South Africa	7.6	British Malaysia	10.4
British Equ. Africa	5.4	Thailand	7.7
Hong Kong	2.7	South Africa	6.8
Ex-Italian colonies	2.7	United Kingdom	5.4

1951	%
British Equ. Africa	15.3
Belgian Congo	9.7
France	6.4
West Germany	5.8
United Kingdom	5.0

Source: *Laniera*, 1952, 1, pp. 15–17.

the UNRRA orders after the war dried up. The era of large purchases of standardized goods in terms of content and colour which were constant over time and which were subject to long-term planning and production based on internal economies of scale was over.

Under the new market conditions, mills with a complete cycle could no longer use all their productive capacity.[16] In order to meet the uncertainty and constantly changing structure and origin of demand (Table 6.5), it was necessary to organize production in a way that was more flexible and could permit a frequent change in the quantity and, even more importantly, the quality of output. In Prato the means for rapidly achieving this objective was to follow the example of the *impannatori* by using external sub-contractors rather than housing all phases of the production process under one roof.[17]

6.5 Productive vertical de-integration and social integration: The emergence of the Prato industrial district

The de-integration of the large woollen factories was not, however, due to only the external factors discussed above. It was instead the result of a combination of those factors with local conditions and first of all with the presence of specialized small firms. The continuous emergence of these small firms since the end of the war had created local markets for the output of each phase of the production cycle (from rag to regenerated fibre and from this to the final product). The availability of an alternative mode of organizing production and the consequent spreading of specialized markets *in loco* made it easy to compare the costs of internal output in each phase with prices charged by the local subcontractors (Coase, 1937).

By the beginning of the 1950s, the major Prato factories not only had the problem of the underutilization of their productive capacity, but their internal labour costs were higher than those in other Italian textile manufacturing areas (PCI, 1954, p. 15; INAIL, 1949–55). In addition, especially for weaving, the prices of external firms were considerably lower than internal costs (see *La realta' economica*, 28 February 1950, pp. 14–17); this was also due to the fact that artisan weavers often worked with the help of family members and used parts of their homes as a workshop (Avigdor, 1961, pp. 84–7).

To these cost differentials we may add the impact of national political change. In May 1947 the PCI and PSI were expelled from the governing coalition and the outcome of the 1948 elections saw the Left cast into the role of a permanent minority (Beccalli, 1974). The outcome was an explosion of labour conflict which caused a further increase in production costs in Prato's larger factories. It is easy to understand why the owners of Prato's large woollen mills decided to 'dismantle' their factories.[18]

This decision was completely justifiable from the point of view of a purely economic calculation. This is especially true if one considers that subcontracting work to one's own ex-employees whose professional skills were well known and using machines often still owned by the factory provided sufficient guarantees of quality and the meeting of deadlines (Williamson, 1985, p. 232). Even if the behaviour of the owners of the larger woollen factories can be easily understood, the reaction of the workers to this process is not so comprehensible. In fact, these workers, the majority of whom were communists and trade union activists, accepted the solution offered them, almost without resistance.[19]

The almost ubiquitous presence of small, specialized firms played an essential role. In the first place, the existence and above all the growth of self-employed workers during times of expansion and recession demonstrated that self-employment constituted an alternative which, at least temporarily, offered an acceptable if not an alluring alternative. Second, as we have already noted above, the development of small firms contributed to the general diffusion in Prato's social culture and even among the workers in the larger factories of a self-help attitude that made them receptive, at least on an experimental basis, to a solution which relied largely on individual initiative and on the ability of the family to provide support and adaptation in case of necessity (PCI, 1954, pp. 9–10). In addition, the proliferation of small firms, both of subcontractors and entrepreneurs, gave the skilled workers forced out on their own the reasonable expectation that they would be able to establish business relations with several customers in the medium term.

Thus, the attempt to explain the end of the 'two circuits' productive structure in Prato simply on the basis of the decisions of a few entrepreneurs, even if they represented the historical nucleus of the local industry is insufficient. The organizational metamorphosis of production was made possible also by the behaviour of workers, behaviour which was influenced by the evolution of local sociocultural attitudes on self-employment and interpersonal economic relations. In fact, these attitudes prevented the radicalization of conflict in response to the mass lay-offs and in promptly redirecting resources (i.e., skills and machinery) no longer used in large mills with a complete cycle into the system of small specialized firms. Despite these developments, it is probable that the dismantling of the vertically integrated firms would not have coincided with the birth of the industrial district – i.e., with the formation of an economically viable unitary local productive system – had it not been accompanied by an appropriate set of public policies.

With the growth of the small firms, it was already possible to see that during the postwar boom the growing density and interactions of interpersonal and interfirm relations contributed to the diffusion of implicit norms on cooperative behaviour which facilitated the coordination of the various phases of the textile production process among different, formally independent participants. The internalization of these norms was for the most part limited to those operators present in the system of specialized small units. With the dismantling of the large woollen mills, however, the system of small firms became prevalent in the local economy, and so norms which permitted such a system to function had to become diffused. The previous structural dichotomy contrasting the vertically integrated large enterprises from the small ones was already disappearing, but the emergence of a single local system of small firms specialized in phases and functions required the contemporaneous diffusion throughout society of a strong sense of communitarian identity and norms of reciprocal cooperation.

It was, in fact, social cohesion and communitarian solidarity which were the principal results achieved by the action undertaken after the first wave of lay-offs by the left-wing local administration. Beginning in December 1949, in fact, the city council of Prato gave the mayor a mandate to create a special commission representing all of the economic groups in the city to examine the problem of local industry and try to come up with mutually acceptable solutions. The work of this commission went ahead until June 1950 when a delegation from Prato left for Rome to present its requests to the national government.[20]

In terms of the immediate objective of helping Prato's local economy, the outcome of the trip was modest. Nevertheless, the creation of the city's commission allowed the Prato administrators to promote the opportunity for different local economic and political groups to converge beyond political divisions on the common problem of defending and developing 'our industry' (Chamber of Labour, 1952, p. 14; PCI, 1954, p. 44). This result, even if it was achieved without a conscious plan, was essential so that the de-integration of the large factories would give rise to the industrial district. The organizational basis of the industrial district model is the division of labour among independent firms interconnected among themselves by a common sense of belonging and trust and thanks to which it is possible to work out a form of coordination in which both cooperation and competition are possible (Piore and Sabel, 1984; Brusco, 1986; Becattini, 1989b; Pyke, 1992).

The institutional support for the birth of the Prato industrial district was not limited to the zeal of the local administration in promoting a sense of community and identification with the textile industry. It was also concentrated on the regulation of competition in the local labour markets, both of self-employed and salaried workers. In fact, the externalization of entire productive phases in the large woollen mills produced an increase in competition not only among the self-employed workers but also between these and the workers employed in the factories. This competition could have produced a decline in the overall living and working conditions of the local community, and such an outcome would have undermined the sense of community which is so important in making the system of small firms function (Piore and Sabel, 1984, pp. 270–1; Scott and Paul, 1990). As a consequence, in January 1950 when thousands of hierarchical relations were substituted by market trans-actions, the Prato left-wing parties and, above all, the PCI created the 'trade union of weavers' which had as its principal goals the subcontracting of external weaving and the prevention of 'misunderstand-ings and competition vis-à-vis weavers employed in the factories' (*Il Nuovo Corriere*, 5 January 1950).

In addition, despite the sudden increase in artisans working in the textile industry, the Prato artisan associations[21] and, in particular, the communist-led one, were able to conduct a lockout in defence of 'fair prices' during the summer of 1952; the lockout took place right after the second wave of dismissals were carried out by the large factories (*Il Nuovo Corriere*, 17 and 25 July 1952; *La Nazione*, 7 July 1952).[22]

The rapid organization of the external subcontractors and the promotion of a sense of solidarity between these and the factory workers (*Nuovo Corriere*, 19 July 1952), which was facilitated by the diffusion of a Marxist subculture (Trigilia, 1985, pp. 87–104)[23] avoided an excess of price competition in the local labour markets. This capacity of limiting the transfer of the costs of restructuring on the poorest segment of the population permitted the keeping of consensus and of reciprocal co-operation. The maintenance of cooperation was essential not only for the birth of the industrial district, but also for its future growth, as cooperation is indispensable to the flexibility and dynamism of the whole system of small firms (Brusco and Sabel 1981, p. 109; Piore and Sabel, 1984, p. 272).

6.6   The take-off of Prato's industrial district and some of its causes

With the dismantling of the largest woollen factories the economic and social transformation of Prato into an industrial district was brought to completion. The metamorphosis was, in fact, the rather casual result of diverse behaviour on the part of local actors in reaction to the crisis of the local industry. The sudden turn of events during the late 1940s and early 1950s placed into question what was considered to be at the time the most modern and advanced part of the city's economy.

Nevertheless, soon after the restructuring, Prato's industrial base began to grow. The spinning capacity increased consistently; the number of carding spindles increased between 1953 and 1963 by 62 per cent in absolute terms, and even in relative terms they went from one-third to over half of the national total (Tables 6.1 and 6.2 and Figures 6.2 and 6.3).

Between 1952 and 1962 exports increased by 526 per cent, representing a change from 32 to 44 per cent of total Italian wool exports (Table 6.6 and Figure 6.4). The number of specialized firms continued to increase. The number of weaving subcontractors that were set-up between 1953 and 1962 was 3,034; new spinning firms during the same period increased by 354; 171 new twisting firms were added; and refinishing firms rose by 112. The same trend was registered by the *impannatori* (+471), rag dealers (+380), firms engaged in the repair and construction of textile machinery (+87) and so forth (CCIAA, register of firms, 1953–1962).

As a consequence of this proliferation of new specialized firms, the role of the large mills in Prato's industrial structure was considerably reduced. The number of units with more than 100 employees which in 1951 – a point in time when a part of the dismantling of vertically integrated mills had already taken place – still employed half of the officially registered workforce. In 1961 this total did not reach 25 per cent; in contrast, the number of local firms with fewer than 50 employees consistently expanded their portion of the workforce. These firms accounted for an increase from 35 to 63 per cent of the workforce in the decade between 1951 and 1961 (Table 6.7 and Figure 6.5).

This rapid development of industry brought great changes in the local pattern of sectoral employment. During the period between 1951 and 1961, industrial employment in the province of Prato went from 62 to 70 per cent, while those active in agriculture slipped from 17 to 8 per cent. In the same year, in Tuscany agriculture still accounted for over 24 per cent of the workforce (Table 6.8). The abandonment of farming, even if not of the countryside, was made easier by the spread of artisan weavers and small subcontracting firms to hamlets and villages over a vast area surrounding Prato. By the mid-1950s, looms and home-based textile work already covered a territory of approximately 220 sq. km. around Prato (Barbieri, 1957, p. 31; see also Figure 6.6).

With the growth of the textile industrial district the social structure of Prato changed accordingly and witnessed a further reduction in the level of

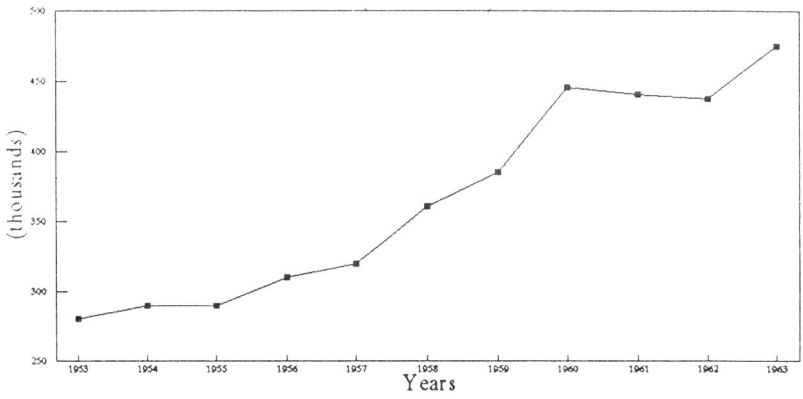

Figure 6.2   Carding spindles in Tuscany on 1 January, 1953–63 (in thousands)

Source: Italian Wool Manufacturers' Association

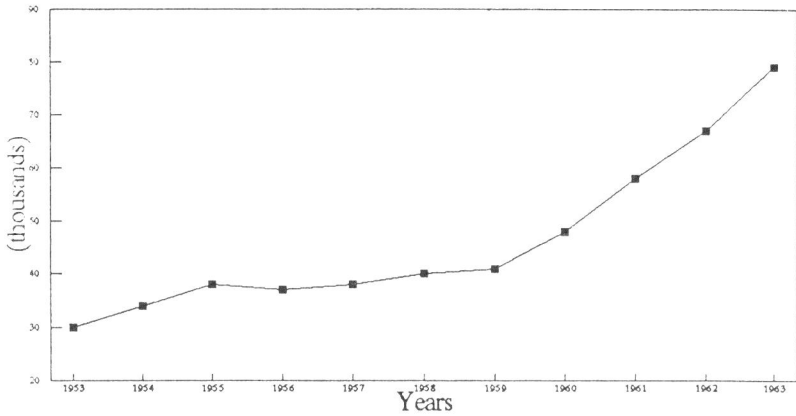

Figure 6.3   Worsting spindles in Tuscany on 1 January, 1953–53 (in thousands)

Source: Italian Wool Manufacturers' Association

Table 6.6   Imports and exports of Prato's industry from 1952 to 1962 and relative
quota of Italian woollen exports (bank payments in million of Italian lire)

Year	Imports	Exports	Prato's percentage of Italian wool exports
1952	15,000	14,000	32.8
1953	17,000	22,000	38.3
1954	18,000	29,000	48.8
1955	19,855	38,182	50.5
1956	23,000	49,500	52.8
1957	35,000	60,500	53.7
1958	22,500	52,200	57.8
1959	27,951	61,000	46.5
1960	29,373	72,982	44.2
1961	28,748	73,484	40.2
1962	39,966	87,644	44.3

Sources: Cols 1 and 2: UIP, 1962, p. 77; col. 3: data calculated by ISTAT and elaborated by
the Italian Woollen Industry Association.

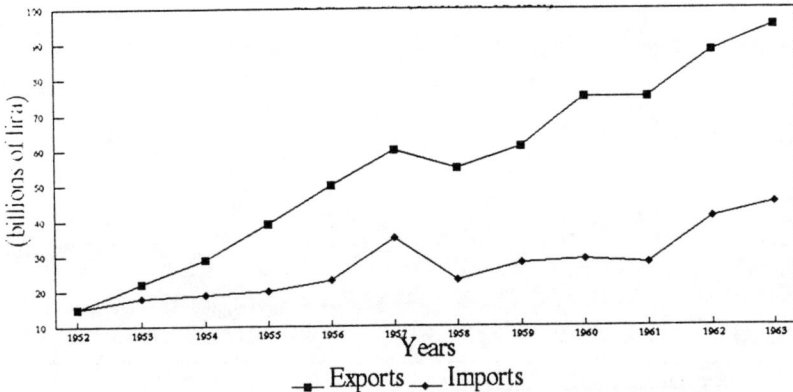

Figure 6.4   Prato's industrial imports and exports, 1952-63 (billions of lira)

Source: UIP, Council Reports, various years

class polarization. There was an increase in self-employment, and despite
the high level of industrialization the percentage of salaried workers fell. In
1951 salaried employees accounted for two-thirds of those active in the
industry. Ten years later the level was down to 61 per cent, and in 1971 it
was 52 per cent (Table 6.9).

Table 6.7   Distribution of firms and workers in textiles in the province of Florence by size (workers per firm), 1951, 1961, 1971 and 1981

	1–10		11–50		51–100	
	No.	%	No.	%	No.	%
1951*						
Firms	805	67.5	284	23.8	51	4.3
Workers	2,433	9.8	6,297	25.3	3,623	14.6
1961						
Firms	5,998	88.4	665	9.8	79	1.16
Workers	13,003	29.3	14,772	33.4	5,482	12.4
1971						
Firms	8,478	88.45	956	10.0	108	1.12
Workers**	16,943	33.0	19,243	37.42	7,455	14.5
1981						
Firms	11,862	88.4	1,427	10.6	89	0.6
Workers**	25,970	42.5	25,674	42.0	6,027	9.9

	101–500		> 500		Total		Average
	No.***	%	No.	%	No.	%	Size
1951							
Firms	48	4.0	5	0.4	1,193	100	20.8
Workers	9,106	36.6	3,385	13.7	24,844	100	
1961							
Firms	49	0.7	3	0.04	6,794	100	6.5
Workers	8,487	19.2	2,454	5.7	44,197	100	
1971							
Firms	39	0.4	3	0.03	9,584	100	5.3
Workers**	6,067	11.8	1,707	3.3	51,415	100	
1981							
Firms	24	0.17	–		13,402	100	4.5
Workers**	3,426	5.6	–		61,097	100	

Source: ISTAT, *General Census of Industry*, 1951, 1961, 1971, 1981.

Notes: * In 1951 the home-weavers' and other subcontractors' work were not surveyed. In 1961, on the contrary, registered artisans were surveyed by the Census.
** Groupings: up to 9; 10–49; 50–99; 100–499; 500 and above.
*** The woollen mills with complete cycles usually employed over 100 workers.

At this point, it is appropriate to ask why the vertical de-integration and the small firm proliferation (which everyone considered at the time to be a declining strategy or at the most a temporary remedy to the crisis) not only persisted but grew capable of sustaining a long period of growth. In the first place, the new organizational structure provided some advantages in

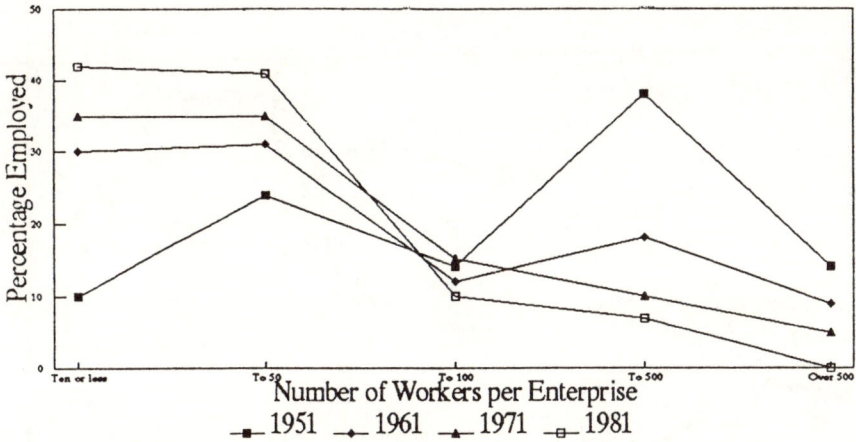

Figure 6.5 Distribution of textile employment by number of employees per enterprise, 1951, 1961, 1971 and 1981

Source: ISTAT, General Industrial Census 1951, 1961, 1971, 1981 – Textile industry in the province of Florence

Table 6.8 Employment by sector of activity in the province of Prato and in Tuscany (by percentage), 1951, 1961 and 1971

Province of Prato*								
Year	Agriculture	%	Industry	%	Other activities	%	Total	%
1951	8,270	17.2	29,895	62.1	9,990	20.7	48,155	100
1961	5,450	8.8	43,469	70.7	12,687	20.5	61,786	100
1971	2,227	3.1	51,349	71.0	18,685	25.9	72,261	100
1981	1,461	1.6	60,230	65.2	30,664	33.2	92,355	100

Tuscany								
Year	Agriculture	%	Industry	%	Other activities	%	Total	%
1951	521,238	39.6	447,198	34.0	347,667	26.4	1,316,103	100
1961	313,680	24.1	572,409	44.0	415,796	31.9	1,301,885	100
1971	145,835	11.5	612,194	48.4	508,212	40.1	1,266,241	100
1981	93,975	6.7	615,484	43.7	698,772	49.6	1,408,231	100

Source: ISTAT, *General Census of the Population*, 1951, 1961, 1971, 1981.

Note: * The province of Prato includes the following townships: Cantagallo, Carmignano (which until 1962 included Poggio a Caiano), Montemurlo, Prato, Vaiano and Vernio.

0   10 km

Vernio

Cantagallo

Bisenzio

Barberino
di Mugella

Usella

il Fabbro

Vaiano

la Briglia

PISTOIA

Montale

Montemurlo

Ombrone

Agliana

Narnali

Coiano

S. Ippolito

S. Marino

Galciana

PRATO

S. Giusto

Iolo

Calenzano

Cafaggio

Mezzana

Sesto
Fiorentino

Tavola

Paperino

S. Maria

Campi Bisanzio

Signa

FIRENZE

Arno

Textile plants

Home-based workers

Boundary between
hills and plains

Figure 6.6 Location of textile plants and home-based workers

Table 6.9 Distribution of those employed in industry and other activities by profession in the province of Prato* (by percentage)

Year	Entrepreneurs, managers and professionals	Self-employed	Salaried employees
1951	12.0	21.6	66.4
1961	10.6	28.2	6.12
1971	17.3	30.2	52.5
1981	25.2	26.9	47.9

Source: ISTAT, *General Census of the Population*, 1951, 1961, 1971, 1981 (data calculated by the author).

Note: * The province of Prato includes the following seven communes: Cantagallo, Carmignano, Montemurlo, Poggio a Caiano, Prato, Vaiano and Vernio.

reacting to the changing market conditions due to its greater flexibility (Storper, 1989). In making use of external producers, firms focused mainly on marketing final products (*impannatori* and small mills) could contemporaneously have made fabrics which were different not only in design and colours but also in production process (Avigdor, 1961, p. 128). In this manner, they had the possibility of widening the range of products offered and of increasing their adaptability to changes in market conditions (Brusco, 1983, pp. 111–12).

In addition, the markets of Western Europe and North America, where Prato's industry had to win customers, not only had their own well-developed textile industry with which the Prato firms had to compete, but they also had a more diversified and variable demand structure than was the case with the old Indian and South African markets. The externalization of the productive phases to local subcontractors permitted the firms selling textiles to specialize in designing a wide range of products, to continually renew their offer in order to satisfy almost any demand, and to respond immediately to a change in tastes and fashion (Barbieri, 1957, p. 26). Moreover, on the basis of the 'principle of accumulated reserves' (Florence, 1957, pp. 50–1), the territorial concentration of firms in the industrial district allowed the system to respond quickly to unexpected fluctuations in demand with a minimum of stockpiles (Barbieri, 1957, p. 27).

Second, because the local system was large, being composed of thousands of firms specialized both in production and marketing, these firms were able to take advantage of the extensive division of labour made possible by the overall dimensions of the system (Marshall, 1879, p. 196). In fact, with a production process which can be broken down so easily and in which the different phases have varying scales of efficiency, it was possible to exploit fully technological change through specialization by phase in units of production serving various customers and using efficient, highly specialized machines (Marshall, 1920; Tani, 1976). With the proliferation of specialized firms, the local market for component products grew; this created new opportunities for further division of labour among firms and for increased standardization of certain components, thus increasing productivity (Marshall, 1923, p. 227; Young, 1928).

Third, the presence of a high level of professional skills among the diverse textile specializations and subsidiary activities – i.e., diffusion connected to the deeply rooted textile culture in Prato and to the local 'industrial atmosphere' (Marshall, 1920, p. 395 and Marshall, 1923, p. 284) – allowed Prato's overall system to innovate its products continuously and to keep itself abreast with technological innovations (Lorenzoni, 1979).[24] With regard to this last aspect, an important role in sustaining the innovative capacity of Prato's industry was carried out by the local mechanical-engineering firms. In fact, the presence of firms specialized in manufacturing textile machinery located in the midst of a local industrial district permitted them to understand and frequently resolve problems arising in the making of new products or in the adoption of new machinery, both designed locally or even elsewhere (Marshall, 1923, p. 603; Russo, 1985).

Another characteristic contributed to the dynamism of Prato's industry and to the diffusion of innovation. It is the continuous creation of new entrepreneurial initiatives stimulated by the opportunities offered on the local markets and by the possibility of cooperation among the diverse specialized firms present in the system.[25] It is due to the capacity of mobilizing considerable initiatives originating from the grassroots and developing their potential that Prato's system succeeded in innovating itself and growing during the 1950s and 1960s.

Last but not least, the predominance in Prato's economy of the specialized small firms system helped to root further the sociocultural factors which had served as one of the bases for its development (i.e., the tendency to self-employment, acceptance of a pattern of behaviour based on reciprocal cooperation, the sense of belonging to a community, etc.) and to generalize it to the wider community. This sociocultural trend along with the extension of local markets for specialized components served to radiate into the system a blend of cooperation and of competition. It was exactly this particular combination of cooperation and competition which made possible and advantageous – lowering the transactions costs within the district – the coordination of the diverse activities through the local markets pervaded by personal ties and communitarian norms rather than through hierarchical relationships, typical of vertically integrated firms.[26]

6.7 Summary and conclusions

We have outlined above some of the causes for the success of the organizational structure which emerged in Prato. For a long time this structure seemed to be unique and specific to Prato because it had no place in the predominant theoretical economic models. In fact, it was necessary for the coming together of a large number of empirical and theoretical studies carried out during the 1970s and 1980s in order to understand that Prato's organizational structure was nothing more than a concrete manifestation of the industrial district model.[27] It is a model of industrial organization which had already been identified in the previous century by the English economist Alfred Marshall (Bellandi, 1982; 1989) but which had been forgotten with the advent of mass production. Nevertheless, we have seen that with the appropriate technological circumstances and market conditions (a modular form of technology and a fragmented and changing demand) it can provide a valid alternative to the organization of the vertically integrated large corporation. This is so because the territorial agglomeration of small and medium-sized enterprises gives rise to a united productive system which, in addition to being rather flexible, is large enough and diversified enough to permit the firms in the system to benefit from economies of scale and scope comparable to those enjoyed by large firms.

For a long time, due to its economic performance, Prato's industrial district was taken as an example to imitate for the encouragement in the development of similar organization forms in other parts of Tuscany and Italy. However, the economic downturn of the 1980s demonstrated that the industrial district as any other organizational model is not safe from crises and the need for innovation. Explaining how Prato responded to the crisis is not the responsibility of this chapter; that responsibility has been assumed by others.

Notes

This chapter draws upon research carried out for the volume: *Prato, storia di una città*, vol. IV, edited by G. Becattini; I participated in this research project along with researchers from different disciplines (history, economics, sociology, geography, statistics and literature) whose contributions will be found in the above cited volume. The views expressed here are the product of the synthesis relative to the decade 1943–53 to which I contributed with G. Becattini, P. Giovannini and P. Absalom, all of whom are thanked for letting me use part of those ideas for this chapter. I have already written on this topic in the essay on 'Prato 1944–1963. Rinascita e trasformazione di un sistema produttivo locale', published in ISRT, *La Toscana nel secondo dopoguerra*, Milan, Franco Angeli, pp. 155–71, 1991.

1. This expression was used in 1911 during a public conference of the Italian Association of the Wool Industry. Cited in Pescarolo (1988), p. 72.
2. An example is the famous merchant Francesco di Marco Datini. Cited in Origo (1957).
3. The only exception was the wool mill, Koessler & Mayer, established in Prato with German capital in 1888 and popularly known for its size as the 'Big Factory, Il Fabbricone'. For an historical account of the textile industry in Prato during the last century and the first half of this century see Lungonelli (1988) and Pescarolo (1988).
4. A nucleus of a textile machine industry had already been created in Prato prior to the war; the industry was mainly composed of small enterprises

specialized in repairing machinery. However, a few of these firms also made new machines. See Silvestri (1954), pp. 34 and 44.

5. The first order was for a total value of £500,000; it was paid for 85 per cent by the exchange of wool and rags and only 15 per cent in cash. Silvestri (1954), pp. 48–9.

6. See Giovannelli (1983), p. 75. All of the statistical information on Prato's textile industries comes from the Unione Industriale Pratese (Prato Industrial Association). This source is certainly accurate but it supposedly underestimates the presence of small and micro firms, especially those newly created and those which did not become members of the Unione.

7. From the autumn of 1945 to the same period in 1947, for example, the city of Prato issued approximately 1,300 licences for setting up new equipment (as opposed to new machinery installed in existing factories which did not need such licences) by individuals entering the textile business. These included as many as 1,177 licences for looms, 130 for warping machinery and 77 for spinning (ACP, Atti del Consiglio, 10 December 1947; Cioni, 1990). During the same period, the activity of the *impannatore* was so common that, according to a newspaper of the day, the door of every house in Prato could have borne the sign 'qui si impanna' or 'an impannatore is at work here' (*L'Impannatore*, 11 May 1947).

8. See *L'Impannatore*, 1, 15, 29 June and 20 July 1947.

9. In 1948 the number of bankruptcies were only ten, even if the promissory notes (*cambiali*) not paid increased by 255 per cent in comparison to the previous year. CCIAA di Firenze, 1947–1948.

10. Italian exports of wool cloth to the Indian subcontinent went from 3,026 tons in 1949 to 450 tons in 1950. *Laniera*, 1951, 5, p. 430.

11. Sources indicate that about 11,000 workers were laid off in addition to the 6,000 fired or suspended from their jobs in the months immediately after the devaluation of sterling. Provincial Council of Florence (1953), p. 50.

12. With the Korean War the demand for Prato's products based on recycled wool increased also because they could be substituted for those made of new wool whose price had leapt 150 per cent in the period between June 1950 and March 1951. *Laniera*, 1951, 5, p. 429.

13. Trade union sources estimate that the number of workers fired or suspended was about 5,000 and those put on indefinite lay-off during the winter of 1951–52 reached 17,000. Provincial Council of Florence (1953), p. 50; Chamber of Labour (1952), p. 4.

14. Even though the great diffusion in those years of self-employment in Prato is recorded by all sources, it is difficult to get a precise count of the number of independent firms and home-based work. According to trade union sources, the number of artisan weavers in 1952 was around 5,000 while in 1947 they accounted for fewer than 1,000 firms (Chamber of Labour, 1952, p. 6) and women engaged in piecework (darning raw fabric) at home rose to over 6,000 at the beginning of the year (PCI, 1954, p. 2).

15. This trend was considered by both the trade unions, dominated by Marxist ideology, and by the entrepreneurs as an unwelcome development – characteristic of economic decline – in Prato's productive structure. See for example, Chamber of Labour, 22 November 1949; *Laniera*, 1951, 11, p. 869.

16. During the first half of 1950, for example, the use of productive capacity in these firms did not go beyond 60 per cent. *Laniera*, 1951, 5, p. 404.

17. For an interpretation of the restructuring of the major woollen firms in Prato in terms of a flexible production scenario, see Lorenzoni (1980).

18. According to the Prato Unione Industriale (local employer association), for the industrial action labelled 'no collaboration', for example, the damage inflicted

on production was estimated to be from 20 to 25 per cent, while during the strikes of a more general character which took place between January 1948 through July 1949 over three million hours of work were lost. UIP, 21 July 1949 p. 2 and pp. 19–20. For an example of the interpretation of the dismantling of these large factories as an anti-union response, see Gregori, 1986.

19. The strikes and demonstrations in protest over the dismissals were mostly limited to the first months of 1950 (Chamber of Labour, typed memorandum, October 1950).

20. The requests of the Prato delegation to the government involved, among others, the awarding of public contracts, compensations for war damages, tax reductions and even diplomatic ties with Eastern European and Chinese governments in order to reopen traditional foreign markets for Prato's production and compensate for the loss of export markets in India and South Africa. See ACP, Atti del Consiglio, 30 December 1949; 15 April 1950; and 7 July 1950.

21. From 1946 Prato had an association which brought together the local artisans irrespective of political coloration. After the 1948 elections and the first lay-offs in the large woollen factories, in March 1950 a split took place which led to the creation of an association of Catholic inspiration.

22. According to the newspapers of the day, the lockout affected 95 per cent of all weavers in the Prato area (*Il Nuovo Corriere*, 25 July 1952). In addition, it should be noted that a regulation of price competition on subcontracted work the subcontracting of weaving and the respect of prices agreed to by the artisan associations and those representing industrialists were requested by the *impannatori* in order to avoid 'unhealthy competition' among those placing orders. *La Nazione*, 15 March 1952.

23. In the 1946 and 1951 elections for representatives in Prato's city council, the parties of the left (PCI and PSI) attracted respectively 63 and 51.5 per cent of the vote of which about 40 per cent went to the PCI. In 1956 the organizational structure of the Prato PCI consisted of 30 party sections, 30 FGCI (Young Italian Communist Youth Federation) groups and 389 cells (Partini, 1992).

24. On the diffusion of innovation and creativity in industrial districts, see Bellandi (1989) and Becattini (1989a).

25. For an understanding of the continuous turnover of firms in the Prato system, one needs to consider for example that in the decade between 1953 and 1962 the register of firms at the Chamber of Commerce had entries for over 6,000 textile units in comparison to 1,900 that ceased operations (CCIAA of Florence, 1953–1962). On the extensive social mobility which manifested itself during those years in Prato see Avigdor (1961), p. 141.

26. On the 'communitarian market' as a governance mechanism of transactions within the industrial district, see Dei Ottati (1986, 1992); on the lesser importance of hierarchical coordination in the presence of communitarian norms, see Williamson (1991).

27. For a reconstruction of the rediscovery of the 'Marshallian district', see Becattini (1987), pp. 7–34.

References

ACP (Archivio del Comune di Prato), Atti del Consiglio, various years.
Avigdor, E., *L'industria tessile a Prato*, Milan, Feltrinelli, 1961.

Bagnasco, A., *La costruzione sociale del mercato*, Bologna, Il Mulino, 1988.

Balestri, A., 'La ricostruzione dell'industria tessile pratese (1944–51)', in Becattini, G. (ed.), *Prato; storia di una città*, vol. 4, Florence, Le Monnier, forthcoming (originally 1990).

Barbieri, G., 'Prato e la sua industria tessile', *Rivista geografica italiana*, 63 (supp.), 1957.

Becattini, G., 'Il distretto industriale marshalliano: cronaca di un ritrovamento', in Becattini, G. (ed.), *Mercato e forze locali: il distretto industriale*, Bologna, Il Mulino, 1987.

—— 'Il distretto industriale come ambiente creativo', in Benetti, E. (ed.), *Mutazioni tecnologiche e condizionamenti internazionali*, Milan, Franco Angeli, 1989a.

—— 'Riflessioni sul distretto industriale marshalliano come concetto socio-economico', *Stato e mercato*, 25, April 1989b.

Beccalli, B., 'La ricostruzione del sindacalismo italiano 1943–1950', in Woolf, S.J. (ed.), *Italia 1943–1950: La ricostruzione*, Bari, Laterza, 1974.

Bellandi, M., 'Il distretto industriale in Alfred Marshall', *L'industria*, 3, 1982.

—— 'Capacità innovativa diffusa e sistemi locali di imprese', in Becattini, G. (ed.), *Modelli locali di sviluppo*, Bologna, Il Mulino, 1989.

Brusco, S., 'Flessibilità e solidità del sistema: l'esperienza emiliana', in Fuà, G. and Zacchia, C. (eds.), *Industrializzazione senza fratture*, Bologna, Il Mulino, 1983.

—— 'Small Firms and Industrial Districts: the Experience of Italy', in Keeble, D. and Wever, E. (eds.), *New Firms and Regional Development in Europe*, London, Croom Helm, 1986.

Brusco, S. and Sabel, C., 'Artisan Production and Economic Growth', in Wilkinson, F. (ed.), *The Dynamic of Labour Market Segmentation*, London, Academic Press, 1981.

CCIAA (Chamber of Commerce), *Bollettini economici della provincia di Firenze*, various years.

Chamber of Labour of Prato, 'Documento sindacale', typewritten document dated 22 November 1949.

—— 'Documento sindacale', typewritten document dated October 1950.

—— 'Relazione', typewritten document, 1952.

Cioni, E., 'Lo sviluppo del lavoro autonomo a Prato nel secondo dopoguerra (1945–1952)', to be published in Becattini, G. (ed.) *Prato; storia di una città*, vol. 4, Florence, Le Mannier, forthcoming (originally 1990).

Coase, R., 'The Nature of the Firm', *Economica*, 4, 1937.

Comune di Prato, *Annuario statistico*, various years.

De Cecco, M., 'La politica economica durante la ricostruzione 1945–1951', in Woolf, S.J. (ed.), *L'Italia 1943–1950: La ricostruzione*, Bari, Laterza, 1974.

Dei Ottati, G., 'Distretto industriale, problemi delle transazioni e mercato comunitario: prime considerazioni', *Economia e politica industriale*, 51, 1986.

—— 'Fiducia, transazioni intrecciate e credito nel distretto industriale', *Note Economiche*, 1/2, 1992.

Florence, P.S., *The Logic of British and American Industry*, London, Routledge, 1957.

Giovannelli, L., *Cambiamento tecnologico e modelli organizzativi. Il caso dell'industria tessile a Prato*, Prato, Edizioni del Palazzo, 1983.

Gregori, G. (ed.), *Per il lavoro e la democrazia. Le lotte sociali a Prato e nella Val di Bisenzio nel secondo dopoguerra – Documenti*, Prato, Camera del Lavoro, 1986.

INAIL, *Notiziario statistico*, 1949–1955.

ISTAT, *Censimento generale dell'industria e del commercio*, Rome, ISTAT 1951, 1961, 1971, 1981.

—— *Censimento generale della popolazione*, Rome, ISTAT, 1951, 1961, 1971, 1981.

Jones, G., 'Transaction Costs, Property Rights and Organizational Culture: an Exchange Perspective', *Administrative Science Quarterly*, September, 1983.

Laniera (monthly journal of the Italian Association of the Wool Industry), various years.

Lorenzoni, G., *Una politica innovativa nelle piccole medie imprese. L'analisi del cambiamento nel sistema industriale pratese*, Milan, Etas Libri, 1979.

—— 'Lo sviluppo industriale di Prato', in *Storia di Prato*, Prato, Edizioni Cassa di Risparmio, 1980.

Lungonelli, M., 'Dalla manifattura alla fabbrica. L'avvio dello sviluppo industriale (1815–95)', in Mori, G. (ed.), *Prato; storia di una città*, vol. 3, Florence, Comune di Prato–Le Monnier, 1988.

Marchi, R., *Storia economica di Prato*, Milan, Giuffrè, 1962.

Marshall, A., 'The pure Theory of Domestic Values', in Whitaker, J. (ed.), *The Early Economic Writings of Alfred Marshall, 1867–1890*, vol. 2, London, Macmillan, 1879.

—— *Principles of Economics*, (Italian edition edited by A. Campolongo, UTET, Turin, 1972), 1920.

—— *Industry and Trade*, London, Macmillan, 1923.

Mori, G., 'Il tempo dell'industria (1815–1943)', in Mori, G. (ed.), *Prato; storia di una città*, vol. 3, Florence, Comune di Prato–Le Monnier, 1988.

Origo, I., *The Merchant of Prato*, London, Jonathan Cape, 1957.

Palla, M., 'Prato tra fascismo e resistenza, 1943–1944', in Mori, G. (ed.), *Prato; storia di una città*, vol. 4., Florence, Le Monnier, forthcoming (originally 1990).

Partini, S., 'Tradizione politica, organizzazione di partito e comportamento elettorale a Prato. Il voto al PCI dal 1946 al 1990', *Quaderni dell'Osservatorio elettorale*, 27, January–June 1992.

Pazzagli, C., 'Le campagne e i contadini fra la permanenza della mezzadria e l'attrazione urbana', in Mori, G. (ed.), *Prato; storia di una città*, vol. 3, Florence, Comune di Prato–Le Monnier, 1988.

PCI (Partito Comunista Italiano), 'Esame del lavoro dei comunisti nelle organizzazioni di massa e prospettive di attivita' nella zona di Prato', typewritten document dated 4 April 1954.

Pescarolo, A., 'Modelli di industrializzazione, ruoli sociali, immagini del lavoro (1895–1943)', in Mori, G. (ed.), *Prato; storia di una città*, vol. 3, Florence, Comune di Prato–Le Monnier, 1988.

Piore, M. and Sabel, C., *The Second Industrial Divide*, New York, Basic Books, 1984.

Provincial Council of Florence, *Atti del convegno per lo studio della crisi tessile pratese*, Florence, Vallecchi, 1953.

Pyke, F., *Industrial Development through Small-firm Cooperation*, Geneva, International Labour Office, 1992.

Riscasoli, E. *L'esperienza migratoria a Prato, 1951–1964*, Laurea thesis, Department of Economics and Commerce, University of Florence, 1984

Richardson, G., 'The Organization of Industry', *Economic Journal*, September 1972.

Russo, M., 'Technical Change and Industrial District: The Role of Interfirm Relations in the Growth and Transformation of Ceramic Tile Production in Italy', *Research Policy*, December 1972.

Scott, A.J. and Paul, A.S., 'Collective Order and Economic Coordination in Industrial Agglomerations: the Technopoles of Southern California', *Environment and Planning*, 8, pp. 179–93, 1990.

Silvestri, S., *Cenni cronistorici sulla Unione Industriale Pratese*, Prato, Unione Industriale Pratese, 1954.

Storper, M., 'The Transition to Flexible Specialisation in the US Film Industry: External Economies, the Division of Labour, and the Crossing of Industrial Divides', *Cambridge Journal of Economics*, June 1989.

Tamburini, L. (ed.), *L'industria di Prato alla prova della guerra*, Prato, Unione Industriale Pratese, 1945.

Tani, P., 'La rappresentazione analitica del processo di produzione: alcune premesse teoriche al problema del decentramento', *Note Economiche*, 4/5, 1976.

Tinacci Mossello, M., 'L'organizzazione del territorio durante la seconda guerra mondiale e la ricostruzione', in Mori, G. (ed.), *Prato; storia di una città*, vol. 4, Florence, Le Monnier, forthcoming (originally 1990).

Trigilia, C., 'Comunisti e piccole imprese', in Bagnasco, A. and Trigilia, C. (eds.), *Società e politica nelle aree di piccola impresa. Il caso della Valdelsa*, Milan, Franco Angeli, 1985.

UIP (Unione Industriale Pratese), 'Relazione del consiglio', various years.

UNRRA, *Survey of Italy's Economy*, Rome, UNRRA, 1947.

Williamson, O., *The Economic Institutions of Capitalism*, New York, Free Press, 1985.

—— 'Organizzazione economica comparata: l'analisi delle alternative strutturali discrete', *Economia e politica industriale*, 70, 1991.

Young, A., 'Increasing Returns and Economic Progress', *Economic Journal*, December, 1928.

7 Case study II: Prato and the textile industry

Marco Bellandi and Marco Romagnoli

The city of Prato and a group of nearby centres in Tuscany constitute one of the three clusters in which we find the concentration of the Italian woollen industry. The other two are Biella in Piedmont and Vicenza in Veneto. Chapter 6 by Gabi Dei Ottati described the metamorphosis of the Prato textile industry during the 1950s. From the 1950s to the mid-1980s the industry underwent a process of significant growth which was interrupted by short periods of crisis. The growth was based on the organization of a complex of new and increasingly numerous small firms and it was sustained by a constant flux of immigrants, at first coming from the Tuscan countryside (Becattini, Chapter 4 in this volume) and then from the Italian south and abroad.

After describing the essential aspects of the model on which was based the growth of Prato's textile industry during the 1960s and 1970s, this chapter will emphasize the more recent developments characterized by the sudden interruption of the quantitative growth, significant changes in the original model, and the rise of alternative models. The question that is posed for the beginning of the 1990s is whether the Prato textile industry finds itself facing a process of metamorphosis.

7.1 The Prato industrial district

The identification of the industrial district

The process of metamorphosis undergone in the 1950s led to the creation of that which was later identified as an 'industrial district' – that is, a socioeconomic and territorial entity characterized by 'complementary activities' conducted within an open community and a set of independent, specialized and small and medium-sized firms operating within a relatively restricted area. Thus we can refer to 'the Prato industrial district' or, in relation to the sectoral vocation of the city, to the 'Prato textile district'.

The spatial delimitation of the Prato district has changed over time. During the 1950s and 1960s the district expanded in the area around Prato. For sake of simplicity, we can trace the boundaries to what is today the province of Prato which includes in addition to the city of Prato the

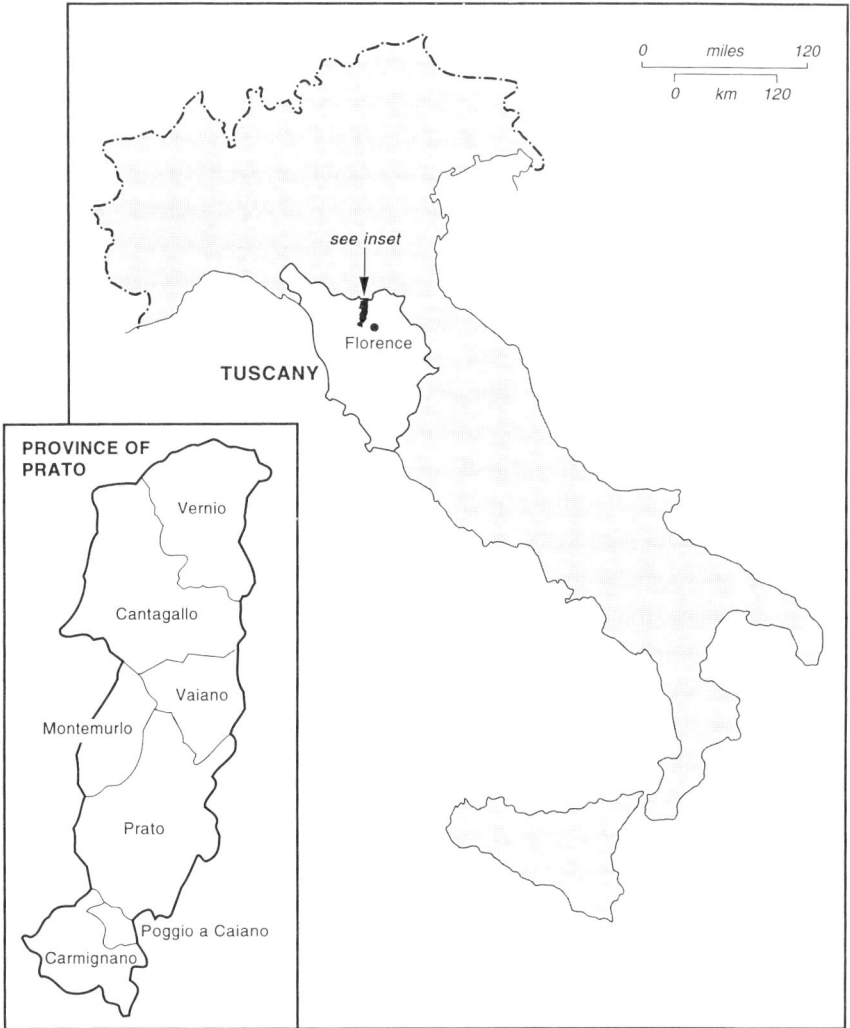

Figure 7.1   The province of Prato

communes of Cantagallo, Carmignano, Montemurlo, Poggio a Caiano, Vaiano and Vernio (see Figure 7.1). The population of this area had doubled in the postwar period and has now reached the level of more than 210,000. The size of the population makes the Prato district the second most important centre of population in Tuscany.[1]

Textile activities tied to those in Prato involve at least partially another six communes in the immediate vicinity: Agliana, Montale and Quarrata in the province of Pistoia and Calenzano, Campi Bisenzio and Barberino del Mugello in the province of Florence. Some of the statistical data will refer to this broader textile area, indicated as the 'Prato textile system' (Balestri, 1990).

The firms

The Prato industrial district is characterized in terms of external image and internal added value by the fact that it is the centre of only one local production system – i.e., textiles – which constitute its primary industry.[2] Despite the crisis of the 1980s, in 1991 Prato's textile industry still employed more than 36,000 workers, equal to 85 per cent of those involved in manufacturing and almost 42 per cent of total employment in the district. There are more than 7,000 textile firms; the average size of the firms is about five workers per firm (Table 7.1). More than 75 per cent of the employees work in firms with fewer than fifty workers.[3]

The Prato textile system, in general, presents a traditional and pre-dominant specialization in carded woollen yarns and fabrics; in 1981 it accounted for 32 per cent of Italian woollen industry employment, 61 per cent of the Italian total in carding spindles, 18 per cent of the combing spindles and 50 per cent of Italian looms.[4] The number of spindles and looms went on increasing up until the beginning of the 1980s (Table 7.2). Already in 1970 the overall total of carded fabric production in Prato surpassed the production of its European competitors (Lorenzoni, 1980).

Other industries more or less connected with the Prato textile system are found in the district. Among those more directly connected are those producting auxiliary services for the Prato textile system such as specialized transportation, computer systems, and complementary industries such as the mechanical-textile one, and the production of plastic accessories, which have their own markets in addition to offering products directly to the textile industry (Table 7.3). Within the Prato textile system we can find other forms of segmentation which will be discussed in greater detail below.

The individual firms in Prato are usually highly specialized in that they operate within single segments or even sub-segments of the production process. Overall, the number of industrial entrepreneurs and self-employed workers in industry is traditionally very high in the district (Trigilia, 1989).

The local institutions

Despite the scale of the immigration (Figure 7.2), at least until a few years ago the unitary image and sense of identification in the district on the part of its members is very strong (see Dei Ottati, Chapter 6 in this volume and Nigro, 1986). Also, the function of financial and manpower support carried out by the extended family has remained strong (Becattini, Chapter 4 in this volume).

Table 7.1 Firms and employees in textile and manufacturing industry Prato Province,* 1961–91

Year	Textile-fashion		Manufacturing industry		Total employed
	Firms	Employees	Firms	Employees	
1961	6,388	38,303	7,447	42,496	51,297
1971	8,740	42,163	9,818	46,898	67,494
1981	11,503	50,216	13,015	56,661	95,471
1991	7,362	36,336	8,649	42,028	92,794
1991/1981 (No.)	−4,141	−13,880	−4,374	−14,633	−2,677
1991/1981 (%)	−36.00	−27.64	−33.55	−25.83	−2.80

Source: ISTAT, *General Census of Industry*.

Note: * Communes of Cantagallo, Carmignano, Montemurlo, Poggio a Caiano, Prato, Vaiano and Vernio.

Table 7.2 The evolution of the Prato textile system*

	1951	1961	1971	1981	1988	1990
Firms[1]	724	7,000	10,600	14,400	14,000[3]	11,800[3]
Employees[1]	21,500	41,000	49,500	61,000	56,000[3]	49,000[3]
Carding spindles[2]	280,000	430,000	600,000	770,000	700,000	400,000
Combing spindles[2]	26,000	58,000	180,000	400,000	450,000	500,000
Looms[2]	5,000	9,000	12,000	13,000	10,000	–

Sources: [1]ISTAT, *General Census of Industry*; [2]UIP Estimates; [3]CERVED, *Survey of Firms*.

Note: * Prato textile system includes textile activities within the province of Prato and six nearby communes: Agliana, Montale, Quarrata and Calenzano, Campi Bisenzio, Barberino del Mugello.

As with many other areas where we find a large number of small and medium-sized enterprises, the Prato district is characterized by a well rooted political subculture. In this case, it has a communist base which has implied a significant freedom of local political practices from clientelistic ties and processes (Trigilia, 1989). Prato's local institutions have traditionally been active and numerous. Without entering into a detailed description of the character and actions of these institutions, two elements have to be taken into account.

In the first place we should remember the relatively cooperative climate of industrial relations within the district up until the most recent years. Trigilia talks about a model of 'flexible compensation'. According to this model: 'The trade unions concentrate on economic-social negotiations . . . tending to compensate for the high level of flexibility. The local government, on its part, contributes with the supply of local services'

Table 7.3 Province of Prato 1971–81. Enterprises and employees, by sector and major economic categories

Sector and class of economic activity	1971		1981	
	Enterprises	Employees	Enterprises	Employees
Agriculture, hunting, forestry and fishing	44	98	49	311
Energy, gas and water supply	13	333	9	449
Electrical industry	9	30	80	645
Manufacturing of which:	10,301	48,093	13,140	56,187
– Metal working, precision instruments	(572)	(2,322)	(818)	(3,306)
– Textile industry	(8,255)	(40,796)	(11,187)	(48,421)
– Shoes, clothing and fabrics for house	(562)	(1,367)	(636)	(1,795)
– Wood and furniture	(259)	(551)	(353)	(1,010)
– Paper, printing, publishing	(50)	(221)	(79)	(360)
– Rubber and manuf. of plastics	(28)	(222)	(91)	(300)
Construction	976	3,737	1,857	4,848
Commerce	4,713	10,028	5,536	14,418
Transportation and communication	562	2,373	1,081	3,320
Banking, Insurance	112	1,010	1,121	4,290
Services	799	1,792	2,147	11,003
Totals	17,529	67,494	25,020	95,471

Source: ISTAT, *General Census of Industry*

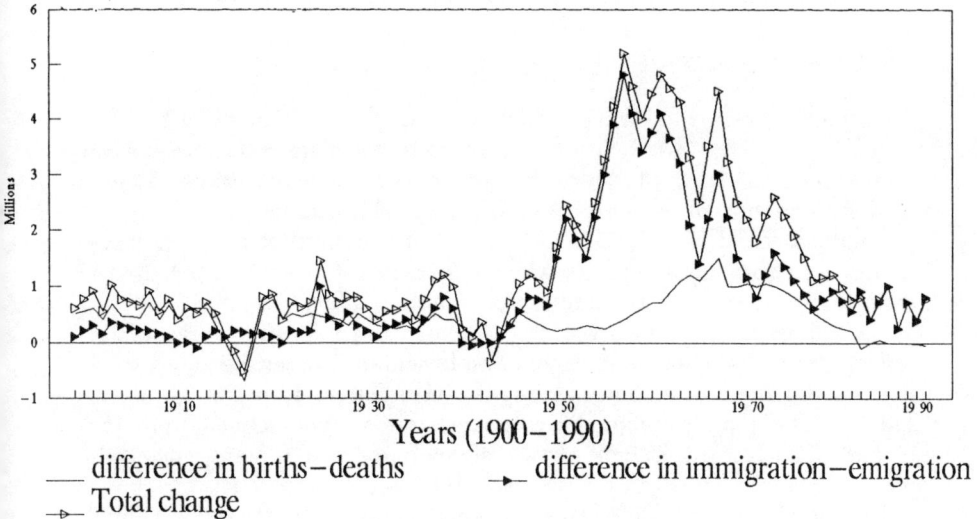

difference in births–deaths   difference in immigration–emigration
Total change

Figure 7.2 Change in the population of Prato, 1900–90

(Trigilia, 1989, p. 327). Another expression of the cooperative climate in industrial relations are the agreements of payment for subcontracting work signed between the local industrial association, Unione Industriale Pratese (UIP), and the local associations of artisans – i.e., Confederazione Nazionale Artigianato (CNA) and the Confederazione Generale Industria e Artigianato (CGIA).[5] Reference can also be made to the work of the 'Permanent Economic Forum on the Crisis of the Prato Textile Industry' (Consulta, 1990). This is a group promoted by the city of Prato in 1988 that brings together local government representatives and representatives from trade unions and entrepreneurial organizations for the purpose of analysing the changes in the system and formulating in response a common strategy.

A second institutional element that needs mention is the increased supply of specialized services offered by many interest groups: from the preparation of applications for social aid and tax declarations for workers on the part of trade unions, to the help with labour negotiations, fiscal rules and legal provisions offered by industrial and artisan organizations. There is also a vast array of commercial and financial services offered by a series of consortia promoted under the sponsorship of entrepreneurial associations. We should also mention the initiatives in the area of environmental protection, urban planning and technological innovation promoted by the cooperation between public and private institutions operating locally and elsewhere (Table 7.4). In general, the supply of services to the system of small industries reinforces the legitimacy of representative institutions and contributes therefore to the solidification of the local social fabric.

7.2   The productive model between the 1960s and 1970s

The production of carded fabrics

The typical Prato productive model that asserted itself in the 1960s was centred on carded wool fabrics. It involved medium and medium-low quality non-standardized fabrics that were sold at moderate prices and used in the production of winter garments usually sold to large-scale markets in the industrialized world (Dei Ottati, Chapter 6 in this volume). These fabrics were produced through an extensive use of recycled wool derived from rags and through the addition of synthetic fibres.

Carded spinning permits the use of textile material with a low level of homogeneity. Through a series of complementary operations, the process prepares for the use of poor quality raw fibres derived from rags or diverse sources. The most common fibre is regenerated wool derived from rags (Figure 7.3). Instead, if the fibres are of good quality and homogeneous the most appropriate procedure is to comb the wool (Figure 7.4).

During the entire 1960s rags, of which Prato is the world's capital, remained the prevalent raw material for the textile processes taking place in Prato and prevalent among the firms with integrated processes which

Table 7.4 Major interventions in support of the development and restructuring of the Prato economy

	Type of organization	Nature of holding	Financial source	Date project initiated	Level of development
1. Support infrastructure					
Infrastructured industrial areas	SPA	–	City, private	End of 1970s	Concluded
Water purification	SPA	Mixed with public majority	City	End of 1970s	Being completed
Transport Centre	SPA		Region	End of 1970s	Work begun
Industrial Aquaduct	Public Body		State–EEC	End of 1980s	Work begun
2. Technological innovation and technological diffusion					
Technical textile	SPA	Mixed majority IMI	Public and private	Mid-1970s	A regime
SPRINT	Consortium	Mixed public majority	ENEA, EEC, Region	1983	A regime
CESIP (engineering study centre)	SRL	Mixed public majority	Region, EEC Univ. private	1992	
CESVIT	Non-profit association	Public	Region, EE.LL.	Mid-1980s	A regime
3. Strengthening of small enterprises					
Promotion consortium	Consortium of firms	Private	State region EEC, private	End of 1970s	A regime
Knitwear service centre	Mixed Consortium	Mixed	EEC, region, City	Mid-1980s	A regime
ASATT Artisan enterprises reaggregation project					
Gulliver	Enterprise Consortium	Private	EEC, region, city	Beginning 1990s	Experiment
Grantessuto	Enterprise Consortium	Private	EEC, region, city	Beginning 1990s	Beginning experiment
Quality centre	SPA	Private	EEC, region, city	1991	
Investment help	–	–	10–20%, EEC and Region		
4. Human resources					
Promolavoro (promotion of new enterprises)	Association	Mixed public majority	Region, EE.LL.	1986	A regime
Professional eduction centre	Public Agency	Region	Region, EEC	Beginning 1970s	A regime
Post-diploma experimental courses	Public Agency	State, city	State, city	Mid-1970s	A regime
International fashion polytechnic	Non-profit association	Mixed public majority	Cities	1985	A regime
Manager education project	–	–	EEC, region	1980s	A regime

Source: IRIS

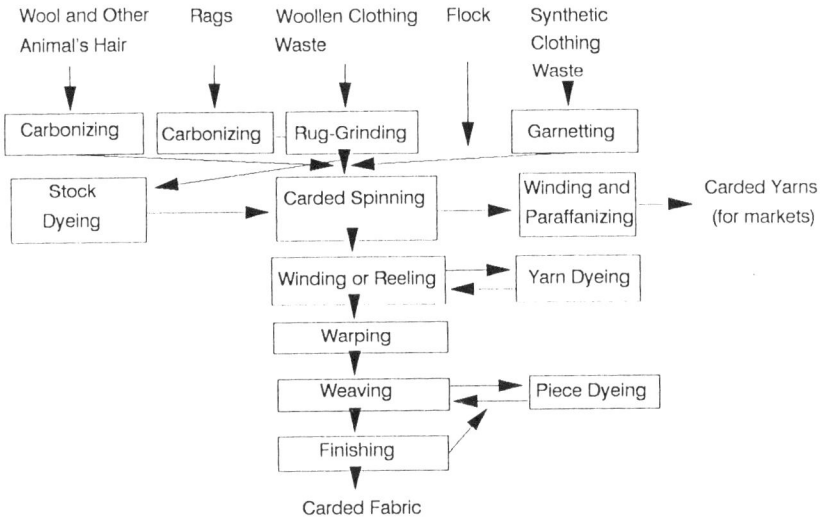

Figure 7.3   Carded fabrics production cycle

Source: SPRINT elaboration

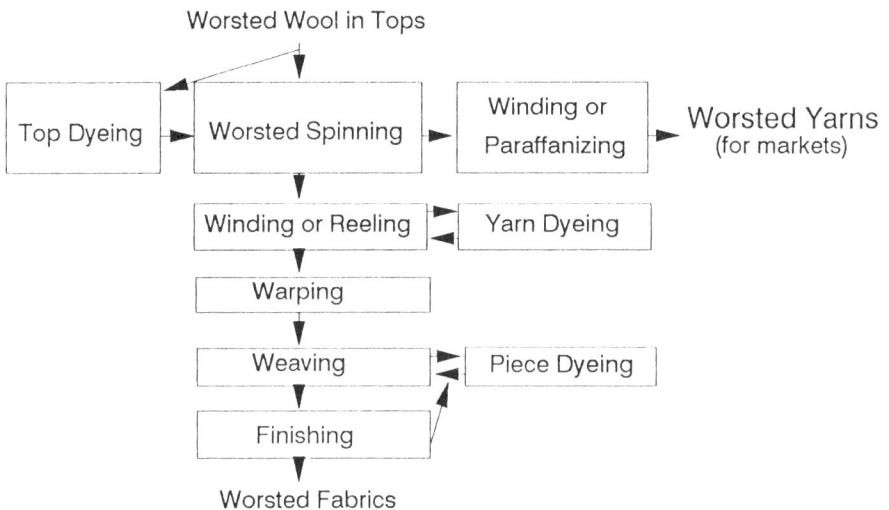

Figure 7.4   Worsted fabrics production cycle

Source: SPRINT elaboration

dominated Prato's industry between the two wars and until the end of the 1950s. Nevertheless, in the 1960s there was a diffusion of chemical fibres mixed in with low-quality natural fibres. The mix allows for a reduction of spun wool and the weight of the material. In addition, the mixed yarns held better than the pure regenerated wool yarns and permitted the use of a vast gamut of colours (Lorenzoni, 1980, p. 515).

Reduced weight, more variety and maintenance of low costs are the bases for the affirmation of the market described above. The reduction of cost is not only tied to the use of low-quality fibres. Keeping costs down and increasing variety of mixes and colours also depend on the ability to develop high levels of specialization, flexibility and innovation through an appropriate division of labour among the manufacturing firms.

Impannatori *and subcontractors*

With regard to the division of labour among firms, the principal distinction is between the 'finishing' firms (*impannatori* and partially vertically integrated woollen mills that concern themselves with the procurement of orders on the national and international markets and the sale of the final product on their own behalf) and specialized subcontractors (*terzisti*) that carry out the major part of the production process.

In the typical model of the production of regenerated wool products the principal specializations of the subcontractors are: the sorting of rags, the *carbonizzo* (carbonizing stove operation), the warper, the weaver, the dyer and the refinisher. Among the subcontractors many are artisans, especially in some phases such as weaving. In other phases – such as spinning, dyeing, and refinishing – the operations are mainly carried out by small industrial firms.[6]

The firms at the end of the production cycle carry out various co-ordination functions: the planning of the products, the acquisition and delivery of the raw materials (rags or textile fibres), the definition of the sequence of subcontractors capable of carrying out certain procedures, the maintenance of good relations with subcontractors and the exercise of control over the production process and quality. At times, these firms also carry out the stocking of the textiles and even some direct manufacturing activities such as the production of samples.

The relationships between the firms involved with refinishing and the subcontractors are often maintained on the bases of face-to-face contacts. Typically, each end-product firm compensates for the variation in the quantity of demand through market relationships with a relatively large circle of occasional subcontractors. However, each firm also has a smaller group of affiliated subcontractors to whom it turns for production of a higher quality than is normally available on the open market, for guarantees on delivery when the subcontracting market is hit by excess demand, or when it needs help in the creation of something new (Bellandi, 1992). *Impannatori* and woollen factories, even if they have design capability in-house, often need the competence of the most skilled subcontractors to complete the design of a new product or organize a new line of production. This is due to the fact that having to deal with production processes that possess a low level of standardization and starting with primary resources that are not standardized, the chances of finding 'holes' in the abstract planning of a new line of production are often significant (Giovannelli, 1983).

The exchange of information with a firm's inner circle of subcontractors is based on a relationship of trust that, in turn, often depends on how the subcontractor assumed his role. It is worth remembering in this context the creation of firms where 'industrialists' (the owners of wool factories and the major *impannatori*) and skilled ex-workers or ex-technicians associate, or the creation of artisan firms on the part of ex-workers and ex-technicians financed by industrialists on the basis of 'reimbursement through sub-contracting work' cited by Dei Ottati in the previous chapter.

This 'going it alone' on the part of technical staff or workers shows, at the beginning, a low level of organizational and financial independence from the industrialists. The level of dependence is tempered by the level of mobility. He who succeeds in surviving – and a lot did survive in the 1960s and 1970s – acquires, over time, autonomy and the more fortunate and capable ones contribute to the renewal of the firms involved in the tail end of the production process, among whom failure is common. On the other hand, if a respected subcontractor begins to systematically fall below the market standard defined by the occasional subcontractors 'the relationship of trust is compromised and those placing orders can turn at minimum costs to other firms' (Trigilia, 1989, p. 295).

The relationships of trust are also upheld, aside from the way that subcontracting firms are born and competition is working, by the local social context: the ease of face-to-face contacts and self-identification with the community facilitate mutual understanding and help to more easily isolate deviant behaviour, even when this is not sanctionable through the market or through legal means (Dei Ottati, 1991). An additional element in stabilizing the relationship of trust is provided by the activities of the representative institutions mentioned above.

Success and the drive towards differentiation

In the 1970s the Prato model achieved a considerable amount of success. Between 1971 and 1981 the number of employees in the Prato textile system increased by 23 per cent (see Table 7.2 above) while in other textile areas in Italy and Europe there were considerable losses in employment and production (Balestri, 1990). Instead, the Prato wool industry quickly increased its levels of quality and creativity for a sector of the fashion industry oriented towards the increasingly rich and sophisticated markets of Western Europe and North America. This involved among other things not only the addition (or exclusive use of) virgin or good-quality fibres but also the use of new and faster machines in one or more phases of the production cycle.[7]

In addition to success there were also forces leading to differentiation. Alongside the firms specialized in organizing the production of carded fabrics and in selling them, there was an affirmation of producers of 'knitwear' and producers specialized in selling woollen yarns that also organized complex webs of subcontractors. In addition to and coherent with pushing upward on the quality scale, there was an increase in the weight of worsted production with an increased differentiation in the fibres utilized (see Table 7.2 above). The division of labour in the production cycle saw the emergence of important nuclei of complementary activities that, in addition to supplying the local textile firms, also had their own autonomous markets. A case in point is offered by the textile machine industry (TEXMA, 1991). These tendencies toward differentiation continued to develop during the 1980s and acquired a greater importance during the periods of crisis: first between 1982 and 1983, and then from 1986 onward as we will see below.

7.3 The change in the 1980s

National and international context

The last decade has been a period characterized by great transformations based on changes in the national and international context and tied to phenomena that have a significant impact on the structure, activities and future of the textile industry and local economy. Even if only briefly, it is worthwhile recalling some of these elements:

- The increase in world trade experienced a strong fall during the mid-1980s.
- The Italian large corporations regained their flexibility in relation to public support policies, a change in the social climate, and the massive introduction of new electronic technology.
- On the other hand, the Italian small firms lost the protection of flexible exchange rates, saw their profit margins shrink and experienced an increase in debt and obligation to pay social costs.
- For the textile industry the 'fashion factor' – that is, the capacity to differentiate products in order to satisfy the variety and variability of tastes and lifestyles of consumers – became an important factor in purchasing products and influencing the market. Success in the fashion industry depended on the capacity to find for each product the right balance among stylistic innovation, intrinsic quality and price.
- The process of international specialization and redistribution of textile production made it possible for some industrialized countries, such as Germany, to reaffirm their production capacity and competitiveness in the international textile trade.[8]

Table 7.5 Fabric exportation on the part of Prato's textile industry

	1982	1985	1986	1987	1988	1989	1990	1991
Value in billions of lire								
Yarns	168	309	249	234	228	252	222	206
Fabrics	811	1,864	1,604	1,552	1,748	1,711	1,663	1,903
of which:								
Wool fabrics	(369)	(754)	(673)	(648)	(675)	(746)	(774)	(917)
Textile fabrics MM*	(411)	(989)	(797)	(708)	(830)	(736)	(646)	(756)
Other textile articles	71	101	96	242	147	180	175	152
Knitwear	582	700	789	810	699	681	753	782
Textile machines	n.a.	63	71	85	76	122	103	111
Total		3,037	2,809	2,923	2,898	2,946	2,916	3,154
Index on basis of 1985 = 100								
Yarns	54.4	100	80.6	75.7	73.8	81.6	71.8	66.7
Fabrics	43.5	100	86.1	83.3	93.8	91.8	89.2	102.1
of which:								
Wool fabrics	(64.3)	(100)	(89.3)	(86.0)	(89.6)	(98.9)	(102.6)	(121.6)
Fibre fabrics MM*	(41.6)	(100)	(80.6)	(71.6)	(83.9)	(74.4)	(65.3)	(76.4)
Other textile articles	70.3	100	95.0	239.6	145.5	178.2	173.3	150.5
Knitwear	83.1	100	112.7	115.7	99.9	97.3	107.6	111.7
Textiles machines	n.a.	100	112.7	134.9	120.6	193.7	163.5	176.2
Total		100	92.5	96.2	95.4	97.0	96.0	103.9

Source: ISTAT, IRPET, Confindustria.

Note: * MM = Man-made fibres.

Prato's textile industry during recent years

In this context, from 1986, there was a fall in Prato's exports (Table 7.5) which represented in the past approximately 60 per cent of local production. The fall in exports was particularly serious for textiles containing mixed fibres with a prevalence of low-cost and low-quality synthetic fibres mixed with wool. There was instead a positive trend in textiles made from good-quality natural and artificial fibres, in which Prato held international market shares reaching 80–90 per cent (CENSIS, 1989).

The contraction of exports between 1984 and 1989, the increase in the importation of yarns (Balestri, 1990), the decrease in volume at the national level in the production of carded fabrics (Figure 7.5), and the drop in the use of electrical energy among Prato's textile firms (Figure 7.6) witness an overall reduction in the volume of Prato's textile production. All of this, tied to the increase in productivity levels (see note 7), produced a considerable drop in the workforce. According to provisional data from the most recent industrial census, between 1981 and 1991, the reduction of employees in industrial jobs amounted to 13,800 jobs (–27 per cent), while there was a decline of 4,100 industrial firms and artisans. For the Prato district it represents the first reduction in firms and employees after thirty-

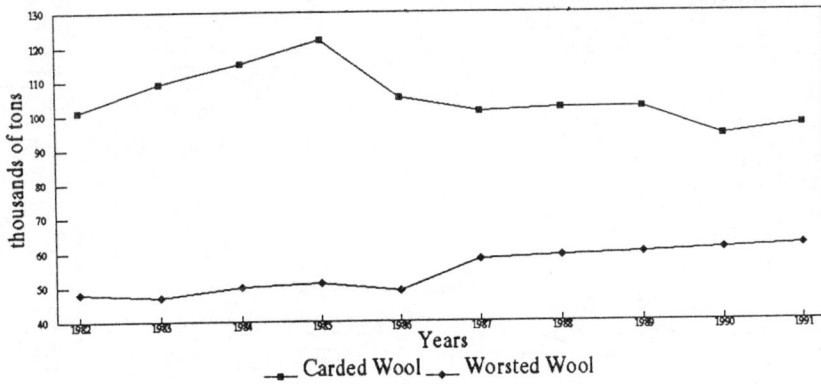

Figure 7.5   National production of carded and worsted woollen fabrics, 1982-91
(thousands of tons)
Source: IRIS elaboration of data from Italian Wool Manufacturers' Association

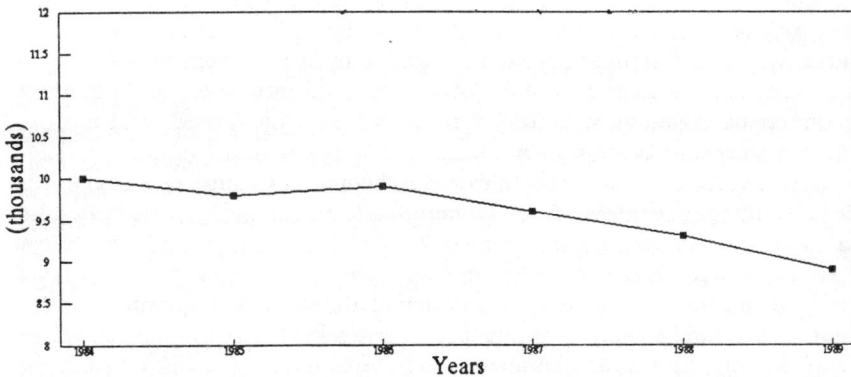

Figure 7.6   Electrical energy consumed by the textile industry of Prato, 1984-89
(Kwh 10[3])
Source: IRIS elaboration of ENEL data

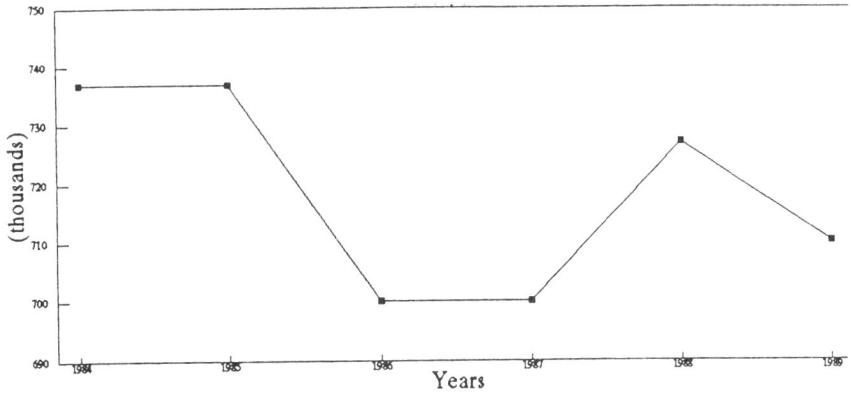

Figure 7.7 Number of electricity users in Prato's textile industry, 1984–89

Source: IRIS elaboration of ENEL data

five years of strong and uninterrupted growth. This is the reason why when the crisis arrived it caught everyone by surprise and unprepared.

The need to restructure the productive structure of Prato was heralded in 1982. The pick-up in exports in the following two years spurred by the strength of the dollar led everyone to forget these first signs of crisis and slowed down realization of the true dimensions of the difficulties which began to manifest themselves in earnest after 1986. As is shown by the drop in the number of textile firms using electricity (Figure 7.7), the reluctance to come to terms with the gravity of the situation and the structural characteristics of the crisis slowed down the search for a reconversion strategy and possible intervention strategies by institutional forces.

In 1982 a consistent number of unemployed were produced, and the number was to increase during the second half of the decade (Table 7.6). Academic studies as well as analyses carried out by local institutions have traced the causes of the crisis to external factors – as mentioned above – as well as internal characteristics of the productive apparatus. In particular the following factors are highlighted: the fall in the dollar and the drastic reduction of the North American market; the change in lifestyles and types of consumption which penalize the demand for heavy products as is the case with carded woollen products; the erosion of the cost advantage of Prato's products; the new competitiveness of the larger textile firms and the excessive fragmentation and reduction in the size of Prato's firms which caused diseconomies and limited the adoption and full use of technological innovations.

In addition to these, many other factors could be added to the list, and some of these would not be of secondary importance. It would be interesting to evaluate the incidence of elements such as economic policies,

Table 7.6 Number of persons looking for work in the Prato province and those on temporary lay-off (hours)

Year	Looking for work	Temporary lay-off ordinary	Temporary lay-off extraordinary
1981	1,695	820,479	84,260
1982	3,876	1,221,591	115,859
1983	6,356	1,762,080	277,598
1984	5,386	386,766	655,903
1985	5,072	177,423	331,358
1986	5,709	723,943	355,816
1987	7,142	1,524,287	836,450
1988	8,292	586,338	1,725,025
1989	7,754	593,714	642,785
1990	5,942	910,213	142,908
1991	5,970	693,280	511,604

Source: UPLMO, INPS, *Annuario Statistico*, Comune di Prato, 1992.

for example, and in particular the cost of borrowing money which is an additional factor provided by the crisis that afflicted the major local bank.[9] The importance of the credit factor in the running of small firms which are often endowed with a low capital stock can be evaluated on the basis of partial indicators, such as in the last two years, the bankruptcy of a few firms well placed in the market and with a substantial number of orders; or long delays in payments for subcontracted work. This type of problem becomes particularly important during times when it is necessary to undertake restructuring/rationalization of firms that cannot be resolved without an adequate level of investment.

The novelty of quantitative reduction

In the past the decline in certain types of Prato's textile products was always preceded or accompanied by the birth and then development of new typologies of textiles. This was the manner in which the progressive losses in the low-cost and low-quality sectors of production were compensated in the 1960s with knitwear and in the 1970s with new fabrics. This was the means by which there has been a slow and constant restructuring of the local textile system with an uninterrupted increase in sites and employees, always in contrast with the tendency at the national and European level which saw production cuts and falls in employment levels.

Even in the 1980s new types of production were introduced. But this was evidently not sufficient to avoid delivering the first real shock to the district's industry and a permanent reduction in enterprises and workers for the first time in the last thirty-five years.

7.4 The readjustment

The product strategy of the finishing firms and the organization of production

By the mid-1980s Prato found itself facing a challenge posed by the significant and permanent reduction in the demand for carded woollen products. The reaction proceeded along two paths: the accentuation of differentiations also within the confines of the textile industry and an increased attention to the quality of the product and service to customers (Balestri, 1990).

If we consider that many of Prato's new fabrics require worsted yarns or artificial and synthetic yarns not produced locally and that many of the renewed carded fabrics require light yarns that do not permit the use of recycled wool, then the speed of adaptation in the type of production is evident from the following figures. The value of imported yarns increased between 1985 and 1989 by 60 per cent, accounting for an increase in the total of imported textile material from 27 to 50 per cent. During the same period, imports of rags declined in value by 58 per cent (Bellandi and Trigilia, 1991, p. 126). Even though Prato remained the leading centre in the world for the production of carded wool, it was no longer possible to refer to a carded products monoculture of the district.[10] Let us examine the process of adaptation in the district.

In a recent study on a few end-product firms, 'selected among those with the highest level of production, capacity for innovation, and ability to be industry leaders in Prato', there emerges an overview of the production strategies adopted by individual firms (Bellandi and Trigilia, 1991, p. 128). Some are still specialized in the offer of traditional products (heavy carded fabrics); others are oriented towards textiles which are new for Prato and sometimes even new for the international market (e.g., imitation fur). Finally, there are firms which produce diversified textile products. They accompany the more or less traditional carded products with a pre-ponderant amount of worsted fabrics. Some Prato entrepreneurs have developed over time a strategy of differentiation, or one of specialization in new products. They now complain that due to the crisis in the carded products market other entrepreneurs are invading their turf and through a quick adaptation of productive capacity run the risk of spoiling the new market.

Thus, the rapid differentiation of Prato textiles seems to result from a decline in typical specialized production activities and an increase in activities both of producers specialized in new products and of diversified operators. The presence of a few innovators has served as a point of reference for imitators who have quickly adapted to the situation (Bellandi and Trigilia, 1991, p. 148).

Among the firms successfully following the various production strategies are those undertaking a change in their organization strategy. In particular, among the producers of traditional products there is the search for an increase in the intrinsic quality of the fabrics that seems to require a more stable relationship with subcontractors, based on organizational links such as the ownership of shares in the enterprise. The relationship with occasional subcontractors seems to be on the decline.

Vertical integration is more diffused among the firms specialized in the production of new types of fabrics. This is the case for imitation furs and synthetic fabrics (Zagnoli, 1993). Among those who have chosen diversification strategies, there seems to be an advantage in what could be defined 'external vertical integration'. The yarns are generally purchased abroad, but there is a noticeable reinforcement of organizational and financial ties with subcontractors in the weaving and refinishing stages, through the creation and extension of 'groups', i.e., a set of firms tied together by a common capital holding (Berardi and Romagnoli, 1984, pp. 90–1; Giovannelli, 1983, pp. 151–3).

While an excess of integration can damage flexibility, for the adjustment to quantity variations attachment to the traditional disaggregation would seem to impose in the short run excessive constraints to the adjustment to new products and quality standards. The problem is that an organizational balance as the one proposed requires cultural and organizational resources which take time to manifest themselves (Bellandi and Trigilia, 1991, p. 147). Despite the lack of targeted empirical data, it seems plausible to hypothesize that the major part of the adaptive behaviour in the textile system was concerned with strategies of diversification. This, however, given the lack of diffusion of the necessary managerial resources to create the organizational links could have been introduced through buying yarns and raw fabrics in markets outside the district and subcontracting to occasional local subcontractors the remaining phases of production, thereby, reducing to a minimum the overall involment of finishing-firms in the production process (NOMISMA, 1989). All of this can justify the continuation of a situation of difficulty for many end-product firms and especially for an extensive group of subcontractors.

Subcontracting strategies

We cannot exclude the existence of a difficult situation even with regard to the subcontracting firms more connected to the stronger finishing firms. A lot worse is the situation of subcontractors who remained outside of this inner circle and who are excluded also from the phases of refinishing which have experienced during recent years a rapid increase in demand.[11]

Outside of these circles, and therefore especially among the artisans, the penalization of subcontractors must have been particularly harsh, both in terms of reduction of demand and its fragmentation. There is in effect a significant reduction in the number of artisan firms of 25 per cent between 1986 and 1990. Their overall presence among the total number of firms in the textile sector declines from 72 per cent in 1986 to 64 per cent in 1990 (SPRINT, 1991).

The search for solutions to escape the difficulties described above followed in large part traditional lines: attempt to increase flexibility and reduce costs. The strategy was followed with skill in the attempt to raise levels of efficiency, which were already high, without radical innovations. This response certainly served to reduce the immediate negative consequences of a serious situation, but it may also have delayed even more the elaboration of a reorganization strategy in response to the change in the production process.

The exasperation of price competition produced contradictory effects on the productive capacity which continued to increase up until the mid-1980s.[12] If the latter has been to a certain extent reduced, this has not always taken place through the expulsion of the marginal firms but often through the sacrifice of the more innovative firms (NOMISMA, 1989; Consulta, 1990). In effect, even among the artisan subcontracting firms there was an attempt to make progress in the area of investments and technological innovation. For these firms the level of debt represented another element of rigidity, given that they were tied to a level of turnover that would guarantee profit margins to cover the interest on loans in addition to an adequate return. This was a problem which did not involve firms with old equipment which had already depreciated and been paid for.

In this context an important role is played by public policies in support of productive activities and restructuring of the sector. It is important to underline that the restructuring of the productive apparatus has been analysed by a variety of local actors: organizations representing entrepreneurs, industrialists and artisan, workers and local government. In particular, the initiative taken by the Prato communal government to create the Consulta Economica for the definition and formulation of a common response to the crisis. The discussions also saw bargaining and stipulation of accords among the participating parties.

According to the strategy elaborated by the various components participating in the Consulta Economica, it was necessary to intervene in, on the one hand, the reduction of productive capacity through the closure of the marginal and obsolete units of production[13] and on the other support for productive investments oriented not so much towards the modernization of technology as towards a partial reaggregation of productive processes within the firm. The restructuring should also have been supported by the payment of unemployment compensation to maintain salaries and favour job mobility through retraining schemes.

The activities of the Consulta are unique in industrial democracy at the local level. The thick web of relationships created between the productive members of the Prato industrial district and diverse levels of government, from the region to the national government and to the European Community, only served to provide partial responses. Also for this reason the coming into effect recently of law 317/91 'Intervention for the innovation and development of small enterprises' has created great interest and represents an innovation. It is an instrument which can at least in part contribute to the resolution of the problems. The more interesting and innovative aspect is represented by the recognition of the district and therefore of its specificity also in terms of the formulation of policies (Becattini et al., 1992). In addition to the possibility of financing the drawing down of obsolete equipment, the law provides for interventions in favour of the consortia and therefore an important incentive to reinforce the ties between firms.

7.5 City and district

New sectors

The regular growth of a productive system goes together with the stability of certain basic characteristics that define the typology of the principal products, contacts with external markets, the division of labour among firms, international and local technology of production, and key skills. These characteristics are affirmed in the industrial district outside the control and direction of any single strategic centre. We are dealing here with a multiplicity of institutions whose role in relation to private operators is more one of persuasion and aggregation and offer of services rather than control and direction. Decentralization can be seen as a decisive limitation to rapid change in one or more structural characteristics of the system. What has happened in Prato during the last few years does not contradict this view. Nevertheless, it suggests some caution in drawing hasty results.

The Prato experience suggests an alternative way of viewing the recent developments. First, the logic of decentralization in a local productive system such as the Prato textile district seems to produce continuously new organizational and productive opportunities. Second, that a few of these opportunities can become the nuclei of alternative models of behaviour in relation to the dominant ones. Third, that there remains a strong push towards imitative innovation even in periods of crisis. Then, the phenomenon of rapid change in the characterizing elements of the productive system can be explained by the coming together of the multiplicity of models and a situation by which human and material resources are freed from adhering to the dominant model. The redundant resources can be reorganized, even if with difficulty, on the basis of imitation and adaptive behaviour provided by alternative models of behaviour.

This vision does not imply that the substitution mechanisms permit a rapid recovery of the conditions (in terms of number of firms and employees) which existed before the crisis. On the other hand, the lack of certain strategic resources, such as for example managerial skills, contribute to explain difficulties and disequilibria in making the adjustments or even false starts and failure. In effect, for the entirety of Prato's textile industry a full recovery is certainly not possible in the short run. Nevertheless, the compensatory mechanisms can operate not only within the textile industry but also between the textile industry and other productive sectors.

In effect between 1986 and 1991 the drop in the number of local textile firms has been in large part compensated by the increase in firms active in the areas of transportation, banking, commerce, and to a lesser extent in the mechanical and construction sectors (SPRINT, 1991, p. 14). The result which emerges is reassuring. It remains to be verified whether the consolidation of the current differences in organization and productive structures are compatible with the conservation of the traditional capacity of aggregation and direction of community energies and competences by the Prato textile industry.

The labour market

Data on the loss of over 13,000 jobs in the textile industry in the decade between 1981 and 1991 demonstrate that the local labour market finds itself in a difficult situation. The first major modification of the area's labour market is provided by the presence of a high level of unemployment which has become by now structural in nature. This has influenced prospects and attitudes towards the job market. Young people seem to have, for example, responded to the crisis by delaying their entry in the job market by seeking a higher level of professional training and orienting their search toward sectors other than the textile industry. For example, there has been an enormous increase in the number of students attending higher secondary schools while there has been a decrease in those enrolled in classes dealing with the textile industry. The transfer rate between compulsory schooling (lower secondary) to upper secondary education which at the beginning of the 1980s was below 60 per cent has almost reached 100 per cent.[14] In this manner, there has been a drastic reduction of 'early entry' into productive activities and, therefore, of learning on the job which had been the most common form of professional training for the artisans and of reproduction of the typical skills necessary in the textile industry.

Other factors have also attenuated the negative repercussions on employment of the fall in demand for labour in the industry. First of all, we should remember the increase in tertiary employment (Table 7.1) and the ageing and low level of reproduction of the local population.

The reproduction of a stock of unemployed represented something new and disturbing for an area which for a long time had only known full employment. But we have to consider that simultaneously with the increase in unemployment there has been an increase in the number of females looking for work. The increasing female component has softened the social impact of unemployment; since female workers have lower levels of expectation and less resistance towards unemployment.

It should also be remembered the increased flexibility in the use of the labour force, for example with the extensive use of work-study contracts and short-term employment. In addition to these structural elements, then, policies designed to maintain standards of living have served to ease tensions and favour job mobility. Trade union sources estimate that between 1986 and 1990 there were approximately 500 early retirements and workers receiving unemployment compensation (Cassa Integrazione Guadagni Speciale) and special unemployment schemes have during the last period remained stable at around 2,000 a year (see also Table 7.6 above).

The changes in the 1980s have therefore profoundly modified and are still modifying the local labour market. The decade closed with a further drop in employment but without raising the level of social conflict. On a more general level, Prato remains in a strong position in regional and national rankings in terms of available income and quality of life. Indicators, such as the level of savings and number of jobs in the banking industry, point in this direction.[15] Even the increase in population through a positive rate of influx demonstrates the continued capacity of Prato to attract immigrants. Overall, the Prato area still seems to maintain its capacity to absorb additional labour and continues to demonstrate a considerable vitality.

Infrastructures

The high level of industrialization of the area and the intensity of the urbanization process which accompanies it have over time produced serious urban and environmental problems. In particular, there is a lack of sufficient water resources due to the enormous increase in consumption but also due to the pollution of ground water and the water-bearing stratum close to the surface.

The continuous increase in industries and population has caused the irregular and discontinuous diffusion of productive units within the city and increasing congestion of the road system. The combination of productive activities along with services and residential uses compromised the possibility of restructuring the industrial plants.

This has produced an accumulation of progressive diseconomies that weigh heavily on the local productive system and the environmental and social viability of the area. Water and land not only became more scarce and, therefore, most costly, but development also requires increased investments to recuperate local resources. During recent years, the commitment of the city has been significant. Prato's system of water filtration and purification is one of the most advanced in Europe, and in the short run the lack of water can be compensated by the opening of the industrial aqueduct and the use of recycled water.

The reorganization and reallocation of productive activities in specifically prepared areas as foreseen by Prato's urban plan has proceeded more slowly. The public–private consortium – Co.Ge.Tra. SpA – created to facilitate the transfer of firms to the industrial area had limited resources and therefore only with difficulty was able to govern the complex reorganization of land use in Prato, which had to take account of the large number of firms involved, their small size, and at time the lack on congruence between their ownership and the ownership of the building in which production took place.

With the reorganization of productive activity in the textile industry, we see a dismantling of industrial buildings and zones that reinforces the need to manage the process. The re-balancing of the economic structure given the reduction in the monosectorial quality of the textile industry and the growth of service activities constitutes an opportunity and a challenge for all of the forces present in the area. It involves, in fact, on one hand, completing the infrastructural network in the area (roads, railways) and, on the other, the localization of metropolitan structures qualifying the urban nature of the area – such as the exposition centre, the transport terminal, some university centres and other cultural centres.

The new activities, the services in support of production, and culture tied to the potential for growth of tourism and the requalification of the most traditional tertiary sector represent additional points of support in the transition, already well underway, of the factory-city into a more complete city.

The requests that are directed towards the local government by those involved in production and by the population at large have these aspects in common: the requalification and efficiency of services, the guarantee of primary resources through the training of human resources and massive investments in infrastructures. This last commitment will be difficult for local government officials in the short run due to the financial difficulties faced by the public sector in Italy.

The difficulties highlighted do not seem to have cancelled out the advantages produced by the district. This has been confirmed by various sources and especially by the entrepreneurs who stress the importance of being located in this area where 'the network of external economies' still sustains today the competitive advantage of enterprises (IRPET, 1991).

7.6 Conclusions: a variety of possible outcomes

The mechanism for change inside and between sectors cited above is capable of producing a variety of results. On one hand, the increase in other manufacturing and tertiary sectors with their own markets can constitute a condition useful for accommodating the reduction of the quantitative importance of the textile system within the district. Such a reduction is still consistent with the presentation of the dominant role of the textile system within the district thanks also to its capacity to adjust organization models, quality standards, and product typology. With a lack of substitutive opportunities of employment for redundant local factors there would not be the same incentives to maintain the local propensity to investments and to mobilize local entrepreneurial and productive energies.

The same alternative mechanisms cited above can, in abstract, have the opposite effect: given the loss of a strongly dominant organizational model, the dilution of the sector's identity and an eventual consolidation of the differences within the textile industry, the unitary image and the sense of identification in the district on the part of its members could erode. In this way the autonomy of the Prato industrial district vis-à-vis the trend of metropolitanization involving the plain area of Florence–Prato–Pistoia would be diminished (Giovannini, 1990).

We have seen in discussing the labour market that the mechanism for sectorial transformation – in addition to other social mechanisms in the district – seems to have effectively contained the tensions created by adjustments within the system. On the other hand, as we have seen in discussing infrastructure, the loosening of the monosectoral nature of the district offers opportunities, physical and economic, to restructure the city for purposes of supporting the qualitative growth of the textile sector. Following this scenario Prato could insert itself into the creation of a greater metropolitan area with its own urban identity characterized by the textile industry.

The support of such a development will depend very much on the strategies of the textile firms. In particular it will depend on the number of firms that have started down new roads of development or have innovated traditional processes, their ability to bring along others, and the viability of the imitative strategies permitting containment of the problems of unemployment and the restructuring of the artisan sector.

An understanding of the advantages of operating the textile industry within the district is, as we have seen, very much alive and tied to an acceptance of its existing limits[16] and already represents a strategic gain. But this strategy is not sufficient if it is not sustained by a resurgence of the traditional ability of the local government to provide direction and by adequate policies from the regional as well as national and community levels of government.

Notes

We would like to thank Carlo Trigilia for permission to use the results of a research project coordinated by him on the Prato textile industry (Bellandi and Trigilia, 1991).

1. The province of Prato was created in 1991 in recognition of a diffused and strong request for separation from the province of Florence. During the 1960s and 1970s the area now corresponding to the province of Prato constituted a largely self-contained labour market (Sforzi, 1990).
2. It is therefore an industrial district characterized by a primary industry, as is the case in many other important industrial districts in Italy (Sforzi, 1990; Porter, 1990, pp. 155 and 443).
3. CERVED data referring to 1990 and published in SPRINT (1991).
4. Data from the Italian Wool Association.
5. We are referring to, for example, the agreement between the trade unions and UIP of 21 July 1987; the agreement between the artisan organizations and UIP on 'Payment scales for sub-contracting artisan firms of 9 January 1991;

Unitary Document of the Artisan Organizations of Prato and Pistoia, 28 February 1989; agreement among artisan organizations–trade unions–UIP on 'Measures for the revitalization of the Prato area'. 3 July 1991.

6. According to law N. 443 of 8 August 1985, an artisan enterprise is understood to be one managed directly by the owner, the main focus of its activity must be in the productive process, and it must not employ more than twenty-two workers.

7. The use of more modern machines moved from 25 per cent in 1975 to 74 per cent in 1985 (CCS, 1986). The transition from a *telaio meccanico a navetta* to a *telaio a proiettile* involves the potential increase of 50 per cent in productivity in spinning and 88 per cent in worsted products (NOMISMA, 1989).

8. The 1980s saw a renewed commitment in industrialized countries towards the textiles-clothing sector. Even if investments abroad register a lower level than in other manufacturing sectors, there is an increasing role played by new forms of production with the affirmation of joint ventures, licensing and productive franchising, the sale of technology, etc. The role of developing countries in the international trade has been contained while competition among industrialized countries has increased (Farnesi and Pozzana, 1990).

9. By the mid-1980s the Cassa di Risparmio of Prato had a deficit of approximately 1,500 billion lire, forcing the Bank of Italy to intervene in order to avoid bankruptcy. From that moment on there was a drastic tightening of credit and an increase in the lending rate.

10. A few estimates place the weight of carded products on the overall value of textile production in Prato at 40 per cent at the end of the 1980s (Balestri and Toccafondi, 1992, pp. 81–2). This study also affirms that at the end of the 1960s the weight was around 90 per cent.

11. The investments required in these phases are in general so high that their insertion into the consolidation strategies discussed above is not easy.

12. According to some estimates, for example, between 1975 and 1985 the number of weaving machines went from 13,000 – with a ratio of 1 to 3 between mechanical and automatic machines, to 10,000 units with a relationship of 3 to 1. A certain overabundance of productive capacity is a structural datum tied to the need to make simultaneously available more options and operative specializations and technologies. In the growth up to 1985, however, this excess was 'expanded' beyond reasonable limits by the policy of the local Cassa di Risparmio.

13. The firms that were supposed to cease production and destroy their machinery were estimated to be around 1,150 artisans employing 2,000 workers in addition to over 75 industrial spinning units with about a thousand employees. A similar result seems to have been reached through the tough selection process carried out by market forces.

14. *Annuario di Statistica del Comune di Prato*, various years.

15. *Bollettino Statistico della Banca d'Italia*.

16. The understanding that there is the need to increase the quality of the product and improve service to clients seems to be widely accepted (Balestri and Toccafondi, 1992, p. 45).

References

Balestri, A., *Cambiamento e politiche industriali nel distretto di Prato*, Milan, Angeli, 1990.

Balestri, A, and Toccafondi, D., *Le trame dello sviluppo*, Prato, Edizioni Pratofortuna, 1992.

Becattini, G., 'The Marshallian Industrial District as a Socioeconomic Notion', in Pike, F., Becattini, G. and Sengenberger, W., *Industrial Districts and Interfirm Cooperation in Italy*, Geneva, International Institute for Labour Studies, 1990.

Becattini, G., Leon, P., Sforzi, F. and Sgobba, G., 'La piccola impresa di fronte alla legge 317/91', *Il Ponte*, 4, 1992.

Bellandi, M., 'The Incentives to Decentralized Industrial Creativity in Local Systems of Small Firms', *Revue d'Economie Industrielle*, 59, 1992.

Bellandi, M. and Trigilia, C., 'Come cambia un distretto industriale: strategie di riaggiustamento e tecnologie informatiche nell'industria tessile pratese', *Economia e Politica industriale*, 70, 1991.

Berardi, D. and Romagnoli, M., *L'area pratese tra crisi e mutamento*, Prato, Consorzio Centro Studi, 1984.

Brusco, S. 'A Policy for Industrial Districts', in Goodman, E. and Bamford, J. (eds.), *Small Firms and Industrial Districts in Italy*, London, Routledge, 1990.

CENSIS, *Imprenditorialità e nuovo sviluppo nella provincia di Firenze*, Rome, Censis, 1989.

Consorzio Centro Studi (CCS), *Relazione annuale sulla economia e l'occupazione nell'area pratese*, Prato, CCS, 1986.

Consulta Economica Permanente, *Analisi e proposte per un piano integrato di interventi per la crisi tessile pratese*, Prato, CEP, 1990.

Dei Ottati, G., 'The Economic Bases of Diffuse Industrialization', *International Studies of Management and Organization*, 1, 1991.

Farnesi, P. and Pozzana, G., *Il sistema produttivo toscano della moda. L'evoluzione recente nel contesto internazionale*, Florence, IRPET, 1991.

Giovannelli, L., *Cambiamento tecnologico e modelli organizzativi. Il caso dell'industria tessile di Prato*, Prato, Edizioni del Palazzo, 1983.

Giovannini, P., 'La costruzione sociale del distretto e le sue trasformazioni', in Perulli, P. (ed.), *Le relazioni industriali nella piccola impresa*, Milan, Angeli, 1990.

IRPET, *Indagine sulle imprese toscane del gruppo moda. Relazione conclusiva*, Florence, 1991.

Lorenzoni, G., 'Lo sviluppo industriale di Prato', *Storia di Prato*, Prato, Edizioni Cassa di Risparmio e Depositi di Prato, 1980.

Nigro, G., 'Il caso Prato', *Storia d'Italia. La Toscana*, Turin, Einaudi, 1986.

NOMISMA, *Prospettive del conto terzismo nel quadro dell'evoluzione del modello pratese*, Bologna, NOMISMA, 1989.

Porter, M., *The Competitive Advantage of Nations*, London, Macmillan, 1990.

Sforzi, F., 'The Quantitative Importance of Marshallian Industrial Districts in the Italian Economy', in Pike, F., Becattini, G. and Sengenberger W. (eds.), *Industrial Districts and Inter-firm Co-operation in Italy*, Geneva, Internation Institute for Labour Studies, 1990.

Signorini, L.F., 'Grandi e piccole imprese negli anni ottanta: la ristrutturazione dell'industria in un'analisi di dati di bilancio', *Temi di discussione*, Banca d'Italia, 157, 1991.

SPRINT, '1° rapporto sul sistema economico pratese 1990', (edited by A. Balestri), Quaderni di SPRINT, Prato, 1991.

TEXMA, *Industria meccanotessile*, Prato, 1991.

Trigilia, C., 'Il distretto industriale di Prato', in Regini, M. and Sabel, C. (eds.), *Strategie di riaggiustamento industriale*, Bologna, Il Mulino, 1989.

Zagroli, P., *Percorsi di diversificazione dei distretti industriali: Il caso di Prato*, Turin, Giappichelli, 1993.

8 Case Study III: Santa Croce in context or how industrial districts respond to the restructuring of world markets

Ash Amin

The literature on industrial districts seems to have reached something of an impasse. On one side the proponents of industrial districts sit around their camp fires, supposedly wild eyed with enthusiasm, talking flexible specialization and post-Fordism. On the other side are a series of supposedly grim-faced critics, shouting destructive comments about globalization and corporate networks from out of the mist. This chapter is an attempt to break out of this often acrimonious impasse. We want to take the emergence of new localized industrial complexes seriously, but we want to set them firmly within a context of expanding global corporate networks.

Accordingly, the chapter is in four parts. In the first part, we will summarize the key arguments of the localization thesis which predicts a return to industrial districts; and some of the major criticisms that have been made of the claim that there is a resurgence of the regional economy on a pervasive scale. In the second part, we will attempt to reformulate the localization and globalization theses so as to provide a space for local agglomeration within growing global production filières. In particular, we will want to focus on Marshall's idea of industrial atmosphere, indicating a set of socio-cultural characteristics which are still crucial in global production filières and which can lead to a degree of localization. The third part of the paper attempts to illustrate these and other contentions via a consideration of the history of one industrial district: Santa Croce in Tuscany, which has become a Marshallian industrial district of the old kind over the last twenty years. Finally, in the fourth part, we address some of the local economic development policy implications of the previous parts of the chapter.

8.1 The localization thesis

The most powerful case for the possibility of a major return to the regional economy comes from a group of writers speculating on the rise of locally agglomerated production systems out of the crisis of mass production. What is envisaged, to put it somewhat reductively, is a return to a division of labour between self-contained, product specialist regional economies as first conceived by Adam Smith at a national level. This is a thesis which draws upon the work of Michael Piore and Charles Sabel (Piore and Sabel, 1984; Sabel, 1989), Allen Scott and Michael Storper (Storper and Scott, 1989), Paul Hirst and Jonathan Zeitlin (1989, 1991) and others borrowing the concepts of 'flexible specialization' or 'flexible accumulation',[1] to describe the transition to a new era of vertically disintegrated and locationally fixed production.

The key argument is that the irreversible growth in recent decades of consumer sovereignty, market volatility and shortened product life-cycles, requires production to be organized on an extremely flexible basis. Size, scale, hierarchy, vertical integration and task dedication on the part of machinery and employees, are deemed to be too inflexible to turn out short runs of better quality and differentiated goods with the minimum of time and effort. Instead, the market is said to require decentralized coordination and control; the 'de-verticalization' of the division of labour between independent but interlinked units; numerical and task flexibility among the workforce; greater reliance on innovation, ingenuity and skills; the deployment of multi-purpose and flexible tools and machinery; and the elimination of time and wastage in supply and delivery.

Such a change is said to be particularly evident in industries which face pronounced volatility and product innovation in their niche markets. Examples include electronics, designer clothing, craft products and other light industrial consumer products. In organizational terms, the new market circumstances are said to require a radical transformation of the production system towards flexible intra-firm and interfirm arrangements which can simultaneously combine the economies of scale, scope and versatility.

This change, it is argued, implies a return to place – a dependence on locational proximity between different agents involved in any production filière. Agglomeration is said to offer a series of advantages upon which a system of vertically disintegrated production can draw. Echoing the factors first identified by Alfred Marshall in his work on small-firm districts in Lancashire and Yorkshire during the nineteenth century, these advantages are said to include the build-up of a local pool of expertise and know-how and a culture of labour flexibility and cooperation resulting from dense social interaction and trust; lowered transport and transaction costs; and the growth of a local infrastructure of specialized services, distribution networks and supply structures. Via the consolidation of particular product specialists in different regions is anticipated a federation of self-contained regional economies, each with its own cumulative causation effects drawing upon strong external economies of agglomeration.

Empirical verification of this thesis comes from the claim that over the last few decades the most dynamic and competitive examples of industrial restructuring have been 'Marshallian' in their spatial dynamics. The examples which are quoted have now become almost too familiar. They include high-tech, R&D and innovation-intensive areas such as Silicon

Valley, Boston, the M4 corridor, Grenoble and other successful techno-poles. They also include industrial districts in both semi-rural contexts such as those in the Third Italy regions and as well as those in inner-city environments (e.g., motion pictures in Los Angeles, the furniture industry in inner London), in which networks of specialist small firms produce craft or quality consumer goods. Finally, also cited is the example of areas such as Baden–Württemburg in Germany, where leading-edge large companies (e.g., Bosch) are said to rely on local subcontracting and supply networks for their flexibility and innovative excellence.

The significance of this thesis should not be underestimated, equating, as it does, industrial renovation with territorial development. The cited examples are very real cases of success, and their experiences could inform policy measures in other areas. The novel conceptual aspect of the thesis is (re)discovery of the locational importance of patterns of linkages and the formation of interfirm relationships, notably in relation to the exchange of information and goods between buyer and seller and its influence on linkage costs. The new literature makes the interesting proposition that negotiations involved in producing and exchanging certain types of commodity are less conveniently carried out at a distance. Customer-specific supplies, for instance, are often based on extensive technical cooperation between the seller and the buyer. Therefore such cooperation requires reliable and rapid communication, usually best conveyed through personal contacts. Production of customized goods and services under conditions of 'dynamic' competition, the hallmark of the post-mass production economy, will therefore tend to bring with it agglomeration and local networking.

To anticipate a pervasive, perhaps even total, return to local production complexes in the post-Fordist economy is nonsensical, for a number of reasons.[2] First, it is inaccurate to refer to the conditions and areas cited by the localization thesis as the only examples of success. Others, must surely include the reconsolidation of the major metropolitan areas such as London, Milan, Frankfurt and Paris as centres of growth, through their magnet-like pull on finance, management, innovation, business services and infrastructure. Reasons related to their status as core metropolitan areas and size as centres of consumption have far more to do with their economic success than the rediscovery of Marshallian tendencies. Should any citation of success not also include the resurgence of major provincial cities such as Birmingham, Turin and Grenoble, which have managed to carve out a niche as intermediate centres of agglomeration within global financial, corporate and service networks? Indeed, why not also include, as an example, the growing concentration of wealth in certain rural areas characterized by an odd combination of capital intensification in agriculture, the decentralization of offices and service industries and in-migration by commuters looking for a pleasant lifestyle? These additions to the geography of 'post-Fordist success' have little in common with the logic of flexible specialization.

Second, in proposing local agglomeration as the symbol of a future regime of capital accumulation, the localization thesis effectively rules out the possibility of transformation and change within the very areas cited as examples of post-Fordist growth. These areas, too, are likely to evolve and, perhaps, fragment internally, in much the same way as did for example Alfred Marshall's cutlery district in Sheffield in the course of the twentieth century. Evidence of such change is already apparent in 'mature' production complexes such as Silicon Valley, now being drawn into a wider spatial division of labour as a result of intense inward investment by overseas multinational corporations, and the export of assembly and intermediate production functions respectively to areas of cheap labour and growing market demand. Some Italian industrial districts, too, are undergoing change, as local linkages begin to replace external ones, owing to either the threat of takeover of local banks by foreign financial institutions, or the increase in international rather than local intra-firm and interfirm linkages (see section on Santa Croce below as well as Amin, 1989; Bianchini, 1990; Harrison, 1990).

Third, taking the ingredients for local success identified by the localization thesis seriously, it has to be concluded that the proliferation of localized production complexes is likely to be restricted by the fact that these ingredients are not readily transferable to other areas. Local containment of the division of labour requires a gradual build-up of know-how and skills, cooperative traditions, institutional support, specialist services and infrastructure. These not only take time to consolidate, but also escape the traditional instruments of spatial policy owing to their ephemeral and composite nature (Amin and Robins, 1990). In addition, there remains the problem that 'new' growth cannot, as on a *tabula rasa*, sweep aside local traditions which might resist such change (Glasmeier, 1991). The dismal failure of strategies to promote technopoles in different European less-favoured regions (LFRs), as well as efforts to encourage greater local networking among and between small and large firms within the depressed industrial regions bears witness to this difficulty.

A final problem with the notion of a pervasive spread of local production complexes is related to the observation made by a number of critics that there is no conclusive evidence of the demise of Fordist principles of mass production and consumption and of the multitude of labour processes which coexisted under Fordism (e.g., customization, batch production, mass assembly, continuous flow). The idea of a clean break between one macro-system dominated by one way of doing things and another regime with its own distinctive organizational structure, is too simple a caricature of historical change and a denial of the ebb and flow, the continuity and discontinuity and the diversity and contradiction that such change normally suggests (see Gertler, 1988; Sayer, 1989; Thrift, 1989). Sensitivity to diversity is particularly essential when it comes to the analysis of the geography of production. Depending on the labour process in an industry, the organisational cultures of the players involved, the nature of the areas in which activity is located and the market or macroeconomic circumstances surrounding individual sectors, a diversity of industrial geographies can be produced, with each offering different options of the spectrum between locational fixity and global mobility.

The emergence of new localized production complexes to conclude this section, should be noted seriously. But, this cannot become a basis for assuming, as two observers have done, that 'the mode of production, has in a sense, gone back to the future', with 'local economies . . . already on the march' (Cooke and Imrie, 1989, p. 326). If localities are on the march, it is, if anything, as argued in the section below, to the tune of globalizing forces in the organization of production; a process in which local territorial integrity is far from guaranteed.

8.2   A reformulation: global networks

So far we have followed a fairly standard critique of the current literature on the resurgence of local economies. The literature has rather limited analytical power, most particularly because of a tendency to cling to a model which is locally based and which does not therefore recognize the importance of emerging global corporate networks. In this chapter we will want to retain the notion of 'localization' but we want to relocate the account in two ways. First, we will want to consider industrial districts and local complexes as the outgrowths of a world economy which is still rapidly internationalizing and which is still a world of global corporate power. Second, against an incipient economism in explaining the strengths of localized production, in order to provide a reformulation of the significance of local networking, we will want to build on Marshall's work on 'industrial atmosphere', trying to analyse why such an atmosphere might still prove central in a world economy where transactions are increasingly indirect. In other words, we want to cross the new international political economy with the new economic sociology.

We take it that an important shift has occurred in the 1970s and 1980s and that this is a move from an international to a global economy. This global economy has many characteristics of which four are particularly important. First, industries increasingly function on an integrated world scale, through the medium of global corporate networks. As a consequence, the control that multinational corporations (whether foreign or domestically owned) exert over employment, investment and trade has continued to grow in most developed economies through the 1980s and into 1990s.

Second, corporate power has continued to advance, so that the new global industries are increasingly oligopolistic; progressively cartelized. This intensifying concentration is best seen in the various merger booms around the world in the 1980s. For example, the EC saw a massive 25 per cent increase in the number of industrial mergers across a wide range of sectors (Jacquemin, Buiges and Ilzkovitz, 1989), leading to an increase in seller concentration levels, increasingly on an international rather than only a national scale.

But, third, and importantly, today's global corporations have themselves become more decentralized through increased 'hollowing out', new forms of subcontracting, new types of joint ventures, strategic alliances, and other new 'networked' forms of corporate organization. Thus corporations increasingly resemble 'flattened hierarchies'. However, there is little evidence to suggest that operational and organizational decentralization has resulted in a similar degree of devolution of power and control. 'Hollowing out' for example, has led to forward vertical integration by market leaders in order to secure stategic control over markets and distribution networks. New developments in subcontracting also, have often led to preferred status being bestowed on fewer suppliers linking them more tightly into corporate hierarchies, and threatening the survival and growth of other suppliers. Strategic alliances, too, appear to be global partnerships between major oligopolies seeking to share markets and R&D costs. In other words, some form of centred control still exists, and in the hands of global corporations, thus suggesting that new developments like those noted above may well represent simply an extension and sharing of power beyond the boundaries of the individual firm, among key actors in a value-added network, rather than a genuine spread of authority to smaller or local players in corporate networks (Amin and Dietrich, 1991).

Further, it is by no means clear that these new developments are local phenomena or even have inevitable localized consequences. Increasing corporate integration may well be accompanied by increasing *geographical* integration, as more and more places are drawn into, or excluded from, the web of global corporate networks. Thus, against the benefit that the operational status of sites within these networks might be more complex and more autonomous than that of sites trapped in rigid (Fordist) intra-corporate hierarchies. The fact remains that they are still locked into a global corporate web and therefore not restricted to local ties. In other words the sites might be relatively autonomous but they are not free agents.

Fourth, and finally, there is a new, more volatile, balance of power between nation-states and corporations, which we might call 'short-run corporatism'. The nation-state's ability to intervene in the world economy has been weakened because states have been 'hollowed out' (Held, 1991), and because states are often internally divided. But corporations also find it difficult to impose a strategic direction on the world economy for reasons such as the unstable nature of business alliances and the contradictory interests embedded in individual industries (and even, sometimes, individual firms). The result is the increasing prominence of cross-national issue coalitions 'uniting fragments of the state, fragments of particular industries and even fragments of particular firms in worldwide networks' (Moran, 1991, p. 133).

The net result of these four developments has been the growth of increasingly integrated global production filières orchestrated and coordinated by large corporations. But, because these filières are more decentralized and less hierarchically governed, there are in fact a number of very considerable problems of integration and coordination. Three of these, each related to the other, stand out.

The first problem is one of *representation*. Information has to be gathered and analysed about what is happening in these filières. But, the benefit of advances in global communications and information-processing capacity, to the growth of a globally oriented business press (Kynaston, 1985) and a whole industry of industrial research and analysis, is a two-edged one. It has produced a massive increase in the quantity and even the quality of information, but the problems of how that information is interpreted and who has access to the interpretations remains: indeed it is probably more pressing. There is *a growing interpretive task*. What can be said is that the 'stories' that are circulated about a global production filière and how they are scripted, constitute that filière's understanding of itself. Indeed new work in 'economic sociology' (e.g., Adler and Adler, 1984; Block, 1990; Zukin and Dimaggio, 1990) suggests that the only way of making sense of large and complex economic systems is through the formation of social cliques within which these stories circulate. This point related to those of Giddens (1990, 1991) and Strange (1988, 1991) who have pointed out that what they call 'expert systems' or 'knowledge structures' have become a critical part of the global economy and these systems or structures are increasingly asymmetric.

The second problem is one of social *interaction*. Global production filières are not just social structures, they are sociable structures. There is constant social interaction within them. Indeed this is one of the ways in which they are able to be understood. Interaction promotes particular discourses and taps into particular knowledge structures. Perhaps one of the most misleading articles of the early 1980s was Offe and Wiesenthal's (1979) where they suggested that the capitalist class is a monological entity. Of course, capitalists have many advantages but they are still dialogical beings. In particular, social interaction is still needed to gather information and to tap into particular knowledge structures, to make agreements and coalitions, and to continually cement relations of *trust*, of implicit contract (Marceau, 1989). New or heightened forms of corporate interaction, like joint ventures and strategic alliances, have made social interaction more rather than less central to many aspects of corporate life.

The third problem is one of tracking *innovation*. The problem is how to keep up levels of product and process innovation in a decentralized system (especially when the pressure to produce more products has increased) and, perhaps more important still, how to market products successfully in the early customized stages when they can succeed or fail and when a small critical mass of customers is needed. In turn, success depends critically on representation and interaction since the stories that are told and who they are recounted to influence a product's chance of success.

Thus the world economy may have become decentralized, but it is not necessarily becoming decentred. Centres are still needed, even in a world of indirect communication, for three reasons related to the problems above regarding representation, interaction and innovation.

Centres, in the first place, are needed to represent, that is to generate and disseminate discourses, collective beliefs, stories about what world production filières are like. These discourses are constitutive of the direction in which industries and corporations can go – whether we are talking about new fashions in design or products or new management trends (like strategic alliances). They are the understandings industries make of themselves. As well, centres are needed as points at which knowledge structures, many of which carry considerable social barriers to entry, can be tapped into. Often such centres can constitute a local knowledge structure which has 'gone global'. In other words, these are centres of *authority*.

Second, centres are needed to interact, i.e., to act as centres of sociability, so gathering information, establishing or maintaining coalitions, and monitoring trust and implicit contracts. Third, they are needed in order to develop, test, and track innovations. Centres produce a discursive mass sufficient to help generate innovations; contact with numerous knowledgeable people identifies gaps in the market, new uses for technologies, and so on. In the case of certain products (e.g., financial products), development occurs in close liaison with most who are the potential sources of reward. Centres are associated to provide sufficient mass in the early stages of innovation. Their social networks provide rapid reactions, and an initial market. The success or failure of products, especially in the early stage, can depend upon the stories told about them. Finally, centres are still needed, to some at extent at least, to keep track of innovations; that is, as judges of their success.

These have to be *geographical* centres, that is, place-bound communities in which the agglomeration and interaction among firms, institutions and social groups acts to generate and reinforce that 'industrial atmosphere' which nurtures the knowledge, communication and innovation structures required for retaining competitive advantage in a given global production filière. In other words, the localization of the functions of the 'head', contributes towards resolving problems outlined earlier facing global cooperate networks.

To be sure, this form of localization is quite different from the older and more familiar habit of the vertically integrated, hierarchical firm to concentrate its strategic functions, its 'head', in headquarters located in major metropolitan cities. In contrast to this latter example of 'tight-encasement' of the 'head' within a closed corporate, neo-Marshallian nodes in global networks act, as it were, as a collective 'brain', as centres of excellence in a given industry, offering for collective consumption, local contact networks, knowledge structures and a plethora of institutions underwriting individual entrepreneurship (see Peck, 1991; Todling, 1991; Tornqvist, 1991).

Such 'socialization' of the functions of the head, amounting to the 'valorization' of a local community, itself as an active factor serving to help local industry to maintain industrial supremacy, appears to be of particular relevance in industries characterized by knowledge-based competition, rapidly changing technological standards and volatile markets. All three are conditions of a greater spread of costs and risks among individual agents, as long as continuity in the flow of information, goods and services between firms, institutions and social groups is maintained. This is precisely the advantage which Marshallian nodes are able to offer – an industrial atmosphere and infrastructure which firms, small and large, isolated or interconnected, can dip into as and when required.

8.3   Marshall in Tuscany: leather tanning in Santa Croce Sull'Arno

Santa Croce is a small town in the lower Arno Valley, forty kilometers east of Pisa, which specializes in the production of medium to high-quality cured bovine leather for predominantly the 'fashion' end of the shoe and bag industries. There are only two other major leather tanning areas in Italy: Arzignago in the Veneto, which is dominated by a small number of large, vertically integrated and highly mechanized tanneries, oriented towards the furnishing and upholstery industry; and Solofra in the south (Campania), which specializes in less-refined, non-bovine, cured leather for the clothing industry. The lower Arno Valley accounts for about 25 per cent of national employment in the leather and hide tanning industry.

In Santa Croce, an area no larger than 10 sq. km., are clustered 300 artisan firms employing 4,500 workers and 200 subcontractors employing 1,700 workers. The real figures are probably much higher as the latter capture only those firms officially registered respectively with the Santa Croce Association of Leather Tanners and the Association of Sub-contractors. In 1986, the combined turnover of these 500 firms was £860 million (one-tenth of which was that of the subcontractors). On average, the area derives 15 per cent of its sales revenue from exports, almost 80 per cent of which are destined for the EC. Although the share of exports has been growing, the industry is still heavily dependent on the Italian market, particularly upon buyers in Tuscany, who account for over 40 per cent of the domestic market.

Twenty years ago, Santa Croce was not a Marshallian industrial district. There were many fewer firms, production was more vertically integrated, the product was more standardized (albeit artisanal) and the balance of power was very much in favour of the older and larger tanneries. Today, Santa Croce is a highly successful 'flexibly specialized', small-firm, industrial district, which derives its competitive strength from specializing in the seasonally based fashion wear niche of the industry. Typically, market conditions in this sector – e.g., product volatility, a very short product life-cycle, design-intensity, flexibility of volume – demand an innovative excellence and organizational flexibility which Santa Croce has been able to develop and consolidate over the last two decades by building upon its artisan strengths.

The booming demand for Italian leather fashion wear in the 1970s and 1980s provided the occasion for area-wide specialization and growth in the output of cured leather. That such growth was to occur through a multiplication of independent small firms supported by a myriad of task-specialist subcontractors, was perhaps more a result of specific local peculiarities than an outcome of the new market conditions. Opposed to the highly polluting effects of the tanning process – Santa Croce is one of those places in which you can recognize the Marshallian 'industrial atmosphere' by its smell – the local leftist administration was unsympathetic to factory expansion applications and also refused, until very recently, to redraw the structure plan to allow for more and better factory space. This, together with the strong tradition of self-employment and small-scale entrepreneurship in rural Tuscany, effectively led to a proliferation of independently owned firms, scattered in small units all over Santa Croce. Two further encouragements to this process of fragmented entrepreneurship were, first, the preference of local rural savings banks to spread their portfolio of loans widely but thinly to a large number of applicants as a risk-minimization strategy and, second, the variety of fiscal and other incentives offered by the Italian state to firms with fewer than fifteen employees.

This initial, and somewhat 'accidental', response to a situation of rapidly expanding demand was gradually turned into an organizational strength capable of responding with the minimum of effort and cost to new and rapidly changing market signals. The tanners – many of whom call themselves 'artists' – became more and more specialized, combining their innate 'designer' skills with the latest in chemical and organic treatment techniques, to turn out leathers of different thickness, composition, colour and design for a wide variety of markets. The advantage for buyers, of course, was the knowledge that any manner of product could be made at the drop of a hat in Santa Croce.

The small firms were also to keep costs down without any loss of productive efficiency through different mechanisms of cooperation. One example is the joint purchase of raw materials in order to minimize the buying price. Another is the pooling of resources to employ export consultants. The main device for cost flexibility, however, has been the consolidation of an elaborate system of putting-out between tanners and independent subcontractors (often ex-workers). The production cycle in leather tanning is composed of fifteen to twenty phases, of which at least half are subcontracted to task-specialist firms (e.g., removal of hair and fat from the uncured skins, splitting of the skins, flattening and drying). Constantly at work, and specializing in operations which are most easily mechanized, the subcontractors have been able to reduce drastically the cost of individual tasks at the same time as providing the tanners with the numerical flexibility demanded by their market. This articulate division of labour among and between locally based tanners and subcontractors – combining simultaneously, the advantages of complementarity between specialists and competition between the numerous firms operating in identical market niches – is perhaps the key factor of success.

But other factors have also played their part. One is area specialization. Santa Croce, like other industrial districts, past and present, is a one-product town offering the full range of agglomeration and external economies associated with local excellence along the entire filière of activities associated with leather tanning. In the area, there are the warehouses of major international traders of raw and semi-finished leather as well as the offices of independent import agents, brokers and customs specialists. There are the depots of the major multinational chemical giants as well as locally owned companies selling paints, dyes, chemicals and customer-specific treatment formulas to the tanners. There are at least three savings banks which, consistently, have provided easy and informal access to finance. There are several manufacturers of plant and machinery, tailor-made for the leather-tanning industry, and there is a ready supply-base for second-hand equipment and maintenance services. There are several score of independent sales representatives, export agents and buyers of finished leather in the area. The local Association of Leather Tanners, the Mayor's office, the bigger local entrepreneurs and the Pisa offices of the Ministries of Industry and Trade also act as collective agents to further local interests at national and international trade fairs. There are several international haulage companies and shipping agents capable of rapidly transporting goods to any part of the world. There is, at the end of the value-added chain, a company which makes glue from the fat extracted from the hides and skins. There is, finally, a water purification depot collectively funded by the leather tanners, the effluence of which is sold to a company which converts the non-toxic solids to fertilizer. No opportunity is missed in Santa Croce.

The entire community in Santa Croce, in one way or another, is associated with leather tanning. This provides new opportunities, through spin-off, along the value added chain, which in deepening and refining the social division of labour, guarantees the local supply of virtually all the ingredients necessary for entrepreneurial success in quality-based and volatile markets. To use the language of neoclassical economics, over and above firm-specific and asset-specific advantages, exists an area-wide asset which individual entrepreneurship draws upon. This 'valorization' of the milieu is a product of the progressive deepening of the social division of labour (vertical disintegration) at the local level. The area not only produces specialized skills and artisan capability, but also powerful external economies of agglomeration and a constant supply of industry-specific information, ideas, inputs, machinery and services – Marshall's 'industrial atmosphere'.

Thus far, the success of Santa Croce as a Marshallian industrial district has been ascribed to two broad sets of factors. One is the 'fortuitous' combination, since the early 1970s, of new market opportunities (the fashionwear sector) and a minimum set of inherited local capabilities (leather tanning skills, a craft culture and so on). The second is the progressive vertical disintegration of the division of labour and its local containment.

There is also a third factor which has come to play a key role in safeguarding the success of the area. This is the institutionalization, at the local level, of individual sectional interests (e.g., the Association of Tanners, the Association of Subcontractors, savings banks, the Mayor's office, trades union branches, etc.), as well as a sense of common purpose which draws upon Santa Croce's specialization in one industry and the intricate interdependences of a vertically disintegrated production system. Not only has this prevented the growth of rogue individual profiteering which might destabilize the system of mutual interdependence, but it has also created a mechanism for collectivizing opportunities and costs as well as ensuring the rapid transmission of information and knowledge across the industrial district.

The 'collectivization of governance' has been of particular importance for the industrial district in recent years, as it has tried to cope with new pressures. By the mid-1980s, a honeymoon period of spectacular success for virtually all enterprises was coming to an end. This was the result of growing competition in institutional markets from fashionwear-oriented tanneries in south east Asia, a decline in demand from the Italian footwear industry, big price increases coupled with shortages in the availability of uncured skins and hides, and new costs attached to the introduction of environmental controls on effluence discharge. These are problems which have affected the entire community; problems which different interest groups have not been able to resolve individually. Resulting collective responses have ranged from joint-funding by the tanners of an effluence treatment plant and multi-source funding (involving tanners, subcontractors, a local bank and the regional authorities) of an information service centre which offers advice on market trends, management skills and information technology, through to frequent and heated debates on new trends affecting the industry, in the bars of the central piazza. How successful these efforts will be is as yet unknown. What matters, however, is that Santa Croce continues to possess a local institutional capability to respond collectively and swiftly to new market pressures and to steer the evolution of the industrial district in a particular direction.

This said, however, there is already some evidence to suggest that, into the 1990s, the organization of industry in Santa Croce will be 'post-Marshallian', that is, less locally confined and less vertically disintegrated. Increasingly, the trend is for tanners to import semi-finished leather, owing to difficulties in obtaining uncured hides and skins. If this practice becomes the norm, more than half of the production cycle will be eliminated from the area, to the detriment of locally based hide importers, subcontractors and chemical treatment firms. There is also a threat of 'forward' internationalization of the division of labour. A handful of companies – the oldest and the most powerful – have begun to open distribution outlets overseas as well as tanneries, usually through joint ventures, in countries either producing hides and skins or promising growth in their leather-goods industries. They have also gone into the business of selling turn-key tanneries for the East European countries; a development which stands to threaten Italian tanneries, including those in Santa Croce, if the finished leather is imported by the domestic leather goods industry.

The risk, then, is that Santa Croce will come to perform only specific tasks in an internationally integrated value-added chain, thus threatening a shake-out of firms dependent upon tasks no longer performed locally. Through a narrowing of functional competencies, the area's industrial system will become less vertically disintegrated. Such a narrowing runs the risk of threatening the institutional synergy and richness of activity which, hitherto, has secured the area's success as an industrial district. It is also possible that, with functional simplification and the offer of larger and better premises more recently by the local authority in its new structure plan, the larger tanners will seek to internalize individual production tasks more than before. Initial signals of such a development include the recommendation by the Associations of Tanners and Subcontractors that transfers to the new industrial zone involve horizontal mergers, stricter loan scrutiny by banks of applications for business start-ups and the grouping of firms into business consortia in order to maximize firm-level scale economies in such activities as purchasing and marketing.

If the twin processes of internationalization of the division of labour and vertical integration at the local level become the dominant trend, Santa Croce will lose its current integrity as a self-contained 'regional' economy. But, and this is the point, it will continue to be a central node within the leather-tanning industry. Twenty years of Marshallian growth have made Santa Croce into a nerve-centre of artisan ability, product and design innovation and commercial acumen within the international, fashion-oriented, leather goods filière. This unrivalled expertise will guarantee its survival as a centre of design and commercial excellence, even if the activities of the hand are reduced or internalized. The open question is whether without the 'hand', the head will lose its might or successfully engineer a transition into other industrial ventures.

8.4   Conclusion

The argument of the first half of the chapter is that there does not appear to be any inexorable trend towards the localization of production. This is not to deny that trend towards vertical disintegration may have become more pronounced than in the past. Nor is it to play down the significance that 'networking' may have in encouraging the resurgence along Marshallian lines of some regions as self-contained units of economic development. Against this, however, it has to be stressed that networking is also a global phenomenon, one which has come to coexist with, rather than replace, more orthodox forms of internationalization. Contemporary organizational change is very much a process of layering of new global corporate networks upon old international production hierarchies.

In this age of intensifying global hierarchies and global corporate networks, with both, as proposed in this chapter, representing a reworked centralization of corporate command and control, it can only be a truism to propose that local economic prospects are becoming more dependent upon global corporate organizational forces. In such a context, it is difficult to think of localities as independent regional economies which participate freely, as the Marshallians would have it, in a global system integrated only by trade.

But, then, what of the argument that an integral component of globalization is more localization of corporate activity, as companies turn decentralization and localization proximity into key conditions for flexibility and innovation? It cannot be denied that the growth of networking could lead to greater functional and operational decentralization down the corporate hierarchy as well as greater reliance on local external linkages for profitable production. However, and this is the point, the rediscovery of place is only occurring in a quite restricted set of localities, and efforts to encourage Marshallian growth in other areas, through the formation of highly localized production systems, are likely to fail. The examples of Santa Croce and the City of London illustrate only too clearly that the conditions for such growth are difficult to capture through even the most innovative policy measures, *unless certain basic structures are already in place*. These include a critical mass of know-how, skills and finance in rapidly evolving growth markets, a sociocultural and institutional infrastructure capable of scripting and funding a common industrial agenda, and entrepreneurial traditions encouraging growth through vertical disintegration of the division of labour.

Collective intervention, both private and public, may be able to build upon and manipulate these basic structures, but it cannot generate them. Such an awareness of the limits of policy interventions is, in our view, important. Otherwise, typically Marshallian efforts to regenerate local economies through locally regulated ventures such as efforts to strengthen links between firms and between business and other local institutions such as training colleges, development authorities, etc., run the risk of doing little more than legitimizing a false belief in the possibility of achieving solutions for what are global problems beyond local control.

Somewhat bleakly then, we are forced to conclude that the majority of localities should abandon the illusion of the possibility of self-sustaining growth and to accept the constraints laid down by the process of increasingly globally integrated industrial development and growth. Concretely, this may simply amount to pursuing those interregional and international linkages (trade, technology transfer, production, etc.) which will be of most benefit to the locality in question. It may also involve – and on this point, the literature on industrial districts is helpful – upgrading the position of the locality within international corporate hierarchies and networks by improvements to a locality's skill, research, supply and infrastructure base in order to attract 'better quality' branch investments.

This, of course is not much of a solution. On the other hand, it has to be stressed that today even the neo-Marshallian nodes of global corporate networks are finding it difficult to retain their status. Furthermore, it has to be noted that the stakes for achieving the status of a node at the apex of an international filière are truly high, and discounted to the vast majority of local areas which either lack or have lost the social and cultural infra-structure for innovation and transaction-rich competition. *Plus ça change* in the post-Fordist economy?

Notes

1. These two concepts, it should be noted, are not interchangeable. Flexible specialization is a concept deployed to describe transformations in the production process stimulated by new technological, skill and market developments. In contrast, the term flexible accumulation, drawing upon the regulation approach developed in France as well as a recent essay of David Harvey (Harvey, 1989), refers to a broader macroeconomic design for the twenty-first century transcending the 'Fordist' regime of accumulation which was built upon the pillar of mass consumption, mass production and Keynesian regulation of the economy.
2. Some of the exponents of the localization thesis, for example Allen Scott and Michael Storper (Scott, 1991; Storper, 1991) have begun to talk of the future, in their more recent work, as a complex juxtaposition of local and global production networks. However, this development still does not draw them sufficiently far away from the localization thesis to warrant a reformulation of their position in the debate on the geography of flexible accumulation.

References and bibliography

Adler, P. and Adler, P. (eds.), *The Social Dynamics of Financial Markets*, Greenwich, CT, JAI Press, 1984.

Amin, A., 'Flexible Specialisation and Small Firms in Italy: Myths and Realities', *Antipode*, 21(1), pp. 13–34, 1989.

Amin, A. and Dietrich M., 'From Hierarchy to "Hierarchy": The Dynamics of Contemporary Corporate Restructuring in Europe', in Amin, A. and Dietrich M. (eds.), *Towards a New Europe?*, Aldershot, Edward Elgar, 1991.

Amin, A. and Robins K., 'The Re-emergence of Regional Economies? The Mythical Geography of Flexible Accumulation', *Environment and Planning D: Society and Space*, 8(1), pp. 7–34, 1990.

Bianchini, F., 'The "Third Italy": Model or Myth?', mimeo, Centre for Urban Studies, University of Liverpool, 1990.

Block, F., *Post-industrial Possibilities*, Berkeley, University of California Press, 1990.

Cawson, A., 'Varieties of Corporatism: the Importance of the Meso-level of Interest Intermediation', in Cawson, A. (ed.), *Organised Interests and the State*, London, Sage, pp. 1–21, 1985.

Chapman, S., *The Rise of Merchant Banking*, London, George Allen & Unwin, 1984.

Cooke, P. and Imrie, R., 'Little Victories: Local Economic Development in European Regions', *Entrepreneurship and Regional Development*, 1(4), pp. 313–27, 1989.

De Cecco, M., *Money and Innovation*, Oxford, Blackwell, 1987.

Driver, S. and Gillespie, A., 'Spreading the Word? Communications Technologies and the Geography of Magazine Print Publishing', *Newcastle PICT Working Paper I*: Centre for Urban and regional Development Studies, University of Newcastle, 1991.

Dunning, J.H. and Morgan, K., *An Economic Study of the City of London*, London, George Allen & Unwin, 1971.

Gertler, M., 'The Limits to Flexibility: Comments on the Post-Fordist Vision of Production and its Geography', *Transactions of the Institute of British Geographers*, 13, pp. 419–32, 1988.

Giddens, A., *Consequences of Modernity*, Cambridge, Polity Press, 1990.

—— *Modernity and Self-Identity*, Cambridge, Polity Press, 1991.

Glasmeier, A., 'Technological Discontinuities and Flexible Production Networks: the Case of Switzerland and the World Watch Industry', mimeo, Department of Geography, University of Texas at Austin, 1991.

Harrison, B., 'Industrial Districts: Old Wine in New Bottles?', Working Paper 90-35, School of Urban and Public Affairs, Carnegie Mellon University, Pittsburgh, 1990.

Harvey, D., *The Condition of Postmodernity: An Inquiry into the Origins of Cultural Change*, Oxford, Blackwell, 1989.

Held, D., 'Democracy, the Nation State and the Global System', *Economy and Society*, 20(12), pp. 138–72, 1991.

Hirst, P. and Zeitlin, J., 'Flexible Specialisation and the Competitive Failure of UK Manufacturing', *Political Quarterly*, 60(3), pp. 164–78, 1989.

—— 'Flexible Specialisation vs. Post-Fordism: Theory, Evidence and Policy Implications', *Economy and Society*, 20(1), pp. 1–56, 1991.

Ingham, G., *Capitalism Divided*, London, MacMillan, 1984.

Jacquemin, A., Buiges, P. and Ilzkovitz, F., 'Horizontal Mergers and Competition Policy in the European Community', *European Economy*, 40, CEC Directorate-General for Economic and Financial Affairs, May 1989.

Kynaston, D., *The Financial Times. A Centenary History*, London, Viking, 1985.

Leyshon, A. and Thrift, N.J., 'European Integration and the International Financial System', *Environment and Planning A*, 24, 1992.

Marceau, J., *A Family Business? The Making of an International Business Elite*, Cambridge, Cambridge University Press, 1989.

Moran, M., *The Politics of the Financial Services Revolution*, London, Macmillan, 1991.

Offe, K. and Wisenthal, J., 'Two Logics of Collective Action', pp. 67–115 in Zeitlin, M. (ed.), *Power and Social Theory*, Greenwich CT, JAI Press, 1979.

Peck, J., 'Labour and Agglomeration: Vertical Disintegration, Skill Formation and Flexibility in Local Labour Markets', mimeo, School of Geography, University of Manchester, 1991.

Piore, M. and Sabel, C.F., *The Second Industrial Divide*, New York, Basic Books, 1984.

Pryke, M., 'An International City Going Global', *Environment and Planning D: Society and Space*, 9, pp. 197–222, 1991.

Rajan, A., *Create or Abdicate?*, London, Witherley Press, 1988.

—— *Capital People*, London, Industrial Society, 1991.

Sabel, C.F., 'Flexible Specialisation and the Re-emergence of Regional Economies', in Hirst, P. and Zeitlin, J. (eds.), *Reversing Industrial Decline? Industrial Structure and Policies in Britain and her Competitions*, Oxford, Berg, 1989.

Sayer, A., 'Post-Fordism in Question', *International Journal of Urban and Regional Research*, 13(4), pp. 666–95, 1989.

Scott, A.J., *New Industrial Spaces: Flexible Production Organisation and Regional Development in North America and Western Europe*, London, Pion, 1989.

—— 'The Role of Large Producers in Industrial Districts: A Case Study of High-technology System Houses in Southern California', *UCIA Research Paper in Economic and Urban Geography*, 2, February 1991.

Storper, M., 'Technology Districts and International Trade: The Limits to Globalisation in an Age of Flexible Production', mimeo, Graduate School of Urban Planning, University of California, Los Angeles, 1991.

Storper, M. and Scott, A.J., 'The Geographical Foundations and Social Regulation of Flexible Production Complexes', in Wolch, J. and Dear, M. (eds.), *The Power of Geography: How Territory Shapes Social Life*, Winchester, MA, Unwin Hyman, 1989.

Strange, S., *States and Markets*, London, Pinter, 1988.

—— 'An Eclectic Approach', pp. 33–50 in Murphy, C.N. and Tooze, R. (eds.), *The New International Political Economy*, Boulder, Lynne Rienner, 1991.

Thrift, N.J., 'The Fixers: the Urban Geography of International Commercial Capital', pp. 203–33 in Henderson, J. and Castells, M. (eds.), *Global Restructuring and Territorial Development*, London, Routledge, 1987.

—— 'The Perils of Transition Models', *Environment and Planning D, Society and Space*, 7, pp. 127–9, 1989.

—— 'The Perils of the International Financial System', *Environment and Planning A*, 22, pp. 1135–7, 1990.

—— 'Doing Global Regional Geography', in Johnston R.J. and Hoekveld, J.A. (eds.), *Regional Geography*, London, Routledge, 1990.

Thrift, N.J. and Leyshon, A., 'In the Wake of Money', in Budd, L. and Whinnster, C.S. (eds.), *Global Finance and Urban Living*, London, Routledge, 1991.

—— *Making Money*, London, Routledge, 1992.

Todling, F., 'The Geography of Innovation: Transformation from Fordism Towards Post-Fordism?', mimeo, Institute for Urban and Regional Studies, University of Economics and Business Administration, Vienna, 1991.

Tornqvist, G., 'Swedish Contact Routes in the European Urban Landshape', mimeo, Department of Social and Economic Geography, University of Lund, 1991.

Zukin, S. and De Maggio, P. (eds.), *Structures of Capital, The Social Organisation of the Economy*, Cambridge, Cambridge University Press, 1990.

Part III

The Specialization of the Tuscan Economy

9 The background, conditions and image of quality agricultural production in Tuscany

Reginaldo Cianferoni

9.1 Historical roots and the importance of Tuscany's polycentric territorial structure

Tuscany presents in its entirety a healthy polycentric territorial structure that is the product of a continuum whose origins are located in the distant past. Initially, between the twelfth and fifteenth centuries, the protagonists of Tuscany's polycentrism were the flowering city-states engaged in commerce. Florence was subsequently able to impose its control over the other Tuscan city-states (Pisa, Siena, Lucca, Arezzo) through the strength of its economy and even military conquest, but Florence's domination never succeeded in snuffing out the ability of the other Tuscan cities to revive themselves economically or in impeding the emergence of an autonomous artistic expression in architecture, sculpture and painting. Then, with the formation of the Grand Duchy, illuminated princes from the Medici and Lorena families were able – from their location in the regional capital – to favour the development of the other major Tuscan cities, encourage the growth of the minor and numerous other urban centres in the region, and the rapid launch of the new city of Leghorn.

In this context, an important role was played by the numerous small rural towns which had understood fairly early the necessity of detaching themselves from the powers of the feudal lords and codifying what at the time constituted democratic and autonomous city statutes. In addition, between the thirteenth and sixteenth centuries a system of share-cropping (introduced above all by the merchants) emerged in Tuscany as a common form of land tenure.[1] Another original characteristic of the Tuscan territorial structure was the density of the population present in the countryside. In 1861 55.2 per cent of the Tuscan population still lived in scattered rural housing. These scattered housing nuclei were arranged in groups of farmhouses located in the middle of a share-cropping holding. The rural housing stock was built by unknown rural bricklayers who authored a 'made by hand' architecture, but there were also farmhouses built by artists. Given that every twenty to thirty holdings belonged to one noble landowner, the countryside was also characterized by a less dense network of great villa-farms housing the sumptuous residences of the nobility along with the residences of the farm administrators (*fattori*) – the hired personnel of the farm – and the accompanying wine cellars, olive-mashing facilities, and storage facilities. In most cases the villas were surrounded by parks and gardens.

This particular territorial structure was not substantially changed by the creation of the modern Italian nation-state. The moderate Florentine nobles interested in conserving traditional ways held important positions in the new centralized national government created under Itaiy's consti-tutional monarchy. The moderate political forces in Tuscany which had the most important role in the events leading to Italian unity were determined to achieve unification on the basis of protecting local interests, norms and traditions. Many Tuscans, among whom we find Lambruschini and Capponi, initially supported the ideal of an autonomous Tuscany within a regionalized Italian state. Ricasoli, who at the beginning of unification had defended with vigour Tuscan autonomy, changed his mind when he became prime minister after the death of Cavour. In a speech to Parliament in 1861 he affirmed: 'I confess that I was also for a time a supporter of the regional system', while now '[I am] convinced [that] for the good of Italy we must centralize power on the part of the [national] government'. Nevertheless, he (with the support of the other political moderates) was able to effectively defend – even in the centralized system – personal interests and represent the wider interests of the Tuscan land-holding class and, at the same time, preserve the provincial and communal autonomy which was part of the cultural framework expounded by the moderate wing of Italy's political leadership represented by Capponi and Lambruschini.

The situation was not very much different during the fascist period, even if Tuscany was one of the regions most penalized by the autarkic policy that emphasized the production of wheat to the detriment of high-quality products typical of the region such as wine, olive oil and high-quality livestock production. The fascist policy deepened the crisis which had already become manifest during the post-First World War period of the structure of Tuscan farm holdings, and the policies enacted by the fascist government in favour of share-cropping and the large landed estates could do little to compensate for the negative impacts of autarky.

In the 1950s the centuries-old socioeconomic structure of the Tuscan countryside appears to have undergone a severe blow after the irreversible crisis of the share-cropping system which led to the exodus of a large number of share-croppers from the countryside.

However, an analysis of the data shows that this was not an accurate representation of what happened. There was only a temporary reduction in residents in the scattered housing sites in the countryside while the network of small and medium-sized towns retained its resident population with only a few losses. The large cities underwent an increase in population in the periphery and in the 'urbanized countryside' in the metropolitan hinterlands, but the increases were kept within limits. Even with a diverse territorial distribution of the population, the polycentrism of Tuscany was maintained and succeeded in consolidating itself during this phase of tumultuous economic growth. The miracle, if we can call it that, was due to the diffusion of light industry and its ties to local activities formed by small and medium-sized enterprises. In reality it was not a miracle; it was not a phenomenon which could not be rationally explained because it was perfectly in line with the original characteristics and origins of the region cited above.

In this regard it is useful to remember that share-cropping was one of the causes, maybe the most important, of the late industrialization of the region. Tuscan landowners in leasing their lands to share-croppers did not have the incentive of moving their investments towards industrial activities which in other countries with the growth of an urban proletariat led to severe social conflict. The end of share-cropping in the 1950s released a large number of individuals into the market possessing a variety of skills and with a great capacity for organizing small enterprises, especially those based on family structures. This was a necessary condition for the development of diffused light industry which characterized Tuscany and the other regions where share-cropping had a significant presence and only one region in the country (Veneto) where share-cropping was not present.

In conclusion, Tuscan polycentrism has survived and has reinforced itself despite the profound economic and social changes derived from recent industrialization and the significant changes in the territorial distribution of the population in the region. These changes have taken place within the cities (even the small ones) due to an internal migration within short distances from the outer housing complexes in the countryside to the city centres. The shift in population has led to a noticeable increase in the concentration of population but also to the formation, especially in the plain areas, of development poles which are the centre of focus for a number of communes. In contrast, there are areas which could be defined as 'isolated and depopulated' which are generally located in mountain or high hill areas. The housing complexes in these areas have undergone a process of re-aggregation, especially in proximity of concentrations of small and medium-sized firms, large cities, and areas of great environmental significance.

The re-aggregation process is a phenomenon which only rarely is tied to the re-establishment of the economic viability of the farms on the part of professional farmers. Instead, it is usually related to the restructuring of old farmhouses as new residences, first of all in areas close to productive activities and then in more distant areas. All this is made possible by the reduction in travel time through the use of motor cars and improvements in the road system but also owing to a re-evaluation of country life, especially in restructured farmhouses providing all modern facilities while conserving all their architectural and landscape characteristics.[2]

The demand for these farmhouses on the part of professionals, highly educated individuals and those, in general, belonging to the middle and upper classes has increased greatly and has provoked a subsequent, considerable increase in market values. This trend determined – at least in the areas of major environmental attraction – a profound change in the socioeconomic characteristics of the inhabitants of these dispersed farmhouses which were at one time the residences of poor farmers. The rich nobles who lived or vacationed in their countryside villa-farmhouses represented a small minority. Now, the minority in these areas is represented by the ex-share-croppers and full-time farmers while the majority is characterized by wealthy and upper-class residents.

The change in the structure of ownership of rural farmhouses is an important phenomenon which only in part was rationalized and provided legal backing by a regional law, N. 10, passed in 1975. However, we need to underline the role in the transformation of the rural areas of what Becattini (1975) has called the 'urbanized countryside'. The urbanization of the countryside immediately surrounding the cities has come about as the result of hundreds, if not thousands, of separate private decisions not regulated by an urban plan. On the ground, the structure of the urbanized countryside has produced a network which is at times so dense with new roads, houses and factories producing a mix of urban and rural elements that it has not always produced positive results.

An improvement has been registered, at least for the new initiatives, during the 1970s and 1980s as a result of better communal urban plans that have foreseen and carried out new residential construction located in appropriate urbanized areas, even in the absence of industry in the immediate vicinity. In these cases, the residences have a low income characteristic, but there is no lack of new, high income residential buildings located in the countryside where the local urban plan has permitted their construction. The most recent data from the 1991 census of the population and housing shows the extent of new construction in many rural towns during the last decade though the phenomenon was also present in previous decades. Recent construction has allowed these new areas to meet the demand for housing, but the results have not always been implemented in harmony with the environment. The structure of the demand has often prevented the re-use of a number of older, small urban centres.

Despite the changes described above, it is possible to affirm that the traditional territorial structure of Tuscany can be considered a valuable environmental and historical patrimony worthy of being protected. This affirmation is based on both objective data on the presence of an historical artistic patrimony that is irreplaceable and unequalled in the world and on the accounts of life in Tuscany by artists and writers of every era and of every nationality which have given the region an important position in the 'historical-literary imagination' of mankind, a role which in terms of different forms and structures finds widespread support although often only within the tourism sector.

9.2   The territorial distribution of economic characteristics

The existence of a Tuscany which can be considered in its fundamental territorial nucleus a composite environmental and cultural whole does not detract from the polycentrism and from the considerable territorial articulation of its economic characteristics. It is necessary in this regard to make use of the results of a research project on the Tuscan foothills undertaken and sponsored by the Accademia dei Georgofili. The hills constitute the skeletal structure of the region in terms of expanse of territory and resident population.[3] At present, the data presented here serve only to explain how important are the differences and how the various territorial typologies we have discussed highlight the problems to be resolved and the policies that need to be adopted.

Tuscany contains areas characterized by *emigration and isolation* covering almost all of the high hill and mountain areas in which the number of residents has been significantly eroded and in which there has been a lack of industrialization. The level and quality of agricultural production in these areas is low. However, the quality of the natural environment and rural setting is quite high, and there is no lack of cultural attraction produced over the centuries. This is the case where share-cropping was dominant and at the time when agricultural production was the primary economic commodity. According to the data in Table 9.1, these high-hill and mountain areas account for one-fifth of the Tuscan territory, but the residents of these areas represent only 3.1 per cent of the population. The population is distributed in fifty-six small communes with an average population of 1,930. Between 1951 and 1991, the resident population was halved, and the losses of inhabitants continued unabated during the last decade with a further loss of 8.8 per cent of the resident population.

A substantially different pattern of population migration characterizes the areas where quality agriculture is the dominant economic force. These are areas of considerable interest because they represent the type of development which should become the goal in Tuscany. This is, for example, the type of agriculture present in the Chianti Classico area which is oriented toward quality products and the development of services related to the natural environment and the tertiary sector. In certain areas, we find the presence of industry, but the presence of quality agricultural products is the most important element. The latter may not be entirely correct in terms of number of people employed but it certainly is for the contribution that the production of quality agricultural products makes to the protection and improvement of the environment and natural landscape.

The areas – which, for the reasons we have already discussed, are the most exposed to exploitation are the ones that cover the largest part of the region's territory. These are the areas where light industry is most diffused. Here, we can distinguish two sub-areas: the *industrial district* and the *industrialized countryside*.

In the former, industrialization assumes its largest presence and reflects the specialization in one particular sector (for example, textile products in the Prato industrial district) in which numerous small firms operate and are characterized by a logic of specialization in separate phases of the manufacturing process. As a whole, the industrial district represents a flexible

Table 9.1 Socio-economic typologies of Tuscan communes*

Characteristics and Indicators		Tuscany	Total	Industrialized		Tertiary sector	Emigration	Residential
				Heavily	Moderately			
1 Communes		287	107	61	46	40	56	84
of which:								
plain		(36)	(20)	(15)	(5)	(9)	(0)	(7)
plain-hill		(55)	(25)	(10)	(15)	(5)	(4)	(21)
hill		(112)	(43)	(24)	(19)	(16)	(24)	(29)
hill-mountain		(25)	(8)	(7)	(1)	(6)	(4)	(7)
mountain		(59)	(11)	(5)	(6)	(4)	(24)	(20)
2 Territory	ha	2,298,414	732,176	402,467	320,709	402,697	475,714	696,827
	%	100.0	31.5	17.5	14.0	17.5	20.7	30.3
Population								
3.1 Residents 1991		3,510,114	1,186,983	533,507	653,476	1,593,398	108,075	621,658
	%	100.0	33.8	15.2	18.6	45.4	3.1	17.7
of which:								
plain	%	35.4	34.6	38.5	31.4	45.4	0.0	17.6
plain-hill	%	21.7	26.3	14.8	35.7	17.5	8.2	25.8
hill	%	30.6	31.1	36.1	26.9	25.5	46.6	40.2
hill-mountain	%	7.4	4.1	8.6	0.5	10.4	7.3	6.1
mountain	%	4.9	3.9	2.0	5.5	1.2	37.9	10.3
3.2 Res/sq. km.		153	164	133	204	396	23	89
3.3 Res/51–81	%	+11.1	+25.4	+15.9	+34.5	+17.1	–50.6	–1.8
3.4 Res/81–91	%	–2.0	+1.9	+1.8	+2.0	–5.3	–8.8	+1.1
4 Housing 81–91	%	+10.3	+12.6	+12.8	+12.4	+8.0	+9.4	+12.6
Industry								
5.1 Employees 91		483,092	264,440	150,116	114,324	156,951	7,428	54,273
	%	100.0	54.7	31.1	23.7	32.5	1.5	11.2
5.3 Emp. Ind/Res 91	%	13.8	22.3	28.1	17.5	9.9	6.9	8.7

5.4	Employes/Firm	%	6.1	6.2	7.0	5.4	7.2	3.5	4.3
5.5	Emp. Ind/Res 81–91	%	-3.1	-5.0	-5.0	-5.0	-2.3	-2.8	-2.6
5.6	Emp. Ind 81–91	%	-19.9	-16.7	-13.6	-20.5	-23.1	-35.1	-22.0

Tertiary

6.1	Employees 91		822,567	214,140	93,072	121,068	497,766	13,955	96,706
		%	100.0	26.0	11.3	14.7	60.5	1.7	11.8
6.3	Emp. Tert/Res 91	%	23.4	18.0	17.4	18.5	31.2	12.9	15.6
6.4	Emp. Tert/Res 81–91	%	+5.1	+4.7	+4.7	+4.7	+6.8	+2.4	+3.1
6.5	Emp. Tert 81–91	%	+25.2	+37.8	+39.0	+36.8	+20.8	+11.7	+25.9

Farms and agri. labour

7.1	Farms 1990	ha	928,948	295,826	156,142	139,684	158,686	179,759	294,677
		%	100.0	31.8	16.8	15.0	17.1	19.4	31.7
7.3	Agricultural labour		99,021	34,943	18,120	16,822	23,743	11,372	28,963
7.4	Agricul. lab/Res 91		2.8	2.9	3.4	2.6	1.5	10.5	4.7
7.5	Agricul. lab/100ha		10.7	11.8	11.6	12.0	15.0	6.3	9.8

Overall employment

8.1	Emp. Totals/Res 81–91	%	+2.0	-0.3	-0.3	-0.2	+4.5	-0.4	+0.5
8.2	Emp. Totals 81–91	%	+3.7	+1.2	+1.0	+1.3	+6.2	-10.7	+3.1
8.3	(5.3 + 6.3 + 7.4)	%	40.0	43.3	49.0	38.6	42.6	30.3	28.9

Source: Calculated by the author based on data from the Census of the Population, Industry and Commerce of 1951, 1981 and 1991 (provisional); provisional data from the 1990 Census on Agriculture; data from the Agriculture and Forestry Department, Tuscan Region, on the morphological classification.

* The classification of the communes was based on the dominant socioeconomic characteristic observed. The break-off points were based on the regional averages which were the following:
– Highly industrialized communes: where the index in 5.3 is above 20%.
– Moderately industrialized communes: where the index in 5.3 is above 16%.
– Tertiary communes: where the index in 6.3 is above 23.4%.
– Communes with emigration and isolation: where the relationship in 3.3 is inferior to –40% and the relationship in 3.4 is below zero.
– Residential communes: where the index in 8.2 is inferior to 28% or the index in 8.6 is inferior to 34%.
The morphological classification of the communes (plain, plain-hill, hill, hill-mountain, mountain) is based on the altitude and the slope of the ground.

system capable of realizing economies of scale and quickly adapting to changes in the marketplace.[4]

In the latter (industrialized countryside) light industry has become diffused with the support of complementary local activities without assuming the characteristics of an industrial district. In general, in these areas we do not find the necessary specialization and dominance by one line or type of production.

As a whole, these two forms of industrialized areas represent one-third of the population and a smaller portion of the region's territory. As will be discussed below, the delineation of industrialization involves strong rural economic areas in the region as well as strong metropolitan centres with industrial economies.

The area with the largest population is the one, according to the parameters in use, we have classified as *tertiary*; it covers only forty communes (17.5 per cent of the region's territory) in which, though, reside 45.4 per cent of the Tuscan population. We find in this category all of the provincial capitals and the large cities (excluding Prato which falls in the industrialized category) and those of medium size which are important from the point of view of tourism (i.e., communes located in areas of mountain and seaside tourism).

Last, but not necessarily least important, the *residential countryside* which we have already mentioned above and which is located in proximity of the major urban, tertiary areas, industrialized communes, and parts of the region (even those not so close to urban centres) dedicated to the use of the natural environment. These communes total eighty-four in number. They cover 30.3 per cent of the territory and account for 17.7 per cent of the region's population.

9.3   Characteristics of the economic activities

Agriculture

To the first profound changes in the structure of agriculture created by the crisis of share-cropping, other structural changes have been added by the widening of the market within the European Community. During the last decade, the widening of the market has already forced out of production a great part of the standardized Tuscan agricultural products such as wheat and other cereals and some livestock production which in the past were common in even difficult mountain and hill terrain given the availability of cheap labour. Aside from a few limited areas on the plain, Tuscany does not physically have any possibility – with the present level of available technology – of being competitive vis-à-vis the large plain areas of northern Europe in the production of grains and extensive livestock farming. This form of competition will become increasingly stiff with the adjustments of the system of protection created by the EU vis-à-vis external competitors.

Fortunately for the region, a large part of the Tuscan countryside finds itself in an advantageous position in the growing of quality products derived from leafy plants (especially grapes and olives). The production cost of these quality products is higher than those produced on a standardized basis, but it is compensated by the higher prices that a large segment of consumers with medium-high or even low salaries are willing to pay for them. In addition, in some parts of the plain due to the favourable environmental conditions and the skills of the entrepreneurs, an extensive plant nursery and floriculture industry has developed.

Another resource available to the many agricultural farms in the region is represented by the old and beautiful rural buildings which, as we have already observed, are no longer necessary for agricultural pursuits. The former farmhouses are highly appropriate buildings for the conduct of agritourism activities by local farmers or for sale at high prices as primary residences or holiday homes. Profits from these sales can then be used to finance agricultural activity and, at times, to make up for the losses that are often incurred in agricultural production.

The flexibility in the use of the rural housing resources is made possible by the 'beautiful agrarian landscape' of Tuscany that even if compromised in some parts still provides stimulation for new initiatives aimed at its restoration or improvement. The generalization also applies to foreign buyers of Tuscan residences and those generally interested in environmental tourism, agritourism, open-air recreational sports, and other pursuits suitable to a country setting. The upsurge in investment and interest in country living has also created an incentive for the sale of quality agricultural products directly to the consumer, thereby avoiding the middlemen who have often reaped the major part of the profits derived from quality agricultural goods.

In support of these favourable conditions, we have seen the development of an agriculture which in addition to producing quality foodstuffs undertakes to provide tourism services, food and drink, and commercialization of products directly to the consumer. In this manner, the profits return to the farmer and help to support his/her effort to preserve the natural environment of the rural areas.

The quality products, in addition to providing goods to an active local market, present an additional market advantage over the national and international competition, especially when these quality products can be adequately marketed though the adoption of appropriate policies. Competition in quality agricultural products does not fit the model for standardized products which are subject to strong challenge from outside producers based on price level. Competition in standardized products has forced producers to lower their costs to a minimum through the adoption of the most efficient and innovative technologies and being less sensitive to whether the innovations in technologies or products administered to boost agricultural production are detrimental to the environment.

It is, therefore, indisputable that great care must be used: in the development of quality agricultural products and services favoured by

Tuscany's natural environment, in taking into account the interests of entrepreneurs and, above all, in responding to the public need to conserve, improve and appreciate the environment. The Tuscan model of agricultural development needs to take into account the structural characteristics of the farms. It is not possible to provide here all of the details of such structures; we will limit ourselves therefore to providing only a few of the essential elements.[5]

The capitalist farms which seemed to be the inheritors of a great part of share-cropping have lost their importance. In general, they have become concentrated in the areas of production emphasizing quality agricultural goods while those who have concentrated on standardized agricultural products have run into considerable difficulties. Many of these producers do not achieve their proper objective of realizing a profit. Their ability to stay in the market is based more on the orientation toward 'consumption' – that is, satisfying the need for recreation in a wider sense that is tied to residing in the countryside rather than producing for a specific market (Dei Ottati, 1990).

A second and even more important category is represented by farms run by professional farmers.[6] The number of these farms has declined, though the same may not have happened in terms of land tilled. A number of these small farms have turned to residential pursuits which will be discussed in greater detail below. The move away from agriculture is a tendency which derives from the fact that agriculture is less profitable than other economic activities. One of the consequence of this trend is that the young do not continue to pursue the agricultural activities of their parents and therefore impose limits on the ability of the agricultural enterprise in adapting to a shift in exigencies.

The changes taking place in agriculture and in the economy in general are reflected in the increase in the number of farms with a residential component and engaged in other complementary rural-based activities. In relation to the latter, we find the development of a type of agriculture which, in other terms, can be labelled as one whose objectives are also recreational and residential; it is closely linked to the extra-agricultural activities which provide almost all of the income and it assumes different forms from a social and spatial points of view. The expansion of these new forms of economic activity centred around the farm have taken place almost everywhere, but they are more present in some communes (referred to here as 'residential') where it is the most important form of landholding. It is necessary to distinguish the residential form of agriculture of the former share-croppers and professional farmers from that of rural settlers from the urban areas – that is those families who have transferred their residences from the cities (even non-Tuscan ones) to the country without possessing any experience in agricultural production. For these types of holdings – but also for all of the others described above with the exception of the large ones – a growing role is played by agricultural service firms which through the supply of machines and labour carry out a number of operations requested by the farm owners.

To complete the overview, it is necessary to add a few observations on a phenomenon which is often discussed, even in political circles, but seldom in an accurate manner: *part-time* (or multiple jobs) in relation to the families and in relation to individuals residing in the countryside. It concerns a phenomenon involving, tangentially, all the preceding categories of farms, beginning with the capitalistic and para-capitalistic ones. Very often, the individual entrepreneur-owners of these farms, exercise economic activity, often highly profitable, in a sector outside agriculture. Often, a part of the hired labour in these farms is carried out on a part-time basis. In relation to the farmer's family the conduct of various activities is usual, assuming that the family is numerous enough to conduct a plurality of activities. Commonly, it is the retired and elderly in the family who are involved in agricultural production while the young are employed in non-farm activities. Even here, in comparison to the past, there has been a radical change. Today, it is easier to find families composed of more than one working unit employed in the same industrial, artisan, or commercial enterprise than is the case in agriculture. Agricultural activity is mostly an individual activity, and no longer predominantly a family concern.

The description of the organizational structure of the farm presented above certainly cannot be considered adequate given the lack of an adequate workforce for the needs of agriculture, in particular when it comes to the production and conservation of natural resources. The lack of a sufficient supply of labour will worsen if it is not possible to increase the return from agricultural pursuits. But we should also not forget that agriculture has a fundamental role to play in the development of an overall integral quality production model.

Industry

From the analyses and observations on industrial activities already presented above, it is necessary to add or underline a few aspects that emerge with great clarity from the ISTAT data collected as part of the 1991 Census on Industry and Commerce (1991b) in connection with the census of the population and agriculture partially presented in Table 9.1.[7] The data in the table are here analysed in relation to a number of characteristics of industry in Tuscany. Despite the current crisis, the trend toward deindustrialization, and the advance of the tertiary sector, light industry is still the dominant sector in the Tuscan model of development.

The most industrialized area consists of 107 communes (of which sixty-one with a high density and forty-six less so) and account for one-third of the residents and 54.7 per cent of those employed in the region. The large communes do not belong to this area, aside from Prato. However, we do find communes which were in the past rural with an average of 11,093 residents. The smallest of these is Radicofani with 1,299 residents (not taking into consideration the very small Ortignano Raggiolo with 804 residents) and the largest, though isolated, is Prato with 165,364 residents. After Prato we find Scandicci with a population of no more than 53,264.

Aside from Prato, then, we are dealing with those towns we have referred to as 'industrialized countryside' and which from the point of view of production constitute the strong economic nucleus of Tuscany. We also find in this area a high incidence of all of the other important variables presented in Table 9.1. First of all, the increase in population which has risen during the last four decades by 25.4 per cent in comparison to 17.1 per cent in the service-oriented communes and the decline in the other geographic areas. During the last decade (1981–90), the population has increased at a lower rate (+ 1.9 per cent) but more than the 'residential' communes where the trend has been negative as has been the case for Tuscany as a whole (−2.0 per cent).

Even in considering the significant increase in the number of personal residences during the last decade (which has been positive everywhere), we find the highest increases in the heavily industrialized areas along with those in the residential communes. Those employed in the tertiary sector constitute significant numbers, but the level of tertiary employment is much higher in the forty service-oriented communes which also account for all of the large cities. There is no doubt that the industrialized countryside makes partial use of the services in the adjacent cities, and the tertiary sector in the largest cities draws an advantage from the demand coming from the communes located in the industrialized countryside.

Agriculture in the industrialized countryside is no worse off than average in Tuscany. The most important indicator is employment per ASU (agricultural surface utilized) which shows that it is higher than the Tuscan average; thus, wine and olive oil production are most concentrated in this area. Such an outcome is not unexpected given the diffusion of part-time labour permitted by the level of industrialization, but also because aspects of high-quality olive oil and wine production activities have served to stimulate some forms of industrialization.

The industrialized communes record the highest level of employment in part due to the patterns of employment of the residents and the added impact of commuters who live in the residential communes but work in the industrialized centres. The residential communes also feed commuters to the tertiary activities of the large cities if they are in the vicinity. Looking at the map of the location of the industrialized communes, it would be possible to observe that they are not distributed over the territory in a scattered fashion; they form a continuous line that goes from the province of Pisa to that of Lucca, Pistoia, a good part of the province of Florence, and Arezzo. Siena can be included in this area due to its northern communes while the southern part of the province, along with the entire province of Grosseto, is involved only on the fringes and on the basis of a few communes. The same is true for the coastal area of the province of Leghorn which has three industrialized communes.

In relation to industry present in the other typologies reported in Table 9.1, it is possible to observe different trends and conditions. In the service-oriented communes involving all the large cities (with the exclusion of Prato), the proportion of those employed in industry is 9.9 per cent, that is, less than half of the total in the communes of the industrialized countryside and a third of those employed in services, but the total numbers involved are quite high given the large size of the population. These towns contain 32.5 per cent of industrial employment in Tuscany. The number of employees per firm is a little bit higher than that found in the firms of the industrialized countryside. Here, we find the headquarters of the largest Tuscan industries and a large number of small artisan activities. The result is a different overall structure of industry vis-à-vis that found in the industrialized countryside.

In the residential communes those employed in industry are in percentage terms lower than those found in the service-oriented communes and the average number of employees is a lot smaller in comparison to all the other categories of communes described above. It seems that here more than elsewhere the dominant industrial form is the small firm.

The areas of emigration register, according to the indicators considered here, the lowest level of industrial employment, and the drop is general in nature and also concerns the tertiary sector and even in some cases agriculture. The latter, even if its accounting of employment is relatively significant in relation to the weak industrial and limited tertiary sectors, is still the weakest in relation to other territorial categories in term of days worked/ASU. This can be explained by the domination of an extensive form of agriculture in mountain areas or in other difficult terrains (for example in the Sienese chalk areas).

The lack of industrial development has negatively impacted on all of the economic indicators reported in Table 9.1. In general, in the weakest economic areas a future based on industrial development is not even thinkable. What may be possible is a development of tourism (in particular agritourism) based on the beauty of the landscape and the presence of artistic/historical treasures. Unfortunately, the ageing of the population trend, more pronounced here than elsewhere, represents a limiting factor even for the development of tourism services.

Finally, we need to comment on the phenomenon of deindustrialization within the confines of the indicator present in Table 9.1. In the decade 1981–91 the rate of deindustrialization in Tuscany is at −3.1 per cent.[8] A part of the reduction can be explained with the transfer to specialized service firms of administrative and commercial functions which were previously conducted by salaried workers inside each industrial firm. This is a fairly common phenomenon and can be considered a positive develop-ment. It is, however, difficult to quantify the exact contours of the pheonomenon accurately. We can be certain that a part of the figure reported in Table 9.1 is attributable directly to pure and simple de-industrialization. The total figure and even the percentage of deindustrialization are higher in the highly industrialized areas. The figure here is −5 per cent, double that in other economic-territorial groupings of communes. Deindustrialization represents an almost silent trend because when small firms close or reduce their personnel no one notices in contrast to what happens when large industries shut down even though the amount of employment accounted for by small firms is on the whole much greater.

The tertiary sector and metropolitan areas

The metropolitan areas in Tuscany have not registered the expansion seen in other regions. The merit (or lack of it) can be attributed to the polycentrism of the region. In addition, the development of advanced service firms seems to be rather modest while the development of tourism and related activities has been very strong. These activities are not tied to the metropolitan function of the city; instead, it is attributable to the existence within these perimeters of historical and artistically rich cities which, despite the limitations in the structure and organization of museums and valorization of works of art, have served to increase their force of attraction among tourists. There is no doubt that the major art centres, along with the minor ones, present significant problems which must be solved immediately. It does not seem, however, that the urban plan recently approved by the communal government of Florence foreseeing substantial increases in the volume of residential space is in line with the prevalent tendencies which foresee an increase in the number of residents in the 'residential countryside' and a fall in the population of Florence. The metropolitan model is, in our opinion, already passé. Urban planning needs to provide added vigour to the polycentric nature of the regional urban structure.[9]

9.4   Conflict and synergy among economic activities

Agriculture and food industry

The recent literature in general economics and agrarian economics in particular places agriculture and the food industry in one integrated agro-food system. In reality, by their very nature, agriculture and the food industry represent two different worlds in which the latter is dominant and has the characteristic of large multinational firms following a multinational and world strategy (Linda, 1988).

Such objectives are substantially in conflict with the strategy of protecting the quality of food products based on characteristics favourable to the place of origin and the professional skills of the agricultural workers. These last two elements have historically guided the consumers in their preferences of products. However, in recent times legislation has been introduced and implemented to provide consumer guarantees of the quality of agricultural products. Two types of guarantees of quality have been foreseen: the 'designation of origin' of the product (DOC, denominazione di origine controllata) and the 'designation and guarantee of origin' (DOCG, denominazione di origine controllata e garantita).[10]

In the multinational food industry the objective is instead that of increasing public awareness of the trademark as a guarantee of the quality of the product which is separated from that of geographic origin of the agricultural product. Multinationals seek to procure the basic agricultural product wherever it can be purchased at the lowest price. The international food industry is the champion of free trade in primary agricultural goods necessary for its production. In this manner, standardized products are produced and commercialized through a substantial investment in the advertizing and marketing of the product, and the advertising campaign usually excludes any mention of the particular origin of the product or of its ties to any local agriculture or culinary culture.

With regard to the latter aspect, the case of olive oil is emblematic. Olive oil produced by Tuscan olive mills is purchased at the present time by consumers at three times the price asked by the firms industrially producing olive oil through the use of 'sophisticated' chemical manipulations and using olives and oil originating in other Italian regions and foreign countries.

Without entering into the details of the conflict between the agricultural firms directly producing olive oil from olive mills and that produced by the multinational companies,[11] if the latter were to prevail then Tuscan olive oil production – which, due to the prevailing natural conditions, produces an oil of high quality not requiring chemical treatment but costing much more than the oil produced for the large multinational corporations – would be forced to disappear causing great economic damage and undermining the structure and characteristics of the Tuscan countryside.

The fact remains that the multinational food industry – irrespective of the particular food sector in which it operates – is, in the final analysis, not supportive of the DOC or DOCG designations because they emphasize the traditional procedure by which agricultural goods are produced and where production takes place rather than the standardized nature of the product itself. Fortunately, for the consumers there are also small and medium-sized food industries tied to the DOC and DOCG type and levels of agricultural production active in the food and drink industry. A number of wine producers in Tuscany participate in consortia created for the defence and marketing of local agricultural production. This should be the case for not only wine producers but also all of those active in the production of olive oil and cheese which are the organized expression of small member farmers in specific areas.

Agriculture and other activities

The conflicts between agriculture and other activities in the use of natural resources – such as water and land – is well known. A similar case could be made in the use of labour which is at the present time the limiting factor in agricultural production and in the production of environmental goods.

Given the shortage, agriculture is always on the losing side because the competing activities are in a better position to increase the compensation of the factors of production used. Such is the case in particular with regard to the return to labour of activities located in the industrial districts, as has been shown in the case of Prato (Cianferoni, 1990).

Nevertheless, among these activities we find synergies that allow agriculture to carry out important functions even under conditions of low productivity as in the case of the 'consumption' and residential farms that survive on the basis of income from industrial and tertiary activities whose presence is tied to the existence of more productive activities than agriculture *in loco*.

Agro-industry and international commerce

The data in Table 9.2, even if they refer only to 1991, allow us to discuss in greater detail and depth a few of the aspects presented above which can be considered structural factors. Results show that the region makes great use of agro-food products imported from abroad because imports are 2.7 times the size of exports and this takes place at a rate significantly above the Italian average.[12] The most important item in the region's exports is wine which alone covers 30 per cent of the total (while in terms of agricultural production wine accounts for 13.4 per cent); it is followed by olive oil with 12 per cent (in comparison to 3.1 per cent of agricultural production) and flowers and plants with 11.9 per cent. The other products, as reflected in the data in Table 9.2, represent on an individual basis small contributions but together account for 46 per cent of the total. The data allow us to affirm that in the agro-food industry Tuscany is a great importer of standardized products from abroad while its exports involve the sale of high-quality goods. The latter, however, takes place in limited quantities in relation to the potential capacity of the region. The case of olive oil is quite instructive.

The Tuscan oil industry imports olive oil from abroad and from southern regions in Italy, and after undergoing chemical treatment and purification to improve its quality considerably the oil is sold on domestic and international markets. In addition, it seems that at least on the basis of sale price the exports involve the shipment of large quantities of poor quality olive oil. What is certain is that the olive oil produced by the crushing of olives in old olive mills and the lack of chemicals in the production processes contains a number of qualities beneficial to the body. This oil is particularly appreciated by Tuscans, but it is not well known in other countries or even in northern Italy. Despite the fact that the dietary qualities of the oil have been widely recognized by scientists and specialists working in the field of dietary science and the analysis of the relationship between foods and health, the use of traditionally produced Tuscan olive oil is not widespread. Several ways of improving the situation have been attempted, such as the soon to be applied DOC designation to olive oil

Table 9.2 Agro-food exports and imports, 1991, (in tons and millions of lire)

Product	Exports			Imports			Difference	
	Quantity	Value	%	Quantity	Value	%	Value	%
Wine	35,542	195,622	29.6	2,736	10,190	0.6	+185,432	+16.8
Olive oil	21,231	80,221	12.1	49,365	186,971	10.6	-106,750	-9.7
Other oils and fats	21,685	16,428	2.5	40,091	38,035	2.2	-21,607	-2.0
Grain	129	143	0.0	430,824	127,694	7.3	-127,551	-11.6
Corn	62	281	0.0	11,274	5,196	0.3	-4,915	-0.4
Orzo, avena and others	249	540	0.1	8,071	2,512	0.2	-1,972	-0.1
Tropical fruit	119	135	0.0	46,561	34,445	2.0	-34,310	-3.1
Other fruit	4,087	6,029	0.9	6,623	9,946	0.5	-3,917	-0.3
Seeds, oil seeds	–	2	0.0	78,569	36,778	2.1	-36,776	-3.3
Coffee	2	24	0.0	6,670	14,876	0.8	-14,852	-1.4
Tobacco	8,230	24,088	3.7	7,362	48,966	2.8	-24,878	-2.3
Fresh flowers, plants	56,869	78,755	11.9	15,006	48,266	2.7	+30,489	+2.8
Animals, livestock	635	2,852	0.4	36,658	109,739	6.4	-106,887	-9.7
Meat	2,715	7,747	1.2	37,140	202,971	11.6	-195,224	-17.7
Fish	2,208	8,208	1.3	5,885	40,046	2.2	-31,838	-2.9
Vegetables	2,029	4,455	0.7	54,059	67,040	3.8	-62,585	-5.7
Cheese	262	1,446	0.2	3,698	22,261	1.3	-20,815	-1.9
Cereal flour	203,578	52,597	8.0	2,299	592	0.0	+52,005	+4.7
Pasta	59,965	73,284	11.1	171	402	0.0	+72,882	+6.6
Other	–	107,685	16.3	–	753,902	43.1	-646,217	-60.2
Total Tuscany	–	660,542	100	–	1,760,828	100.0	-1,100,286	-100.0
Total Italy	–	15,044,778	–	–	34,150,745		-19,105,967	

Source: Author's calculations based on IRPET data.

production. It is hoped that the designation will introduce greater transparency in the olive oil sector to the benefit of agricultural producers and consumers. A change in the manner by which the quality of olive oil is documented and guaranteed will hopefully permit the growth of a small but capable Tuscan olive oil industry.

Productive activities and the environment

The environmental issue presents in Tuscany a number of aspects common to all industrialized countries, but it also presents a number of other issues tied to particular aspects of, and conflicts and synergies with, the environment peculiar to Tuscany which need to be discussed at least briefly. The fact that in Tuscany small and medium-sized industries are prevalent is not a positive factor in terms of environmental problems in relation to areas where large-scale industry prevails. What is important (aside from the concentration of production plants in a geographic area) is the type of industry and the type of technology used in the local production process. Although the chemical industry (which is among the most polluting) is not strongly present in Tuscany, there are other industrial activities using chemical products in their production process which are very much present in Tuscan industrial districts such as textiles, leather, etc. Even modern agriculture uses chemical products (fertilizers, insect repellents, and weedkillers), but the average use of chemicals in Tuscan agriculture is a lot lower than that used in other northern regions with a more intense form of agriculture. All of this allows us to affirm that Tuscan agriculture – despite its modest contribution to value added in the region – has an important role in the support of 'integrated quality development'.

9.5 Competition, cooperation and quality

The present economic situation is not currently favourable to Tuscany and there are a number of entrepreneurs and observers who look with some apprehension at the future of the Tuscan model of development, and in particular there are those who fear that the Tuscan system of small enterprises finds itself in a position of inferiority in the context of the consolidation of the European Single Market. This view is summed up in the slogan 'small is no longer beautiful as it once was' expressed by the president of the regional council, Paolo Benelli, in his meeting with the Minister of Industry in the Tuscan Regional Council. Vannino Chiti, the president of the regional government, during the same meeting emphasized that large industry has been consistently dismantled in the region.

According to the author's point of view, the region lacks the conditions for the development of large industries capable of substituting a significant part of the small and medium-sized enterprises in relation to employment and the production of wealth. If such an exchange were to take place, it would undermine the territorial structure and polycentrism of the region with a return of those phenomena of depopulation of the industrialized countryside and a scale of economic and social costs much higher than those registered when the share-croppers left the land. Our thesis is that despite the present recession the Tuscan economy can return to growth if it can take advantage of the products that it produces for internal and international consumption and in which it has a considerable competitive advantage.

We will try to document the basis of this view in the section below. The concept of competitive advantage had been widely used by Becattini (1992) who has made use of research conducted by Porter (1991), according to whom Italy is in a condition of competitive advantage in forty-two homogeneous sub-sectors consisting of a well delineated and articulated system formed by a few products used as food, for consumption, for residences and other semi-worked products and instruments which are well rooted in the economic and social life of Tuscany. The case of the industrial districts is emblematic of this trend because it provides the concerned industries contemporaneously strong competition and a remarkable level of cooperation. Tuscany is well inserted in this overall structure with some notable peculiarities and maybe even with some advantages. In our opinion the concept of competitive advantage can be considered useful not only in explaining the current reality but also in reflecting – keeping in mind the advantages that have already emerged and those which have a potential of emerging – the economic and competition policies that are necessary and appropriate in the case of Tuscany. Porter, in this regard, observes that the single firms should think about 'new and better ways of competition in their industrial niche'. Such research should be based in our opinion on the method of cooperation from within the system of enterprises where we believe, in contrast to what Porter assumes, an important role is played by the ability of public administration to understand, support and favour the most important choices.[13]

Even if it is not completely accurate, a concrete idea of the particular conditions and economic vocations of Tuscany toward the export market can be outlined on the basis of the data presented in Table 9.3. The table highlights the differences in the structure of Tuscan exports vis-à-vis those of Italy in general and of those from Lombardy which is the leading export region in the country.

Aside from the agro-food exports which we have already discussed, the data show that Tuscany is highly specialized in sectors in which Porter asserts that Italy has a comparative advantage. From this perspective, Lombardy which overshadows Tuscany in terms of total quantity of exports does not deviate very much from the Italian average and seems to be less favoured than Tuscany if the opening of the Community and international markets will have the competitive impact foreseen by economists.[14]

On the basis of what we have said in the past, it seems possible to outline what are the already experimented and future competitive advantages of Tuscany:

Table 9.3 Pattern of exports, 1991

Items	Italy		Tuscany		Lombardy	
	%	index	%	index	%	index
Agro-food	7.2	100	3.9	54.2	2.9	40.3
Leather and shoes	5.6	100	16.7	298.2	2.6	46.4
Textile and clothing	12.7	100	26.9	211.8	15.0	118.1
Metal products	6.4	100	12.8	200.0	6.8	106.2
Mechanical	42.0	100	17.9	42.6	45.6	108.6
Chemicals	11.2	100	5.1	45.5	13.7	122.3
Others	14.9	100	16.7	112.1	13.4	89.9
Total	100.0		100.0		100.0	
Total in absolute value (billion lire)	209,747		13,638		64,287	
Index (value of export ÷ population)	3,667		3,871		8,376	

Source: Author's calculation based on IRPET data.

1. the overall view of Italy formulated by Porter referring to the past (the data refer to 1985), applies even more specifically to Tuscany;
2. Tuscany can be considered one whole environmental and cultural good even if it is formed by a system of centres and countryside with considerably different characteristics that have to be protected for the use of future generations. It forms a patrimony that has, and could have an even greater economic value translated into tourism activities. The region's patrimony is also the source of a collective historical and literary image that if properly used can serve as the basis for the profitable sale of regional produced goods and services;
3. in Tuscany the historical, social and internal prospects of the productive structures are high in terms of creating the foundations for a type of production which integrates the quality of the environment as the fundamental prerequisite with the quality of agricultural and industrial products and services provided and therefore is in a position to integrate these products with the quality of life of its residents and of its visitors and the enjoyment of its production by consumers inside and outside of the country;
4. quality is probably the winning card and it is part of the evolution which has been proceeding for a long time in industrialized countries substituting an increasing part of their standardized products with those oriented toward quality items no longer destined for a restricted elite but to larger parts of the population. One could say that these products could be earmarked for all the population if pockets of poverty significantly present in industrialized countries and even more so in the developing ones were eliminated.[15]

9.6 Japanese 'total quality' and integral quality

The concept of quality can be operationalized in a variety of manners. It is important to compare the significance of the meaning that we have attributed to 'integral quality' with 'total quality' Japanese style. On the latter there is an extensive literature because there are many who support the idea that the success of Japanese industry is based on the intensity and originality of its constant preoccupation with qualitative innovations.

Even the most recent industrial studies have led some (Garvin, 1988) to state that 'the 1980s will be remembered in the Western world as the years in which quality was discovered on the part of the manufacturing and service industries'. Quality is the factor to which is attributed the most importance in beating the competition, and this had its most extensive application in Japan. Here, the firms conduct a total control of quality in very part of the production process with the ever-present 'predisposition to improve' which involves directly and totally all of the productive components from management to the workers with the lowest levels of responsibility. Obviously this involves internal mechanisms whose efficacy is greater in Japan than in other countries which, in theory, follow the same principles. Japan is an extremely hierarchical society and the majority of the population is willing to follow such controls inside the workplace. It is well known that Italian society and Tuscany in particular is much different from the Japanese one and maybe is not in a position to compete from the point of view of 'total quality' with the Japanese factory system. It is our opinion though that in the small and medium-sized enterprises quality is tied to the single firms in which the owner works together with the family helpers and the salaried employees and in which there are no hierarchies and the problems with improving quality are often faced collectively even with limited understanding and resources. A fundamental role is allocated to the services made available in the area.

Integral quality is not therefore tied to managerial techniques within the factory but to the territory and to all of the products and services considered as a whole and as part of their overall interaction. This is not a new concept because it has already in large part been received and is at the heart of environmental issues. It is senseless to have cars, machines, watches and other instruments created by total quality and constantly changing techniques if, at the same time, one has to consume contaminated food and live in an environment undergoing constant decay.[16]

9.7 Limits and problems

The trademark of origin and guarantee

The development of agricultural products through the guarantee of the place of origin and the quality products produced by small and medium-sized enterprises requires the guarantee of a trademark granted by a consortium created for the control of products through rules established and enforced by the public administration. For this purpose in the agricultural sector there already exists in Tuscany, but not only in this region, long and widespread experience which has produced divergent results due to the inability of the individual consortia to promote products on the market adequately and to undertake through their own organizations the research necessary to improve the quality of their products. In addition, at least in agriculture, the instrument permitting the safeguarding of prices (though not always usable) is the control of the supply of products on the basis of demand.

There are still in this area a number of legislative and organizational problems that need to be resolved. For example, with regard to olive oil for which a recent law has been passed (Law 169/1992), on one hand the position is advanced of creating one trademark for the region and on the other it is felt to be more important to create different trademarks according to the many differences in quality which are manifest in the region. According to our view, the correct approach would be one focused on the creation of a regional trademark (and not only for olive oil) articulated where the conditions exist into local trademarks overseen by distinct consortia. Such a solution would allow for the exploitation of Tuscany's good overall image but also to take advantage of Tuscan polycentrism and a sound level of competition among the diverse and always high levels of quality.

The consortia given the responsibility of oversight along with their trademarks are one of the most useful outcomes of cooperation among enterprises. These need to be asked to achieve a high level of efficiency, a necessary condition which requires capable managers and a significant level of collective effort which is not always present in all the components.

Is Tuscany a fortunate exception?

We have already said that Tuscany does not have alternatives to the type of development based on an integral form of quality given that it has neither the experience nor the structure to sustain competition in the area of standardized products whose costs have to be constantly reduced. Nevertheless, it is worthwhile remembering that, despite the advantages suggested, the model outlined does not permit the region to become a fortunate exception in a world in which a large part of the population lives in poverty. The pressure applied by these forces would be sufficient to overwhelm any type of barrier constructed to preserve the situation. This is in general the problem that is still posed today by the great imbalances between industrialized countries and the numerous and overcrowded poor states. The fortunate exception cannot even be defended from the point of view of other regions. It is easy to imagine that the success of Tuscany would push the other regions to move along the same path entering in competition on the basis of offering products and services based on integrated quality. It is, however, possible to make the observation that given the differences among the regions in terms of the quality of the environment and the integral quality of the products it is not possible in a strict sense to imitate the products or make exact replicas.

The statement also applies clearly to the DOC food products given their ties to their geographical origin which differentiates quality. The Chianti Classico wine is different from the Brunello of Montalcino even if the grapes and technology used are more or less the same. Also the products destined for personal use and use in the home when they express an art form or the tastes of a particular society differ among themselves. Copies of art works, even if perfect, never have anywhere near the same value as the originals. Competition in art does not come from imitating or reaching the same technical levels but on the basis of creating new and diverse 'schools' capable of achieving even more fame on their own. In our case what is at stake is not great works of art;[17] a good part of environmental goods and quality consumption always needs the creative capacity that can also be created elsewhere where similar prerequisites exist. The reference here is to other Italian regions but it would also apply to other countries. It would be a profound mistake if we were to think that Tuscany can be protected from competition based on quality by depending on a permanent advantage derived from a lower price level for its quality products and services.

Difficulties and opportunities in realizing these objectives

The development of an integrated level of quality can within the limits indicated appear to be a 'book of dreams' at the same level of the old economic planning. Without doubt there are strong forces operating with success in the opposite direction trying to homogenize types of consumption, behaviour and local cultures on the basis of a world standard. These forces belong to the already cited multinational food industry trying to sell a universal trademark against which are aligned the weak action of the DOC and DOCG advanced by the farmers. Nevertheless, the research on cuisine brought forward by experts on local culinary traditions still transmitted from one generation to another is still important even though they may be less appreciated by younger generations. Analogous considerations can be made in relation to national industrial products with a Japanese level of quality where the alternative is a high level of 'use and throw away' form of consumption with the macroscopic consequences of mountains of polluting rubbish which has to be disposed of.

Integral quality is instead linked to the saving of the environment – without this component it cannot be conceived of as integral – that is carried out through various forms of intervention by the public sector but also by enterprises emphasizing the quality of products and services and so implementing spontaneous mechanisms integrated with the environment. The latter would represent a new development because up until now the structures and productive opportunities have operated with a few exceptions in the opposite direction. Thus, actions to conserve the environment have been undertaken by the public sphere and in many cases have assumed a suppressive mode of action.

Is all of this feasible in Tuscany, a region which, as we have attempted to illustrate, starts off with an advantage? The reply to the question is difficult to give because it depends not only on the correctness of the analysis carried out but also on the events and individual and collective behaviour in the future because the variables we need to consider are so numerous and so changeable over time. On the other hand, this chapter has the objective of presenting problems and possible solutions and therefore it lacks quantitatively and temporally based hypotheses that can be referred to in evaluating the types of instruments, forces, and resources necessary to resolve these problems.

Our opinion is, therefore, that in Tuscany it is possible to act with success in the indicated direction. Obviously, this does not involve the need to install a market regime and guarantee a 100 per cent level of integrated quality. We do not need to abolish industrial sectors in which standardized mass production remains because the transformations and hopes for changes cannot take place in the short run. Nevertheless, in our opinion, the material conditions, economic forces, and sociopolitical forces are available to achieve considerable progress.

The major difficulty comes from the existence at the world level but also in the region, of those multinational economic forces and their cultural and political expressions which are oriented towards a lessening of the differences and the original features of the region even if the formal autonomy of the political institutions receive a constant stream of acknowledgement, and we will continue to see the unfolding of ferocious and destructive ethnic conflicts. The result is that the struggle concerning the themes discussed here (as is the case for general issues dealing with the environment) is and will be primarily a cultural battle. This chapter hopes to make a contribution to the struggle.

Notes

I would like to thank Giacomo Becattini who read the first draft of this chapter and consequently formulated suggestions and criticism which I have tried to take into account in preparing this second draft. Nevertheless, it is appropriate to state from the beginning that what appears here is the responsibility of the author. I would like to add that I sought, with maybe too much insistence, the help of Becattini because this chapter owes much to the reading of his essay on competition and cooperation (Becattini, 1992); I have already used his essay to draw inspiration for a short article on agriculture (Cianferoni, 1992) to counter the common and – from our point of view mistaken – pessimism on the destiny of Tuscan agriculture. Despite the fact that Becattini did not conclude his analysis with an optimistic outlook, such is the case here with regard to agriculture and more general issues.
  1. Share-cropping was a form of land tenure where the owner of the land was paid in agricultural produce by the tiller. The tiller thus paid a pre-established

percentage of the 'share of the crop' to the landlord as a form of payment for being able to reside on and work the land.

2. The lack of modern facilities and running water and electricity was one of the causes for the abandonment in the 1950s of the old farmhouses as residences by the ex-share-croppers.

3. According to the old ISTAT classification, two-thirds of the region's territory is covered by hills and accounts for the same portion of the population.

4. In addition to the Becattini, Dei Ottati, Bellandi and Romagnoli, and Sforzi chapters in this volume, see for an earlier discussion of the characteristics of industrial districts Becattini (1987) and on their diffusion in Tuscany Sforzi (1991).

5. For detailed analyses see the cited research project of the Accademia dei Georgofili and the data from the recent ISTAT census of agriculture (1990).

6. We define as a farm run by a professional farmer that in which there is at least one full-time person engaged in agricultural production.

7. The analysis of the data was done by Dr Roberto Pagni and will be published and commented on in the publication of the research findings of the project already cited conducted by the Accademia dei Georgofili.

8. The figure is calculated as the difference between the number of employees active in industry vis-à-vis residents in 1991 and the same calculation for 1981.

9. It is not from the point of view of urban planning a simple question considering the traditional localisms which brought to a halt the past experiment with intercommunal urban planning. From the point of view of a lay observer, I find the views expressed by Mariella Zoppi Spimi (1992) on the urban plan of Florence reported in the newspaper *La Nazione* of 9 August 1992 quite convincing.

10. It is a form of legislation that attempts to safeguard and maintain the quality of high-quality products in the area of wine, olive oil and cheese and other products coming from areas purposely designated and particularly appropriate due to environmental conditions. The highest level of quality is recognized to be DOCG for which there is an explicit *guarantee* through specific controls carried out by public authorities directly on the product to be sold on the market. DOC and DOCG production of Tuscan wine involves 47 per cent of overall production which is the highest in all of the Italian regions. For the DOC production of oil the institutive law of this quality control is recent (1992) and the norms for its operationalization are now being formulated.

11. The issue has been given ample treatment by the press. An important article on the matter is the one published by Magda C. Shiff, 'La Toscana scivola sull'olio di oliva', *L'Informatore Agrario*, 15, 1992.

12. Nevertheless, it is important to underline that the regional breakdown of national imports and exports be done according to the declared place of origin and destination of the individual operations which do not necessarily have to be tied to regional production and consumption.

13. It is asking a lot of our political leaders who in the past as Becattini (1992) has written in relation to Italy, but which could be as easily used in reference to Tuscany, have followed 'analyses profoundly distorted and inspired for the most part on the view that the national peculiarities had to be suppressed and which resulted during the last years in policies to block and obstruct the very process of growth that has manifested itself. The preference has gone to a mistaken industrial policy oriented toward the affirmation of sectors abstractly considered "prestigious" and the basis of a rapid development but which has varied and drifted over time to the point that it has been the cause of a loss of opportunities in extending industrial activities in which the domestic competitive advantage is considerable. One needs to ask what could our small

and medium-sized enterprises in their market segments and districts have been capable of doing had they been able to take advantage of credit, export, exchange, scientific and technological research policies in support of their activities rather than the negative ones introduced during this last period. It could be assumed that the position of Italy in its more favourable markets would be stronger that what it is today'.

14. It can be hypothesized that Lombardy owes its leadership in international trade not only to the role of products produced in the region but to the fact that many enterprises have their headquarters in Milan even when their productive facilities are multinational or interregional in nature or taking place completely outside the region. Tuscany, which does not have such firms, owes its position to its internal productive capacity.

15. Without doubt the techniques of mass production based on the reduction of production costs represent one of the instruments that have permitted the diffusion of mass consumption and the overcoming in industrialized countries of fundamental problems concerned with hunger and the lack of sufficient quantities of foodstuffs. The increase in disposable income has then encouraged an increasingly large part of consumers to transfer demand from standardized goods and services to those of quality. At times, as happens with food products, through a reduction in the quantity consumed. We have seen, for example, the per capita reduction in the drinking of wine. This decline is entirely due to the reduction of common table wine because on the other hand there has been an increase in the consumption of DOC wines. The orientation is therefore 'less but better wine'. Even more significant is the trend in the consumption of vegetable fats: first, a strong increase in the consumption of seed oils and a relative decline in the use of olive oil due to the favorable prices of the former; then, despite the fact that seed oil prices were lower, the consumption of olive oil increased and it increased even more for extra vergine olive oil.

16. In the context of integral quality the quality of food products has an important role. This involves the capacity to correctly respond to the nutritional needs and health where the genuine nature of the products is essential (Pilati and Ricci, 1991) and there is the role of food as a form of satisfaction (Barberis, 1985). The evaluation of this aspect is in large part due to the taste and values that differ from one society to another and from one individual to another. The judgement is therefore subjective in nature. It is possible to refer to quality as it is understood by the Tuscans, by the Lombards or more broadly by Italians, the French, etc. These are the evaluations which in the past were tied to the quality of the local cuisine which was in turn tied to the characteristics of the local agricultural products. At the time of multinational food industries and their vast marketing strategies these territorial differentiations tend to decline and even disappear causing from our point of view negative consequences.

17. Permit us to observe that the cultural climate produced within the context of integral quality and the quality of life would be supportive also of the flowering of new works of art.

References

Barberis, C., 'Le due agricolture: teoria e problemi', *Sociologia urbana e rurale*, 18, 1985.
Becattini, G. (ed.), *Lo sviluppo economico della Toscana*, Florence, IRPET/Le Monnier, 1975.
—— *Mercato e forze locali: il distretto industriale*, Bologna, Il Mulino, 1987.

—— 'Concorrenza e cooperazione: la formula italiana', *Il Ponte*, April 1992.

Cianferoni, R. (ed.), *L'agricoltura e l'ambiente nel distretto industriale di Prato*, Florence, Accademia dei Georgofili, 1990.

—— 'Un nuovo impegno delle organizzazioni economiche agricole fiorentine per la valorizzazione della qualità dei prodotti', *Incontri preparatori della conferenza agraria provinciale fiorentina*, 29 May 1992 (in press).

Dei Ottati, G., 'L'agricoltura da elemento di sostegno dello sviluppo industriale ad attività di "consumo"', in Ciaferoni, R. (ed.), 1990.

Garvin, D.A., 'Avere successo con le otto dimensioni della qualità', *Harvard Espansione*, 39, 1988.

ISTAT, *Censimento generale dell'agricoltura 1990*, 1990.

—— *Censimento generale della popolazione 1991*, 1991a.

—— *Censimento generale dell'industria e del commercio 1991*, 1991b.

Linda, R., 'Strategie di sviluppo delle imprese dell'industria agro-alimentare', Atti del XXIV convegno di studi della SIDEA *Strategie e adattamenti nel sistema agro-industriale*, *Quaderni della Rivista di Economia Agraria*, 9, Bologna, INEA/Il Mulino, 1988.

Pilati, L. and Ricci, G., 'Concezioni di qualità del prodotto ed asimmetria informativa lungo il sistema agro-alimentare', *Rivista di Economia Agraria*, 3, 1991.

Porter, M.E., *Il vantaggio competitivo delle nazioni*, Milan, Mondadori, 1991.

Sforzi, F., 'I distretti industriali marshalliani nell'economia italiana', *Studi e informazioni*, Quaderno 34 (distretti industriali e cooperazione fra imprese in Italia), 1991.

Zoppi Spini, M., 'Intervista sul piano regolatore di Firenze', *La Nazione*, Florence, 9 August 1992.

10 Tuscan culture: between production and consumption

Antonio Floridia

10.1 The historical roots

One of the original and distinctive features of Italian culture is the richness and variety of its urban structure. Italy is a country which arrived fairly late (and badly) to nationhood, and it is a country based on many large and small 'capitals', of small and large urban centres which have lived separate existences during the past centuries. These cities and neighbourhoods are rich in unique features which are expressed in their walls, churches, palaces, towers, paintings and sculpture and which speak to an inner vitality still present in the local culture.

Tuscany is one of those regions in which these Italian characteristics are particularly noticeable. Tuscany is reflective of the pride in municipal autonomy and of the sustained struggles which took place between Florence and the other Tuscan cities until the region was unified under the rule of the Medici. Tuscany is also identified with the precocious and extensive development of textile manufacturing, the fortunes and abilities of the first great merchant bankers, the extraordinary flowering of the Humanistic culture, and a concentration of artistic talent which has rarely been seen in human history.

How can we explain such developments? Were they the result of a fortuitous and unrepeatable combination of elements or were they reflective of more general laws operating in human society? In addition, how do these historical and cultural roots affect modern developments and what Tuscany is today? The identification of some of the factors associated with this historical/cultural patrimony is useful in helping us understand the role and future prospects of contemporary Tuscan society.

It is appropriate for this purpose to consider a few simple notions on the role of the city and the characteristics of an urban economy. The urban geographer P. Smailes (1977) has written that 'an urban community can survive only when the productive structures produce goods at a level higher than what is necessary to maintain the producers and when the means of surplus production are concentrated in specific areas' (p. 9). The concept of surplus production seems to be an important transition point in understanding 'the city as a cultural "good"'. The city is, therefore, not only a 'container' of cultural resources; it is in its own right an assembly of places and spaces which express, conserve, and transmit a specific cultural heritage.

Leaving aside the analysis of how surplus agricultural production, the city and social division of labour developed in the ancient world and how the crisis of the high medieval period and the barbarian invasions impacted on them – it is well known that not by chance did the rebirth of European civilization manifest itself as part of the rebirth of urban conglomerations with the emergence of fortified cities (urban centres characterized by predominant military and political functions), the location of major markets within city walls (urban centres as places where the exchange of goods was concentrated) and the affirmation of the power of the Church through a revitalization of the role of the Church's territorial organization concentrated on the traditional diocesan headquarters. The cities revitalized their role by rallying round the cathedrals and the central markets. In Europe Italy represents the epicentre of this development. 'Everywhere the "monument" (of course, the cathedral) is considered the nucleus and dynamic core of urban growth in cities such as Pisa, Siena, Lucca, Florence as well as in Modena, Parma, Ferrara, Venice . . .' (Argan and Fagido, 1973, p. 735).

Nevertheless, these developments were based on a logical and historical assumption: that the city did not represent all of 'society' and that the social structure of the city did not exhaust all of the possibilities involved in the organization of society. The fact that the city increasingly placed itself as the centre of the maximum expression and concentration of social and cultural wealth was made possible because outside of the city were located the sources of production and food feeding its existence. Of course, Tuscany saw the development of important productive activities within the cities, but the source of the growth of cities remained the concentration within the cities of resources coming from outside, especially those from agriculture. In the case of Florence resources were also derived from the highly profitable commercial and financial intermediation undertaken with success by a number of the city's successful families.

The fact that the city became the place for the maximum concentration of wealth and of culture in society was quickly reflected in the collective consciousness. Giulio Carlo Argan and Maurizio Fagiolo (1973) write, 'there is a difference in form and scale, and it is this difference which makes possible the relationship. This is explained with extreme clarity by Ambrogio Lorenzetti in his fresco "Good Government" in Siena. Between the city and the rural villages there is a continuous osmosis. The city is composed of straight lines arranged in a geometric pattern like a crystal. The countryside is made up of continuously undulating lines' (p. 738). The course of nature can be predicted; urban space can be planned. The city therefore becomes a conscious projection of culture; it becomes a concentration of urban patterns. The city is a place which expresses an identity, a culture, a political project, a style and an ideal of life.

Remaining with the Florentine case (however in form and substance the generalization can be applied to other urban centres), the extraordinary cultural vitality of the city – in particular during the fourteenth and fifteenth centuries – found its roots in a particular combination of economic and political factors and in a mechanism of urban growth which witnessed the affirmation of a particular interconnection among financial wealth, conspicuous consumption, philanthropy, property investments, development of the artistic and artisan trades and the expansion of certain markets. To summarize this interconnection with a slogan, a strong surplus in the balance of payments provided in many respects the economic basis for the flowering of the great Renaissance period in Florence.

In this context an historic event merits a brief mention given that it provides the backdrop to events against which we measure ourselves today. The Black Plague of 1348 represents a watershed. In the previous decades during the time of Dante and Giotto, Florence had 90,000 inhabitants and was one of the largest cities in Europe. After the Plague the city was decimated and underwent a drastic reduction in population. However, as often happens, from great tragedies there often emerges a strong drive for recovery. Those who survived found themselves enjoying a higher per capita income than before. Other factors were also operative: the gradual extension of Florence's control over the rest of Tuscany, the growth of textile manufacturing, and above all the consolidation of the presence abroad of Florentine bankers and merchants. All of these developments led to an intensification of the influx of financial resources from abroad into Tuscany's capital city. In addition, after a phase of growth and the opening of a long period of political stability, military expenditures were also significantly reduced, thus providing the basis for an expansion in internal demand and consumption. Florence, thus, became in addition to a significant manufacturing centre the strategic heart of a vast financial European network: 'the apex of the medieval Italian banking system' (Goldthwaite, 1980, pp. 54–9).

These large influxes of profits and capital which gravitated on Florence through a number of noble families quickly found an outlet in property development and in the expansion of collateral productive activities (theorized by Hirsch in his development 'connections') tied to the great building boom of the Renaissance city. Private commissions turned to the building of great residential palaces. The 'public' and 'religious' commissions (the 'workshops' for the great religious buildings constituted permanent technical–financial structures which through collaborations with the major guilds and corporations built and managed the major public works projects)[1] placed into motion a complex of productive activities – from those associated with the building (brick furnaces and stone quarries) to the decorative trades (interior design, furniture, textiles, jewellery, ceramics and tiles, etc. – that unloaded on the internal market profits originating from commercial and financial transactions undertaken abroad.

Here, we run into an historical issue which has often been raised in the past. As Goldthwaite (1980) notes, 'the significant expenditures on private construction . . . should not be seen as a reallocation of capital from more productive activities. Among those who spent their money in the most conspicuous manner in private residences were successful merchants whose investments did not in the slightest represent an end to their productive activities. For example, Filippo Strozzi had sufficient liquidity to pay for the entire cost of his new palace . . .' Nevertheless, the textile manufacturing sector declined during the fifteenth century with a growing dependence on the needs of the internal market. Tuscan manufacturing did not succeed in putting together the conditions for a capitalist take-off. Locally, conditions were not supportive of the process of accumulation and reinvestment of profits capable of overcoming the significant technological barriers which appeared during this period of history in the development of the textile manufacturing sector. The required technological change took place elsewhere and during a different historical period.

As a result, the financial wealth of Florence was directed toward consumption or toward particular forms of expenditure which contained a significant ambivalence toward ostentatious forms of consumption – expressions of civic ideals and of philanthropy which the humanistic culture would elaborate and legitimize[2] – but also forms of consumption which activated other productive networks, thereby supporting a great tradition of artistic and artisan traditions and creative outputs. All of this produced an accumulated cultural and artistic patrimony consisting of palaces, churches, sculpture, paintings, and decorations which after centuries represents a collective good, a cultural heritage that continues to act on the historical memory as a component element of a self-image and identity but also as an economic resource within development processes which are certainly significantly different from those at their origin. Thus, the cultural richness of Renaissance Florence drew from the interconnection between production and consumption, a birthmark which the city and region still carry.

Naturally, this heredity is not only the product of the mechanisms of production and consumption that we have briefly outlined. The dense network of urban centres that preserve their own original historical structure (not only in the historical centres but also in the entire urban structure) appears as a projection into the present of a complex development whose individuality and identity was created and defended often through bitter conflict. The history of Tuscan society in the centuries when the greater part of its cultural heritage was created is a history of urban hierarchies, of a difficult but never concluded process of forming a regional governing body. Pisa, Siena, Lucca, San Gimignano, Volterra, Pienza and many other cities reflect an urban structure that was enriched through a dialect of conflict and cooperation between centres of power that now and then found an equilibrium but which often reflected the hegemonic role of particular centres. If the urban and architectural legacies are the ones that most directly convey to us a sense of history, in the case of artistic production (and painting in particular) the relationship between centre and periphery plays a fundamental role in understanding Tuscany's cultural heritage. Even in a region like Tuscany, the physical structure and geopolitical divisions constituted both integral part in the diversification among the various urban centres and also a strong attractive force in creating a dialogue and opening contacts between these centres and enriching their experience, culture, and prospects.

As is well known, the history of Italian art is a history of geographically located 'schools' and cities which assumed the role (even if for brief periods of time) of 'centres' in relation to many peripheries. It is not only the major 'capitals' (Florence, Rome, Venice, Bologna) which contend for the top national honour. As with Russian dolls, this game is reproduced at the regional level between 'centres' of varying importance. Tuscany is a land which offers a rich diversity of examples. Why should we find in Roccalbegna, a small town on Mount Amiata between the provinces of Siena and Grosseto three important paintings by Lorenzetti? Why did a great artist paint three large canvases for an isolated, far-away town? The answer to this question

> probably lies in the importance that the Sienese attributed to this small mining town which they had taken over and refounded in the 13th century on the southern outskirts of Sienese territory. The case of these paintings has to be seen in relation to the creation of a new city and the efforts through which a series of incentives were provided in order to persuade citizens of Siena to go and live there. The presence of paintings by one of Siena's greatest painters was a symbol of identity and attraction. All of this is tied to the spread of works of art and artistic commissions which took place in the thirteen hundreds in the cities and towns of the southern Maremma, from Grosseto to Paganico in the area of the more recent expansion of Siena. (Castelnuovo and Ginzberg, 1979, p. 341)

The management, conservation and appreciation of these works of art in a region such as Tuscany also must come to terms with the diffusion of this heritage throughout the region. These works of art need to be catalogued and reinserted into the art circuit of critical acclaim. This is a major problem due to the economic and social context within which this heritage finds itself today.

10.2   Economic return and production

We have already mentioned the structural ambivalence of the economic processes which have produced Tuscany's cultural wealth. On the one hand, there was the stocking and development of opulent consumption and on the other the creation of new markets for artistic and artisan outputs and the extraordinary development of human resources which served as the basis for the tradition of high-quality craftsmanship and productive capacity, a tradition which during the course of the centuries distinguished Tuscan society and which even today provides a certain distinction for products 'made in Tuscany'.

However, the role played in Tuscany by the region's artistic treasures can be viewed today in a critical manner. In short, the cultural heritage of the region has served as the material base for an economic process increasingly emphasizing the profitable tourist trade as against areas of production based on the conservation and management of Tuscany's artistic treasures and the connection between these resources and scientific research, contemporary artistic production, and professional education and training.

Expressed in this manner, the thesis needs a few specifications to be understood. What is the means by which returns dominate over production? This is essentially reflected in one simple observation: the cultural heritage of the region has not entered a productive process; instead, it has wound up providing support for an image of the region which has attracted a large number of tourists. The number, characteristics and patterns of tourist inflows place tremendous pressures on the cultural infrastructure as well as city services, especially in a city the size of Florence. The nature of tourism in Florence and other art centres in Tuscany has significantly compromised the relationship between the conservation, valorization and exploitation of the region's artistic treasures. In short, the great 'capital' endowment of culture accumulated through the centuries has been generally used and consumed without limitation rather than being seen as the bases for the investment of resources and know-how.

A long time has passed since Florence and Tuscany were the highlights in the Grand Tour to Italy undertaken by artists and writers in the search of aesthetic inspiration and literary stimuli. Since tourism assumed a mass dimension, the region has become the object of flows governed in great part by the large, international tour operators. Of course, other types of tourism tied to conventions, business trips and study tours are also present, but the major characteristic of tourism in Tuscany is its short-term nature which is reflected in the data on the average stay in a hotel in the region: 3.1 days for each tourist and 2.3 days in Florence. This is a type of tourism which does not have at its disposal time enough for a critical evaluation, a deeper understanding, and an absorption of the spirit, history and identity of the site. The data in Tables 10.1 and 10.2 speak for themselves.

In 1990, 5,862,508 guests arrived in Tuscan hotels and stayed for a total of approximately 18 million days. Other forms of accommodation – such as rooms, camping, agritourism accommodation, and hostels – brought the total to 7,286,134 (for a total of 31,745,983 days). Foreigners account for over 3 million arrivals and 10 million days of lodging. Naturally, the role of Florence (Table 10.3) is predominant; it accounts for 40 per cent of all arrivals in Tuscany (2,797,166 and 7.5 million days of stay). Siena also accounts for a significant influx (over 750,000 tourists) while the figures for the provinces of Leghorn (900,000), Grosseto (700,000) and Lucca (600,000) are accounted for by the beach holiday season.[3]

It is generally the major artistic centres and Florence in particular which 'suffer' from this presence. It is calculated that 20,000 tourists are added on a daily basis to Florence's population, an influx which is predominantly

Table 10.1   Number of clients in Tuscan hotels, 1990

Province	Italians arrivals	days stayed	Foreigners arrivals	days stayed	Total arrivals	days stayed
Arezzo	184,829	398,655	45,351	110,473	230,180	509,128
Florence	926,308	1,910,887	1,497,927	3,498,953	2,424,235	5,409,840
Grosseto	287,221	985,150	57,791	360,218	345,012	1,345.368
Leghorn	402,925	1,732,201	101,558	558,905	504,483	2,291,106
Lucca	370,654	1,611,668	163,211	654,099	533,865	2,265,767
Massa Carrara	78,572	372,888	27,584	99,724	106,156	472,612
Pisa	241,657	626,531	134,532	329,884	376,189	956,415
Pistoia	414,059	1,637,833	147,946	442,802	562,005	2,080,635
Siena	476,943	1,989,139	213,597	479,671	690,540	2,468,810
Prato	54,454	104,305	35,388	74,047	89,842	178,352
Total for region	3,437,622	11,369,257	2,424,885	6,608,776	5,862,508	17,978,033

Source: Regione Toscana, Giunta Regionale (1992).

Table 10.2   1989 Tourism in Tuscany by type of lodging

Type of lodging	Italians arrivals	days stayed	Foreigners arrivals	days stayed	Total arrivals	days stayed
5 stars	38,815	80,553	73,312	198,665	112,127	279,218
4 stars	718,105	1,679,525	734,533	1,795,263	1,452,638	3,474,788
3 stars	1,497,310	4,206,986	951,052	2,347,043	2,448,362	6,554,029
2 stars	771,161	3,222,152	341,385	955,478	1,112,546	4,177,630
1 star	399,735	1,780,227	264,341	802,697	664,076	2,582,924
Other residential hotels	66,581	501,195	49,612	404,058	116,193	905,253
Total hotels	*3,491,707*	*11,470,638*	*2,414,235*	*6,503,204*	*5,905,942*	*17,973,842*
Rented rooms	254,132	4,381,250	93,870	1,444,029	348,002	5,825,279
Camping	472,117	4,836,714	396,193	1,887,013	868,310	6,723,727
Agri-tourist accomodation	301	1,831	487	3,328	788	5,159
Hostels	15,311	35,581	92,685	202,908	107,996	238,489
Holiday homes	12,380	191,872	7,756	77,930	20,136	269,802
Mountain rest sites	358	2,284	2	2	360	2,286
Other accommodation	23,783	618,764	10,817	88,635	34,600	707,399
Total non-hotel	*778,382*	*10,068,296*	*601,810*	*3,703,845*	*1,380,192*	*13,772,141*
Overall total	4,270,089	21,538,934	3,016,045	10,207,049	7,286,134	31,745,983

Source: Regione Toscana, Giunta Regionale (1991).

Table 10.3   1989 Tourism in Florence by type of lodging

Type of lodging	Italians		Foreigners		Total	
	arrivals	days stayed	arrivals	days stayed	arrivals	days stayed
5 stars	23,772	43,691	60,555	156,337	84,327	200,028
4 stars	320,029	499,660	543,933	1,124,973	863,962	1,624,633
3 stars	372,895	717,953	505,985	1,095,131	878,880	1,813,084
2 stars	189,622	414,887	175,803	447,276	365,425	862,163
1 star	134,844	430,426	185,257	524,121	320,101	954,547
Other residential hotels	5,309	13,189	14,472	29,373	19,781	42,562
Total hotels	*1,046,471*	*2,119,806*	*1,486,005*	*3,377,211*	*2,532,476*	*5,497,017*
Rented rooms	6,657	512,158	5,341	537,224	11,998	1,049,382
Camping	23,480	71,242	134,481	367,785	157,961	439,027
Agri-tourist accommodation	221	1,149	470	3,155	691	4,304
Hostels	5,940	11,744	64,917	144,681	70,857	156,425
Holiday homes	52	149	351	999	403	1,148
Mountain rest sites	0	0	0	0	0	0
Other accommodation	12,070	346,376	10,710	85,121	22,780	431,497
Total non-hotel	*48,420*	*942,818*	*216,270*	*1,138,965*	*264,690*	*2,081,783*
Overall total	1,094,891	3,062,624	1,702,275	4,516,176	2,797,166	7,578,800

Source: Regione Toscana, Giunta Regionale (1991).

concentrated in the city centre. The structures carrying the burden of these flows are the city's monuments which are also under attack by environmental pollution, and those who benefit are the people who work in and live off the tourist industry.

The strong presence of tourists has a profound impact on the overall economy of the city, inflating property prices, rentals, the cost of trading and commercial licences, and the overall cost of living. What in one instance seems to be an undeniable gain, on other occasions can become an unbearable cost on the city. Tourism expenditures undoubtedly increase the demand for goods and services in Florence and in the region (one only has to mention the fashion industry and local artisan trades), but the demand is not spread out evenly. The food industry is, for example, largely excluded. What emerges as the most important is the role of commercial intermediation between local demand by residents and tourists and goods and services produced elsewhere.

The historical-artistic patrimony thus finds itself performing a difficult balancing act, sifting through the contradictions present in the system. On the one hand, actions to preserve this patrimony run into the limitations and inefficiency of the Italian state in dealing with art treasures. The limitation is felt even more in places such as Tuscany where the heritage is so rich and widespread. On the other hand, it is difficult to respect limitations in exploiting these resources economically while at the same time conserving them. In many cases the limits are ignored. Due to the enormous demand the result is the development of a stereotype of the 'beauty' of the city and region in relation to the variety of its historical and artistic fabric. Michaelangelo's *David* and the Leaning Tower of Pisa have become symbols of a quick and voracious brand of tourism around which has developed a large subsidiary industry providing low-quality goods such as fast-foods and cheap souvenirs.

What has helped to create this situation is the economic interests which have been mobilized by the exploitation of the cultural heritage for the tourist industry. The profits and returns to be realized from activities tied to the city's and region's cultural heritage has created a strong coalition of private interests. This social coalition has contributed to the distortion of the use and enjoyment of the artistic treasures within restricted parameters. It has promoted brief tourist itineraries confined to limited parts of the city's historical centre and has paid little attention to reducing the physical burden of thousands and thousands of visitors on a small number of monuments by developing alternative historical and artistic itineraries.

It is certainly true that not everything can be reduced to this perverse dynamic. The art treasures represent for Tuscany a source of wealth and income which is not necessarily tied to an unrestricted exploitation. One only has to think about the number of people who are employed in the management of this cultural heritage (museum guards, librarians, officials of the *Soprintendenze*, archivists, restorers, scholars and researchers, etc.) who represent a complex of knowledge which has not always been put to full use due to inadequate resources and lack of will on the part of the administrative apparatus. Even in the field of subsidiary industries tied to tourism not everything is in bad taste or of an inferior quality.

Nevertheless, the dominant theme of the present analysis is the blatant lack of adequate policies and the weakness of the Italian state in protecting its cultural treasures in the face of the pervasive pressure applied by mass tourism which has increasingly sunk to the lowest common denominator. Mass tourism per se is not the problem; what is a problem is the reduction in the length of stays and the 'look-and-run' tours concentrated on a few but always the same itineraries. This has caused a region such as Tuscany with a rich heritage in art and history to become part of an economic cycle characterized by very little virtue and based on a return derived from the over-exploitation of existing resources. The alternative, which has never been fully developed (but which could and should have been), foresees a valorization of the region's resources in a 'productive' manner.

Take for example the museums. Tuscany is rich beyond measure in museums.[4] Each city and village has at its disposal an historical-artistic heritage that permits it to place the heritage on permanent display. From a variety of studies and surveys (see Table 10.4), one clear datum emerges: Tuscany is the Italian region with the highest number of museums (approximately 13 per cent of the national total). Florence with fifty-one and Rome with eighty-three are the cities with the highest number of museums.

Table 10.4   Museums in Italy

Region & Capital city	A	B	C	D	E	F	totals
Piedmont	17	26	12	9	17	29	
Turin	2	4	4	6	2	5	23
Total	19	30	16	15	19	34	133
V.D'Aosta	2	0	1	3	1	7	14
Lombardia	30	35	12	15	13	35	
Milan	2	11	3	3	1	11	31
Total	32	46	15	18	14	46	171
Trentino	2	10	3	1	7	6	
Trento		2	2	2			6
Total	2	12	5	3	7	6	35
Veneto	18	24	5	9	10	15	
Venice	2	15	2	2		9	30
Total	20	39	7	11	10	24	111
Friuli	5	7	4	4	6	5	
Trieste	1	5	2	3	2	3	16
Total	6	12	6	7	8	8	47
Liguria	12	10		1	1	10	
Genoa	1	8	1	2	3	5	20
Total	13	18	1	3	4	15	54
Emilia-Rom.	36	49	13	12	16	20	
Bologna	1	10	2	10	1	9	33
Total	37	59	15	22	17	29	179
Tuscany	24	51	6	14	15	50	
Florence	2	28	1	5	1	14	51
Total	26	79	7	19	16	64	211
Umbria	9	23	0	2	1	14	
Perugia	1	2	0	1		1	5
Total	10	25	0	3	1	15	54
Marche	15	27	3	4	4	21	
Ancona	2	3				2	7
Total	17	30	3	4	4	23	81
Lazio	37	9	1	1	1	10	
Rome	17	19	11	7	3	26	83
Vatican	9	2			1	6	18
Total	63	30	12	8	5	42	160
Abruzzo	7	9	0	5	2	9	32
L'Aquila		1	0	1		1	3
Total	7	10	0	6	2	10	35
Molise	3	2				1	6

Continued

Table 10.4 *Cont.*

Region & Capital city	Category						
	A	B	C	D	E	F	totals
Campania	20	6	1	4	2	15	48
Naples	3	8	0	7	1	7	26
Total	23	14	1	11	3	22	74
Puglia	28	7	0	3	4	14	56
Bari	3	1	0	2	1	4	11
Total	31	8	0	5	5	18	67
Basilicata	6	1	0	0	0	1	8
Calabria	9	5	0	0	1	8	23
Sicily	26	14	2	9	4	17	72
Palermo	2	2	1	2	1	2	10
Total	28	16	3	11	5	19	82
Sardegna	11	1	1	6	2	5	26
Cagliari	1	3	0	1	2	3	10
Total	12	4	1	7	4	8	36
Italy	366	440	93	156	126	400	1581

Source: *Tutti i musei d'Italia*, Editoriale Domus, 1984.

Notes: A = archaeology; B = art; C = history; D = science and industry; E = ethnography, anthropology F = miscellaneous.

Nevertheless, there are few cases in which, around the museums, we have seen the development of a series of complementary cultural activities capable of enriching the role and functions of the museums or producing the increased financial resources necessary for the management and protection of these structures. As a result, many of the museums located around the region and within Florence (often labelled as 'minor' museums) continue to be ignored by the majority of tourists and survive with difficulty given their ties to the often precarious nature of public financing. There has been a refusal to redirect and differentiate the tourist demand and raise it to a level of understanding that is more informed and aware.

The situation of the well-known museums, such as the Uffizi, is also critical. There is a great danger of overuse of the museum facilities and damage to the paintings through exposure to heat and moisture. There is a scarcity of resources made available to the museum; problems persist in ensuring an adequate form of surveillance and hours of opening; and antiquated bureaucratic norms and legislation prevent an adequate administrative autonomy to permit proper management of such a vast museum complex. It is worthwhile remembering that the 'Grandi Uffizi' project for expanding and rationalizing the exhibition space has been stalled for years, and a comparison with the pace of change that was necessary to complete the new Louvre leaves one saddened and bitter.

In talking about the 'correct method for appreciating' or the 'productive connections' which a cultural heritage can put into motion, we can refer to cultural objectives tied to the growth and diffusion of an understanding that such a patrimony necessitates. There is nothing worse than to think of promoting culture in terms of its subordination to extra-cultural objectives. To think of the cultural heritage as a pretext for the achievement of other objectives, such as those purely economic in nature, is self-defeating.

The use and enjoyment of cultural goods should, above all, be seen as a good in itself. Resources used by the community to protect and develop them constitute a common good, an enrichment of the collective identity which helps to develop an historical memory and an enrichment of the common identity. Art is a resource, and as any resource it can be used, abused, or dispersed; just as it can be developed, protected, and above all reproduced. 'Productive connections' therefore, are those which permit a cultural heritage to continue to live and to encourage the growth of a new culture and a new critical consciousness. When they are tied to the phases of training, scientific research and cultural experimentation they constitute factors for growth.

From this perspective and despite the contradictions apparent in cities such as Florence, the overall evaluation is not necessarily pessimistic. To bring to life an historical heritage means to reintroduce it into the public consciousness, and Tuscany has been able to preserve its heritage and history and make it available to Europe and the rest of the world.

Tuscany is at the centre of well-developed and important facilities in the restoration of art works. It has a university and a number of cultural institutions. The urban centres which are considered historically important are generally well preserved. Entire cities, such as Siena (but one could cite many others), have maintained intact their ancient appearance without losing in the process their modern vitality. We find ourselves in the middle of a cultural heritage that continues to reside between 'production' and 'consumption', between the temptation to exploit immediately the spirit and history that has been passed down through generations and the potential of a real and long-term appreciation which, of course, does not exclude relevant economic implications but which also does not emphasize them beyond the goals of the primary cultural and educational objectives.

10.3 The other aspect of economic return

We referred above to Lorenzetti's fresco as reflecting the relationship between city and country. This reference brings to mind another fundamental theme: the historical patrimony of Tuscany is not only made up of a rich and diversified urban fabric; it is also constituted by a countryside significantly transformed but preserved by man. In this chapter we cannot discuss in detail the history of Tuscan agriculture and how the dominant economic relationships existing there have impacted on the conservation of an incomparable natural environment and in the creation of a natural environment where nature and history intersect. Certainly, the situation cannot be idealized nor can it be generalized. In the areas where heavy industrialization has taken place, the environment has been significantly transformed and 'consumed'; the metropolitan area around Florence is certainly not a good example of urban planning, and a part of the coastline has been ruined by over-construction. Nevertheless, there are still many areas in the region which reflect a conscious conservation effort: from the hills around Florence to the Chianti area and from the countryside around Siena to the Maremma. Given this state of affairs, it is important to understand the social and economic logic that permitted and still permits a conservation of this ecological balance.

If the Tuscan countryside preserves to a large extent its attractiveness, it is certainly due to the merits of a correct territorial planning policy implemented by the political authorities. Good government is a determining element that cannot be underrated, as witnessed by the number of bad examples present in other parts of the country. Nevertheless, this element is not sufficient; it is necessary to consider the peculiar nature of positional goods in the sense that Fred Hirsch (1977) gave to this concept which the countryside and the environment in Tuscany have always assumed.

To understand how cultural and natural resources can be considered positional goods it is necessary to refer briefly to Hirsch's definition of the concept. The basis for the analysis is the reference to the paradox tied to the relationship between the growth of earning power and changes in patterns of consumption: 'as the level of average consumption rises', writes Hirsch, 'an increasing proportion of consumption takes on a social as well as an individual aspect. That is to say, the satisfaction that individuals derive from goods and services depends in increasing measure not only on their own consumption but on consumption by others as well' (p. 2).

We need to introduce here the concept of social scarcity: 'The satisfaction derived from a car or a country cottage depends on the conditions in which they can be used, which will be stongly influenced by how many people are using them' (p. 3). Positional goods are therefore those goods which derive their 'utility' from their social scarcity and from the utility that, in comparison to others, the potential users can gain from them. What is highlighted are the mechanisms of social interaction to which the consumption of certain social goods are connected.

We can immediately understand how this definition of positional goods well fits the case under discussion: living in a beautiful square in an historic centre certainly constitutes a positional good, a form of enjoyment of an historical/artistic good that is intrinsically limited to a few rich and fortunate individuals who own houses there. It risks no longer being so if the same square becomes the destination of an influx of uncontrolled and chaotic hoards of tourists. Another example is living in a house in the countryside with a beautiful view of the Tuscan hills. This represents the enjoyment of a positional good which remains so only if there are enforceable limitations on reproducing the uniqueness and rarity of the good in question (i.e., drastic limits on building other residences, protection of the forest, care in the cultivation of agricultural products, etc.).

Our conviction remains that in Tuscany strong social mechanisms have been operative in protecting the positional value of cultural and natural resources. This is the other side of the gains from tourism. Conservation has produced positive effects when it has prevailed over other aspects of profit in managing these resources: when the comparative advantage represented by the conservation of a particular good was superior to that represented by its exploitation tied to other interests. To refer back to the examples already cited, to live in a beautiful square in the historical centre no longer represents a positional good when the logic of commercial exploitation reigns supreme, such as when a fast-food establishment is opened to cater to the passing tourists or when an artisan is forced to leave his shop due to the rising levels of rents.

We can state that in Tuscany this sort of conflict between different economic logics (on one side, a return concerned with a longer-term view in not undermining the material base of the positional goods and on the other those preoccupied in turning a profit within a shorter period of time) has had different outcomes in various parts of the region. In Florence the logic of the short-term return has prevailed while in other places – such as in the countryside, in the more attractive hill areas, and in the smaller towns – the result has been significantly different.

The Tuscan countryside with its network of small towns and villages with a long history (e.g., southern Tuscany and the Chianti area) has increasingly become the target for significant land and property invest-ments which have also assumed the characteristic of symbolic gestures and carry with them significant levels of social status. We have witnessed the restructuring of many farmhouses; the residences of noble families have been transformed into agritourist establishments. Many small towns which had undergone a long process of decline in their populations have seen the tendency reversed and have become the destination for an elite form of tourism, places of residence or of holiday homes. A main beneficiary of this trend has been agricultural production which has received a stimulus to become increasingly specialized.

The combination of these factors has undoubtedly helped the conser-vation of the environment because the obvious goal of these investments is the conservation of the historical-natural panoramas. While Florence witnessed the creation of a contradictory *modus vivendi* between the historical-artistic legacy and a mass form of tourism typical of large regional capitals, a large part of Tuscany has been able to combine its historical and ecological resources with an investment and development approach which has respected the past.

Of course, there are some dangers in this situation. In particular, the risk in producing a breakdown in the logic of productive investments – that is, the particular return from property investments and the magnetism this historical-natural environment exercises in attracting profits from other sectors – will weaken other productive sectors of the regional economy. In addition, it is possible that there will be a shift in the ownership of land and agricultural property outside the region. In this case property in Tuscany – due to the original aspects of its culture and history – could become a 'sheltered investment' in Italy and Europe (i.e., become a positional good in and of itself).

Other elements of risk exist derived from the creation of a double standard between different parts of the region. One standard could exist in the Tuscany that produces and the other in the Tuscany that consumes; in a similar fashion, we could get a differentiation in the types of consumption patterns in those areas dominated by mass tourism and those dedicated to more 'quality' types of tourism reserved for few individuals. These are the dangers against which a renewed concern with regional planning can provide effective counter-measures.

10.4   The production and consumption of cultural goods

In order to complete the analysis presented above, it is necessary to consider one aspect which we have mentioned in passing on a number of occasions. We have seen how Tuscany's cultural heritage has difficulty in managing the contradictions which exist between commercial exploitation and productive conservation and how the region is torn between possible scenarios emphasizing it as the ideal location for consumption and those stressing the role of its past as providing the necessary base for cultural, artistic and scientific expression.

Risks and opportunities are combined, and a choice of direction requires the implementation of significant policies if the contradictions are to be resolved. Nevertheless, the foundations upon which a new cultural policy can be formulated are real and solid. Aside from the figures already mentioned, data on the level of consumption of cultural services confirm this generalization.

Tuscany is one of the Italian regions with the highest level of consumption and production of cultural goods and services. Though some of these aspects are difficult to quantify and compare across regions, the available data confirm the role of Tuscany as a region possessing a high 'cultural' vocation. The region has a vast number and variety of study centres and cultural institutions which produce as well as conserve culture.

The cultural centres active in the field of music and the theatre are also rich and varied. Tables 10.5 and 10.6 present data on the level of attendance of concerts, the theatre, and the cinema between 1970 and 1990 compared on a regional basis throughout the country. In particular, it is important to note the steady increase in levels of attendance up until 1982 and the levelling off after the drop in 1983 which was less in Tuscany than the national average. The trend and the relative stability of the high levels of consumption are symptomatic of another important datum: the existence of a wide and diffuse market for culture which finds expression in institutionalized and active centres. Periodic shifts in these data might

Table 10.5 Theatre and concert attendance (number of tickets sold per 100 inhabitants)

Region	1970	1971	1972	1973	1974	1975	1976	1977	1978	1979
Piedmont	22	28	32	31	39	35	34	38	41	51
Val D'Aosta	7	16	12	11	14	16	18	17	13	17
Lombardy	31	33	32	37	40	39	42	43	45	46
Trentino	38	39	37	42	39	44	41	47	52	58
Veneto	27	31	29	31	32	34	33	35	41	44
Friuli	41	45	50	50	50	53	46	56	56	63
Liguria	30	36	39	42	47	52	46	54	58	59
Emilia-Rom.	31	34	35	40	46	48	48	51	56	65
Tuscany	**32**	**37**	**38**	**46**	**50**	**53**	**54**	**54**	**59**	**63**
Umbria	19	19	25	23	26	29	26	36	40	42
Marche	18	18	17	22	28	30	29	33	32	34
Lazio	32	36	43	42	42	46	48	50	55	57
Abruzzi	12	11	11	13	14	15	18	21	22	28
Molise	5	6	6	11	9	7	7	10	15	11
Campania	13	16	17	18	22	22	24	25	23	26
Puglia	12	13	14	13	19	23	23	22	23	27
Basilicata	5	5	6	6	8	6	6	7	9	9
Calabria	4	5	4	4	5	5	7	7	7	9
Sicily	17	17	21	20	24	26	29	28	31	32
Sardegna	6	9	8	12	10	15	13	11	17	18
Italy	23	26	27	29	33	34	35	37	39	43

Region	1980	1981	1982	1983	1984	1985	1986	1987	1988	1989	1990
Piedmont	49	52	50	38	38	40	38	44	48	45	45
Val D'Aosta	15	20	27	27	64	26	35	42	58	42	42
Lombardy	53	52	51	46	46	47	50	54	53	52	53
Trentino	65	72	77	68	70	63	70	71	69	71	71
Veneto	53	54	52	43	45	45	47	50	50	49	51
Friuli	62	63	61	58	61	57	58	61	71	67	62
Liguria	62	62	58	50	44	52	50	55	56	55	52
Emilia-Rom.	65	66	68	58	56	57	59	64	71	68	64
Tuscany	**61**	**69**	**68**	**58**	**52**	**53**	**54**	**57**	**58**	**60**	**54**
Umbria	43	45	54	38	39	41	39	42	45	48	42
Marche	40	45	49	32	34	36	37	36	39	39	35
Lazio	68	62	67	57	60	63	64	70	70	62	61
Abruzzi	27	28	32	25	24	29	32	32	36	36	34
Molise	16	20	17	14	16	18	15	16	12	17	17
Campania	27	27	28	24	26	27	28	29	30	29	28
Puglia	25	28	25	20	24	26	23	24	23	22	19
Basilicata	11	12	17	12	17	22	23	21	19	23	23
Calabria	10	11	11	10	13	16	15	17	16	17	16
Sicily	37	33	41	35	37	33	35	35	35	34	36
Sardegna	23	27	34	28	33	37	32	33	38	34	33
Italy	46	47	48	30	41	42	43	46	47	45	44

Source: SIAE.

Table 10.6 Number of cinema tickets sold per inhabitant

Region	1970	1971	1972	1973	1974	1975	1976	1977	1978	1979
Piedmont	10	10	10	10	9	9	8	6	5	4
Lombardy	10	10	12	11	11	10	9	7	7	5
Val D'Aosta	10	10	10	9	9	9	7	6	5	4
Trentino	9	9	9	8	8	7	6	5	5	4
Veneto	9	8	9	8	8	7	7	5	5	4
Friuli	10	10	10	10	10	9	7	6	5	4
Liguria	14	14	14	14	14	12	10	9	7	6
Emilia-Rom.	13	14	14	14	14	13	12	10	9	8
Tuscany	**11**	**11**	**12**	**12**	**12**	**11**	**10**	**8**	**7**	**6**
Umbria	6	7	7	7	7	7	6	5	4	3
Marche	9	9	10	10	10	10	9	8	7	6
Lazio	10	11	11	11	11	10	9	7	6	5
Abruzzi	7	7	8	8	8	8	7	6	5	4
Molise	5	5	6	5	5	4	4	3	2	2
Campania	9	9	10	9	9	9	8	6	5	4
Puglia	12	12	12	12	12	10	9	8	7	6
Basilicata	5	5	6	5	5	5	5	4	3	3
Calabria	5	4	5	5	5	5	5	4	3	3
Sicily	9	9	10	10	10	9	8	7	6	6
Sardegna	7	7	7	7	8	7	6	5	4	3
Italy	10	10	10	10	10	9	8	7	6	5

Region	1980	1981	1982	1983	1984	1985	1986	1987	1988	1989	1990
Piedmont	4	4	4	3	2.6	2.5	2.6	2.4	2.1	2.2	2.1
Lombardy	5	4	4	3	2.2	2.1	2.1	2.0	1.8	1.8	1.5
Val D'Aosta	3	3	3	3	2.3	2.2	2.3	2.2	1.9	2.0	1.9
Trentino	4	3	3	2	1.8	1.8	1.8	1.6	1.3	1.4	1.2
Veneto	3	3	3	3	2.1	2.0	2.0	1.8	1.5	1.6	1.5
Friuli	4	4	3	3	2.2	2.3	2.4	2.1	1.9	1.8	1.7
Liguria	5	5	5	4	3.4	3.2	3.1	2.8	2.4	2.4	2.4
Emilia-Rom.	7	6	5	5	3.8	3.7	3.7	3.3	2.9	2.9	2.7
Tuscany	**6**	**5**	**4**	**4**	**3.2**	**3.0**	**3.0**	**2.6**	**2.4**	**2.3**	**2.3**
Umbria	3	3	3	2	1.7	1.6	1.6	1.3	1.2	1.2	1.2
Marche	5	5	4	4	2.7	2.5	2.5	2.2	1.8	1.8	1.8
Lazio	5	4	4	3	2.8	2.7	2.6	2.3	1.9	2.1	2.0
Abruzzi	4	3	3	2	1.8	1.6	1.6	1.4	1.3	1.2	1.1
Molise	1	1	1	1	0.6	0.6	0.7	0.5	0.3	0.3	0.3
Campania	4	3	3	2	1.7	1.3	1.3	1.0	0.8	0.7	0.7
Puglia	5	4	3	3	1.8	1.6	1.6	1.3	1.1	1.0	1.0
Basilicata	2	2	2	1	0.9	0.7	0.8	0.6	0.5	0.5	0.5
Calabria	3	2	2	1	1.2	1.0	1.0	0.8	0.6	0.6	0.5
Sicily	5	4	3	2	2.0	1.7	1.7	1.4	1.1	1.1	1.1
Sardegna	3	2	2	2	1.4	1.3	1.4	1.3	1.1	1.1	1.1
Italy	4	4	3	3	2.3	2.2	2.2	1.9	1.6	1.6	1.6

Source: SIAE.

Table 10.7 Ranking of Italian regions on theatre and concert attendance

Region	1970	Region	1975	Region	1980	Region	1985	Region	1990
Friuli	41	Friuli	53	Lazio	68	Trentino	63	Trentino	71
Trentino	38	**Tuscany**	53	Trentino	65	Lazio	63	Emilia-R.	64
Tuscany	32	Liguria	52	Emilia-R.	65	Friuli	57	Friuli	62
Lazio	32	Emilia-R.	48	Friuli	62	Emilia-R.	57	Lazio	61
Lombardy	31	Lazio	46	Liguria	62	**Tuscany**	53	**Tuscany**	54
Emilia-R.	31	Trentino	44	**Tuscany**	61	Liguria	52	Lombardy	53
Liguria	30	Lombardy	39	Lombardy	53	Lombardy	47	Liguria	52
Veneto	27	Piedmont	35	Veneto	53	Veneto	45	Veneto	51
Italy	23	Veneto	34	Piedmont	49	**Italy**	42	Piedmont	45
Piedmont	22	**Italy**	34	**Italy**	46	Umbria	41	**Italy**	44
Umbria	19	Marche	30	Umbria	43	Piedmont	40	V.D'Aosta	42
Marche	18	Umbria	29	Marche	40	Sardegna	37	Umbria	42
Sicily	17	Sicily	26	Sicily	37	Marche	36	Sicily	36
Campania	13	Puglia	23	Abruzzi	27	Sicily	33	Marche	35
Abruzzi	12	Campania	22	Campania	27	Abruzzi	29	Abruzzi	34
Puglia	12	V.D'Aosta	16	Puglia	25	Campania	27	Sardegna	33
V.D'Aosta	7	Abruzzi	15	Sardegna	23	V.D'Aosta	26	Campania	28
Sardegna	6	Sardegna	15	Molise	16	Puglia	26	Basilicata	23
Molise	5	Molise	7	V.D'Aosta	15	Basilicata	22	Puglia	19
Basilicata	5	Basilicata	6	Basilicata	11	Molise	18	Molise	17
Calabria	4	Calabria	5	Calabria	10	Calabria	16	Calabria	16

Source: SIAE.

suggest a precarious existence for cultural institutions and centres involved in cultural activities. In particular, in 1990 (see Table 10.7) Tuscany was in fifth place in attendance levels at musical concerts and theatres and in third place in relation to cinema attendance (Table 10.6).

If we look in Table 10.8 at the trends registered at the provincial level, we notice a significant difference in the behaviour of the Tuscan provinces in the consumption of cultural products and services. Florence has a primary role which sees it at the top of the national ranking with a slight erosion of its rank during the last five years and the trend in the provinces of Lucca and Siena are particularly impressive. In 1970 Pisa, Arezzo, Pistoia and Grosseto were ranked fairly low in relation to other provinces in the north-central part of the country and below the national average. Twenty years later Lucca and Siena were respectively thirteenth and fourteenth, reflecting a significant increase in the demand for cultural activities in these two provinces. Even Pistoia in twenty-second position has made significant progress and is now above the national average. Grosseto showed some progress between 1970 (forty-eighth) and 1990 (thirty-fifth).

The role of Florence as the great centre for cultural activities is also confirmed by the analysis of the data in relation to the level of attendance of theatres and concerts in the country's seventeen cities with populations of over 200,000 (Table 10.9). Florence is consistently in second or third place; in 1990 it was surpassed only by Milan and Verona.[5]

In summary, this overview of culture and the activities that gravitate

Table 10.8   Ranking of Italian provinces on attendance of concerts and theatres

Ranking	1970		1975		1980		1985		1990	
1	Trieste	103	Trieste	130	Trieste	126	Trieste	148	Trieste	141
2	Verona	59	Imperia	89	Verona	105	Verona	109	Verona	116
3	Florence	56	Florence	84	Ravenna	100	Rome	80	Bolzano	92
4	Bolzano	54	Verona	73	Florence	95	Florence	79	Milan	82
5	Ravenna	45	Ravenna	71	Rome	84	Bolzano	77	Bologna	80
6	Milan	44	Bologna	59	Parma	81	Milan	73	Rome	76
7	Bologna	42	Milan	56	Milan	79	Bologna	73	Florence	74
8	Rome	40	Bolzano	56	Bolzano	79	Genoa	64	Modena	71
9	Genoa	37	Genoa	56	Genoa	78	Gorizia	64	Ravenna	67
10	Parma	36	Rome	56	Bologna	77	Ravenna	63	Forlì	64
11	Leghorn	36	Turin	49	Forlì	72	Reggio E.	61	Parma	63
12	Imperia	35	Parma	47	Turin	68	Lucca	57	Gorizia	62
13	Ferrara	31	Reggio E.	47	Lucca	66	Ferrara	55	Lucca	61
14	Turin	30	Leghorn	46	Venice	65	Parma	53	Siena	59
15	Rovigo	30	Siena	45	Reggio E.	63	Turin	52	Genoa	58
16	Gorizia	30	Forlì	44	Catania	57	Forlì	51	Turin	58
17	Palermo	28	Lucca	44	Imperia	55	Siena	51	Reggio E.	53
18	Venice	27	Pistoia	44	Siena	53	Cagliari	50	Imperia	51
19	Cremona	26	Palermo	41	Udine	51	Pistoia	48	Trento	50
20	Modena	26	Catania	41	Pistoia	50	Trento	48	L'Aquila	50
21	Catania	24	Macerata	39	Trento	50	Modena	48	Palermo	48
22	Mantova	23	Modena	37	Macerata	49	Palermo	45	Pistoia	47
23	Padova	23	Ferrara	37	Pescara	48	Pesaro U.	45	Savona	47
24	Ancona	23	Arezzo	36	Palermo	47	Catania	44	Perugia	47
25	**Italy**	**23**	**Italy**	**34**	**Italy**	**46**	Savona	44	Macerata	47
26	Como	22	Gorizia	33	Gorizia	46	Venice	43	Catania	46
27	Trento	22	Naples	33	Perugia	44	Imperia	43	Ferrara	45
28	Reggio E.	22	Trento	32	Modena	43	Perugia	43	**Italy**	**44**
29	Macerata	22	Venice	32	Leghorn	42	Messina	43	Leghorn	43
30	Bergamo	21	Ancona	32	Ancona	42	Macerata	42	Pescara	43
31	Udine	21	Rovigo	31	Padova	42	**Italy**	**42**	Cagliari	42
32	Perugia	21	Udine	31	Pisa	41	Leghorn	39	Aosta	42
33	Vercelli	20	Pisa	31	Naples	40	Grosseto	38	Venice	41
34	Brescia	20	La Spezia	30	Massa C.	40	Ancona	36	Messina	40
35	Forlì	20	Perugia	30	Terni	39	Terni	36	Vicenza	40
36	Naples	20	Bari	30	Siracusa	39	Bergamo	36	Udine	40
36	Varese	19	Bergamo	28	La Spezia	38	Naples	35	Grosseto	39
37	Piacenza	19	Padua	27	Pesaro U.	37	Padua	34	Mantova	39
38	Massa C.	19	Piacenza	27	Bergamo	36	Bari	34	Piacenza	38
39	Siena	19	Terni	27	Brescia	36	L'Aquila	34	Sassari	38
40	Pisa	18	Pescara	27	Viterbo	36	Pescara	33	Siracusa	38
41	Arezzo	18	Vercelli	26	Ferrara	35	Pisa	31	Bergamo	37
42	Pistoia	17	Mantua	26	Piacenza	35	Novara	31	Naples	37
43	Pescara	17	Ascoli P.	26	Savona	35	Piacenza	30	Padua	37
44	Alessand.	16	Varese	25	Bari	34	Sassari	30	Pisa	37
45	Pavia	16	Como	25	Vercelli	34	Matera	30	Massa C.	37
46	Pordenone	16	Brescia	25	Grosseto	34	Vicenza	29	Pesaro U.	36
47	Lucca	16	Massa C.	25	Oristano	34	Brescia	28	Treviso	36
48	Siracusa	16	Brindisi	25	Como	33	Taranto	28	Asti	35
49	Vicenza	15	Belluno	24	Treviso	33	Alessand.	28	Cremona	35
50	La Spezia	15	Savona	24	Cremona	33	Ragusa	28	Ancona	33
51	Grosseto	15	Pesaro U.	24	Rovigo	32	Rovigo	27	Novara	33
52	Pesaro U.	15	Treviso	23	Ascoli P.	32	Teramo	27	Alessand.	33
53	Bari	15	Cremona	22	Vicenza	32	Varese	26	Cuneo	32
54	Treviso	14	Cuneo	21	Mantua	31	Asti	26	Teramo	30

Ranking	1970		1975		1980		1985		1990	
55	Asti	13	Pavia	21	Trapani	30	Aosta	26	Brescia	29
56	Savona	13	Pordenone	20	Varese	29	Udine	25	Bari	28
57	Terni	13	Taranto	20	Novara	28	Vercelli	25	La Spezia	28
58	Trapani	13	Novara	19	Messina	28	Arezzo	25	Rieti	28
59	Novara	12	Grosseto	19	Rieti	28	Pordenone	25	Terni	27
60	Cuneo	12	Lecce	19	L'Aquila	28	Chieti	25	Pordenone	27
61	Viterbo	12	Trapani	19	Taranto	27	Massa C.	24	Ascoli P.	27
62	Latina	12	Cagliari	18	Alessand.	27	Viterbo	24	Varese	26
63	L'Aquila	12	Vicenza	17	Arezzo	26	Oristano	24	Arezzo	26
64	Taranto	12	Viterbo	17	Pordenone	26	Como	24	Vercelli	25
65	Brindisi	12	Messina	17	Ragusa	26	Treviso	24	Viterbo	25
66	Belluno	11	Asti	16	Sassari	26	Ascoli P.	24	Ragusa	24
67	Ascoli P.	11	Alessand.	16	Pavia	25	Mantua	23	Como	24
68	Ragusa	11	Aosta	16	Latina	24	Cuneo	23	Salerno	24
69	Frosinone	10	Rieti	16	Cuneo	23	Siracusa	22	Matera	23
70	Teramo	10	Latina	16	Lecce	23	Campobas.	22	Potenza	23
71	Messina	10	Teramo	15	Cagliari	23	Brindisi	22	Sondrio	23
72	Sondrio	9	Foggia	15	Belluno	20	La Spezia	21	Rovigo	22
73	Chieti	9	Ragusa	15	Asti	20	Pavia	21	Latina	22
74	Lecce	9	Sassari	15	Teramo	20	Trapani	20	Benevento	21
75	Matera	9	Agrigento	14	Agrigento	20	Benevento	20	Campobas.	20
76	Aosta	7	Frosinone	13	Campobas.	20	Latina	19	Chieti	19
77	Campobas.	7	L'Aquila	13	Salerno	19	Belluno	19	Pavia	19
78	Foggia	7	Salerno	13	Aosta	15	Salerno	19	Trapani	19
79	Caltanis.	7	Siracusa	12	Chieti	15	Nuoro	19	Belluno	19
80	Enna	7	Matera	10	Brindisi	14	Lecce	18	Cosenza	19
81	Cagliari	7	Caltanis.	10	Enna	14	Agrigento	18	Taranto	18
82	Rieti	6	Enna	10	Foggia	13	Potenza	18	Brindisi	18
83	Cosenza	6	Oristano	10	Matera	13	Rieti	17	Reggio C.	17
84	Sassari	6	Chieti	9	Caltanis.	13	Cosenza	17	Agrigento	16
85	Caserta	5	Campobas.	9	Reggio C.	13	Cremona	16	Caltanis.	16
86	Benevento	5	Nuoro	9	Nuoro	12	Foggia	16	Nuoro	14
87	Salerno	5	Avellino	7	Sondrio	12	Catanzaro	16	Lecce	14
88	Agrigento	4	Reggio C.	7	Cosenza	12	Reggio C.	15	Catanzaro	13
89	Reggio C.	3	Sondrio	6	Frosinone	11	Enna	14	Caserta	11
90	Nuoro	3	Benevento	6	Benevento	10	Caserta	14	Foggia	10
91	Avellino	2	Cosenza	6	Caserta	9	Frosinone	13	Isernia	9
92	Potenza	2	Caserta	4	Potenza	9	Sondrio	12	Oristano	8
93	Catanzaro	2	Potenza	4	Catanzaro	7	Avellino	10	Enna	7
94	Isernia	1	Catanzaro	3	Isernia	5	Isernia	8	Frosinone	7
95	–		Isernia	1	Avellino	3	Caltanis.	5	Avellino	6

Source: SIAE.

around it serve to define Tuscany as one of the Italian (and one could even say European) regions with the highest concentration of cultural activities. Based on its historical roots, Tuscany has a vocation that today suffers from all the inherent contradictions and difficulties but which also represents an invaluable resource, a source of wealth which can be drawn upon in the construction of a higher quality of development.

Table 10.9 Attendance of theatres and concerts in Italian cities with more than 200,000 inhabitants (tickets sold per 100 inhabitants)

Ranking	1970		1975		1980		1985		1990	
1	Verona	150	Verona	190	Verona	260	Verona	302	Verona	333
2	Trieste	111	Florence	159	Florence	194	Florence	182	Milan	191
3	Florence	109	Trieste	143	Milan	164	Milan	166	Florence	171
4	Milan	82	Milan	109	Trieste	140	Trieste	165	Trieste	157
5	Bologna	70	Bologna	92	Turin	125	Cagliari	139	Bologna	139
6	Padua	61	Turin	86	Bologna	125	Bologna	123	Catania	113
7	Turin	51	Catania	81	Catania	112	Padua	103	Turin	109
8	Palermo	50	Genoa	72	Rome	105	Rome	101	Padua	107
9	Rome	49	Padua	72	Venice	105	Turin	100	Cagliari	105
10	Venice	49	Rome	69	Genoa	99	Catania	98	Rome	96
11	Genoa	46	Palermo	68	Padua	98	Venice	84	Venice	83
12	Catania	46	Bari	66	Bari	90	Genoa	81	Palermo	81
13	Bari	41	Naples	62	Naples	78	Bari	78	Bari	74
14	Naples	35	Venice	58	Palermo	72	Messina	70	Genoa	73
15	Taranto	18	Cagliari	40	Cagliari	51	Palermo	69	Messina	71
16	Messina	17	Taranto	27	Messina	44	Naples	62	Naples	70
17	Cagliari	17	Messina	22	Taranto	42	Taranto	41	Taranto	29

Source: SIAE.

Notes

1. For example, the 'workshop' of the Baptistry was managed and financed by the weavers' guild.
2. The humanistic culture profoundly modified the traditional attitudes toward wealth and its projection. In the past there had been a generally critical attitude based on Franciscan sources, but this was replaced by new conceptions affirming and reflecting the new social position of the merchants and bankers. Wealth accumulated in this manner was seen as something that could and should be translated into a public good. At the beginning this new orientation expressed itself through charitable donations, but was soon translated into a 'constructive' process that united the role of the donor into an expression of religious devotion socially expressed and felt. It is sufficient to cite Cosimo de' Medici and his significant investments in the convent and the 'works' of San Marco. Soon after and significantly so, 'the correct use of wealth was no longer confined by charitable works' (Goldthwaite, 1980, pp. 77–83). In this regard we can recall the great private buildings such as the Strozzi palace conceived as an expression of noble private philanthropy. This cultural change finds its theoretical justification in the thought of the great Florentine humanists. There is the praise of the active life (*vita activa*) by Leonardo Bruni for whom the production of wealth is already seen as an intrinsic element of public morality to the conception of architecture as civic life (*attività civica*) proposed by Leon Battista Alberti. The *reputation* of an individual and his honour could and should also depend on the magnificence of the buildings that he owned. And it was due to change that Florence is the city in which the placement of coats of arms and family symbols on the external walls of residences was so diffused. There is no other city in Europe in

which the buildings establish the identity of those who built them in such a conspicuous manner and in such a variety of cases (ibid., pp. 83–90).

3. Data from Regione Toscana, Giunta Regionale (1991, 1992).

4. On the many museums located in Tuscany (275 have been counted), see Department of Education and Culture of the Tuscan Region (1988).

5. In order more accurately to evaluate the role of Florence in relation to a city like Verona we need to keep in mind that attendance of cultural events in the latter is very much tied to the presence of a great structure for cultural events represented by the Arena capable of sitting large numbers for both operas as well as rock concerts. It should also be kept in mind that the ratio between the expenditure or sale of tickets per inhabitant not only involves in the determination of the numerator the resident population but also the surrounding metropolitan and non-metropolitan area. In general, the catch basin for customers is much wider than the city proper. Nonetheless, Table 10.9 provides information that is important in illustrating the level of geographical concentration of the demand, the power of attraction exercised by a city, and the quality and scope of the cultural activities that it is able to make available.

References

Argan, G.C. and Fagiolo, M., 'Storia, storia della città, storia dell'arte', in *Storia d'Italia*, vol. 1, Turin, Einaudi, 1973.

Castelnuovo, E. and Ginzberg, C., 'Centro e periferia', in *Storia dell'arte italiana*, vol. 1, Turin, Einaudi, 1979.

Department of Education and Culture of the Tuscan Region, *Musei e Raccolte della Toscana, Indagine statistica*, Florence, 1988.

Goldthwaite, R.A., *The Building of Renaissance Florence: An Economic and Social History*, Baltimore, Johns Hopkins University Press, 1980.

Hirsch, F., *Social Limits to Growth*, London, Routledge, 1977.

Regione Toscana, Giunta Regionale, 'Il movimento turistico in Toscana: Terzo quadrimestre 1989' in *Informazioni Statistiche*, 5, April 1991.

—— 'Movimento dei clienti negli e sercizi alberghieri in Toscana: Anno 1991', in *Informazioni Statistiche*, 11, November 1992.

SIAE (Società italiana degli autori e degli editori), *Lo spettacolo in Italia, Annuario statistico*, Rome, various years.

Smailes, P., *Geografia urbana*, Venice, Masilio Editore, 1977.

11 Networking and the European Single Market: Tuscany as the vanguard Mediterranean region

Robert Leonardi

11.1 Tuscany's European strategy

In analysing the role of Tuscany in the context of the Single Market created on 1 January 1993, we have to keep in mind the impact of two factors that are operating to change the status quo. The first is the creation of European-level institutions to manage the new market with European-wide rather than national institutions, thus the emphasis in Italy, on the one hand, to meet the criteria for monetary union spelled out in the Maastricht Treaty and, on the other, the need to create a European monetary system equipped with instruments for joint decision-making such as a federal bank. These proposed changes in the structure of decision-making and the new terms of reference for the economies of member states have stimulated political leaders to rethink the structure and nature of European as well as local political institutions as well as the means for interacting in the determination and implementation of policies relevant to the pursuit of economic and social objectives.

The second factor originates from the grassroots. The very existence of the Union and the commitment of member states to work within the confines of the Single Market have already fundamentally affected individual decisions made by citizens, entrepreneurs, and regional and local governments in taking advantage of the opportunities provided by the Union integration process. Integration is no longer only a top-down process; it has, in fact, assumed an increasingly clear bottom-up characteristic that is challenging traditional notions and expectations concerning the pace and nature of European-level policy processes.

Taken together, these pressures for eventual economic and political reform have wide implications for the Union's institutional structure, the formulation of policies for social and economic cohesion, and the role played by sub-national governments at the European level. Tuscany needs, at this point, to identify a European-wide strategy based on its geographic location (i.e., position along the northern coast of the Mediterranean) and the characteristics of its society and socioeconomic structure (which have been amply discussed in the previous ten chapters).

This chapter will discuss the potential role that Tuscany can play within the wider European Union based on a dynamic networking strategy that places Tuscany at the centre of the European stage and as the mobilizing agent for a northern Mediterranean network of regional bodies in the process of creating a new Mediterranean 'core' area as an alternative centre for European economic and social development.

As we have already seen above, Tuscany is well equipped – based on its social and economic development, combined with its intellectual and political resources – to project for itself a vanguard position in Europe. What will be discussed here are the means and reasons for assuming such a position.

11.2 The Single Market and the changing economic geography of Europe

Despite the fact that the full realization of the Single Market is rapidly approaching, it has only been recently that the regions have begun to contemplate their role within a deeper and more intense Community integration process.[1] The potential role of the regions in the new European context will be much larger than it ever was before because the restraining powers of the nation-state in limiting European-wide linkages will disappear. What was before considered to be difficult from an institutional and legal point of view (i.e., to launch the region on transregional projects and maintain institutionalized links with the European Union administrative structure) will now be possible.

The IMP programmes and the reform of the Structural Funds presented the first opportunities for local and regional authorities to be present at the European level. In 1988 the creation of the Council on European Regions and Localities combined with the opening of offices in Brussels by a number of regional and local authorities changed the nature of the linkage system that brought together on a formal basis the Commission with subnational governments and socioeconomic groups at the local level.[2] During the last three years, the combination of a greater organizational presence of the regions in Brussels and the partnership established between the Community, national governments, and the regions in the implementation of the Community Support Frameworks (CSFs) has given a new meaning and imperative to the maintaining of viable ties between the Community and the regions.

With the CSFs and the other initiatives taken by the Community in preparing for the Single Market, the role of subnational authorities has changed substantially; the trend will undoubtedly accelerate with the formulation and implementation of the second round of Community Support Frameworks (1994–99) and the implementation of the provisions for increased economic and political cooperation foreseen by the Maastricht Treaty. The institutional implications of the 1988 reform of the Structural Funds and the realization of the Single Market in 1993 are now joined with a new reality: the pursuit of economic and social cohesion and the formulation of multiregional projects on the basis of an *intra*-EU rather than as an *inter*-state exercise. Cohesion, as an explicit goal of the European Union, changes considerably the role and function of regional and local governments. At the present time, subnational governments enjoy a greater leeway than before in contacting their counterparts in other countries and establishing direct contacts with the European Union (Leonardi, 1994).

With the elimination of national boundaries as barriers to the free flow of goods, services, individuals and capital, the role of national frontiers as impediments to intergovernmental cooperation among Union member institutions has, de facto, disappeared. What were once considered by national governments as 'foreign policy' initiatives (i.e., contacts among subnational units geographically located in different nation-states) have been transformed into 'internal' EU policy: national boundaries can no longer legally impede economic interaction and policy-making within the context of the European Union.

The implications of such a change are immense. Subnational governmental units can cooperate in the pursuit of common economic and social development goals not only along an expanded vertical linkage track connecting the regions with national governments and the European Union but also along the horizontal dimension (i.e., promoting linkages across regional borders). The opportunity of conducting operations on a more horizontal dimension is actively being pursued by the Union in its experimentation with multiregional pilot projects. A primary objective of these projects is to define a new mode of behaviour and orientation that stresses the Union as a whole rather than individual national markets as the necessary reference point for enterprise planning and investment within the context of the Single Market. The shift from a national to a Union frame of reference for economic and social policy-making by public as well as private institutions is a basic building block in the Union's second round of Structural Funds projects, and it represents a revolutionary change in the structure of Union policy-making.[3]

The realization of the internal market now permits the creation of the basis for European-wide interactions by individuals, enterprises, development agencies and subnational governments in the implementation of economic and social policies.[4] The freedom to act within this new European context will allow new economic markets to emerge. Regions in contiguous geographic areas will be free to formulate and administer policies together, aid the forging of contacts between entrepreneurs and sectoral associations operating in the same sector but in different national and regional contexts, and increase the capacity of local and regional authorities concerned with economic development to evolve new policy responses to economic challenges emerging from within as well as from outside the Union. The thesis advanced in this chapter is that the realization of the Single Market coupled with an active programme of networking will help achieve economies of scale *external* to the enterprise but internal to the network that becomes the crucial determinant for the production as well as the information network into which the enterprise is inserted.[5]

11.3   The region as entrepreneur

These new opportunities offered by the Single Market can be realized if the role and objectives of the region are seen in entrepreneurial terms. Changes in the activities of the regions in Italy, Germany, Spain and elsewhere have established the realization that regions are no longer mere administrative appendages of the nation-state but in fact active partners in the regional and local development process. As discussed in a number of the chapters above, the emergence of the Tuscan model or, more in general, the emergence of the Third Italy is based on the active participation of the regional governments in the provision of economic, social, and institutional infrastructure for the evolving local economies.

Thus, the concept of the region as an institutional 'entrepreneur'[6] participating in a proactive manner in development needs to be fully taken into account by EU regional and sectoral policy-makers. Taking a proactive stance on the issue of development is one example of voluntary action by the region that some argue is beyond its statutory responsibilities and an invasion of the realm that should be left exclusively to the private sector. We would argue, however, that in post-industrial economies the lines separating the public and private sector and the responsibilities of public authorities for economic and social outcomes have become blurred and need to be redefined in light of pragmatic exigencies rather than legal or philosophical tracts.

The concept of the region as entrepreneur is based on the a priori existence of a private–public partnership and an ethic for the pursuit of the goal of economic and social development as a common good. According to the notion of regional development as a product of conscious public policy, the role of the private sector is to concentrate on the productive and distributive phases of the economic process while that of the public sector is to mobilize collective goods – such as social services, investment projects, and policy planning. In addition, both sides of the institutional divide are interested in developing and maintaining the national and international competitive edge of local production units through public policies that aid in the continuous re-examination of products, markets, and productive structure.

Where public–private networks and the focus of public policy on the production of collective goods are missing, balanced and diffused forms of economic development have difficulty materializing. There is, instead, a growth of alternative forms and models of economic growth. In many cases we have seen a rise in dependence on growth strategies determined from outside the immediate regional territory. In the past, this has meant development schemes formulated, financed and administered by the central state authorities. The logic of the centralized model emphasizes the role of centralized sources of capital investment, economic infrastructure projects, industrial plants with high levels of capital investment, and public administration as the primary source of non-agricultural employment and the ethic of centralized transfer payments as the primary source for maintaining standards of living and employment.[7]

The dependence on the central government for economic policy and transfer payments is one of the major differences which separates larger from smaller member states in the Objective 1 areas. The latter still depend to a great extent on centralized administrative structures while the former have moved to more decentralized forms of decision-making and administration. We are not necessarily arguing that the role of centralized authorities may be counter-productive to development in underdeveloped areas. Rather, we are postulating the possibility that the decentralization of decision-making power and resources to the subnational level may make a positive contribution to local development above and beyond what is added in terms of expenditures for the running of a new tier of government. The encouragement of local and regional government initiatives in favour of the local economy helps to encourage the evolution of a regional networking pattern that can make an additional contribution to sustaining and even accelerating regional economic development (Leonardi and Garmise, 1993).

11.4   Decentralization and autonomy

Institutional decentralization and policy making autonomy are two of the necessary components in launching an intensive system of regional networking, and these two factors are found in abundant supply among the regions residing on the northern Mediterranean rim. All three member states along the rim – Italy, France and Spain – have devolved, regional forms of subnational government.

The existence of regional governments makes it much easier to mobilize a region's socioeconomic forces through decentralized political structures. In centralized systems the mobilization imperative is left to members of the public administration or private political forces such as political parties and semi-public interest groups and sectorial associations (Greece, Ireland and Portugal). In decentralized systems there is a greater liberty for interplay between public institutions and private groups on the basis of functional specialization and mutual interest. Case studies carried out in France, Germany, Italy and Spain have demonstrated that the role played by public officials operating within autonomous political institutions is quite important in forging links between institutions and socioeconomic forces for the pursuit of collective interests in a planned and transparent manner.

The current system of networking that links regional institutions and social and economic groups in the Community's more developed regions is not based on the subordination of either the groups to the institutions or the public institutions to the groups. It is, instead, based on an autonomous

and mutually reinforcing relationship where the different but complementary needs of the participants in the network are met. From the
perspective of the regional government, it achieves a much greater
penetration of the socioeconomic fabric of society and higher levels of
political mobilization operating through its networks with socioeconomic
groups. The groups are, in turn, given access on an organized and
predictable basis to public decision-making and resource allocation. Thus,
it is in the interest of all of the participants to consolidate, perpetuate and
even expand the network.

11.5 The advantages of networking for the region, Community, and individual

What are the advantages of transregional networks bringing together
regions residing in diverse member states? Networks allow regions to
achieve certain goals that would not be possible if they were to act on their
own. Cappellin (1990) has argued that regional cooperation permits
regions as geographic and economic expressions to achieve six distinct
goals. The first three advantages are: (1) the achievement of economies of
scale not possible through development on an individual basis of infrastructures, research, development, services, etc. in order to overcome size
thresholds; (2) the use of common resources (e.g., rivers, sea, forests, etc.) as
joint ventures in order to avoid the creation of external diseconomies such
as air- and water-pollution; and (3) the common use and development of
geo-economic systems in order to build higher levels of interaction among
regions sharing a common border or geographical territory.

The other three advantages initially apply to more explicitly transregional cooperation networks that attempt to overcome the limitations
imposed by national borders as traditional barriers to the free flow of
goods, services, capital and people between regions existing within different
nation-states. These three advantages are: (4) the reduction of 'transaction
costs' which in past have raised the cost of doing business across national
frontiers; (5) the avoidance of economic conflict and retaliatory measures
that limit the size and scope of mutual development; and (6) the increase
in regional decision-making autonomy from national authorities. All six
goals provide a positive stimulus from the region's point of view in the
planning and realization of networks at the transregional level.

Given the advantages of networking from the regions' point of view, why
should the Community – a European-wide institution – be interested in
promoting transregional networks? The current debate on political union
demonstrates that the building of European institutions through
reinforcement and consolidation of the legislative (providing legislative
powers to the European Parliament) and executive (extending the scope
and powers of the Commission) powers will take a long time. The process
of institution-building in the Community will be gradual and the evolution
of adequate administrative structures to handle the growing responsibilities

for sectorial policies will be realized in the long term rather than the short-term. Therefore, the Commission faces the problem of administering policies devoid of a territorially based administrative apparatus.

The use of networks solves part of this problem by making the policies self-administrating and devolving ultimate responsibility to the regions. Managing policies through networks:

(1) requires a minimal amount of administrative input by the Commission,
(2) provides contact with the grassroots without requiring the intermediation of national administrative structures,
(3) permits direct contact with the 'active socioeconomic forces' operating at the local level,
(4) operates on a Union-wide basis,
(5) expands the capacity to respond to increased demands for participation from new areas and sectors,
(6) provides the possibility of monitoring the progress of programmes on a continuous and efficacious basis,
(7) does not threaten any of the institutional actors at the national or local level,
(8) provides a positive stimulus to reorient the views and frames of reference of local actors away from local and national perspectives to a more European perspective, and
(9) possesses the flexibility of adding on to the structure further responsibilities and/or a greater complexity of procedures and structures in policy-making and implementation.

In sum, networks are the ideal instrument for the implementation of a gradual approach to the creation of a European policy-making community given the lack of a territorial administrative structure.

A similar question can be asked of the individual as a citizen and especially as an entrepreneur. What, then, does the entrepreneur gain by operating through a network system? The answer is provided by identifying what is transmitted through the linkage structure in the simplest kind of intra-regional network. First of all, a linkage system provides information on the regional economy by identifying where skills are located, where complementary productive capacity can be organized, where credit can be accessed and under what kinds of advantageous conditions, and what are the overall plans of the governmental organs on the development of infrastructure, investments, and productive capacity. Second, a network system provides services that are valuable not only for the management of an enterprise but also in keeping up with market and technological trends. Third, a network system provides intermediation at the political level to enter new markets, widen one's horizons, and establish new ventures.

As initially discussed above, participation in a network and taking advantage of its opportunities for the dissemination of information on markets, opportunities, skills, specializations, etc. provide the entrepreneur the opportunity to specialize output for a particular market niche and achieve an external economy of scale through the operation of the network. In a modern economy operating in a highly competitive market, networks can become indispensable mechanisms for the organization of information, production, and distribution, and make an important impact in determining the success and survival of the enterprise.

11.6   Which networks?

Having described the reason why networks exist and the positive contribution that they can make to policy-making and implementation in the European Community, we now turn to the issue of defining exactly what are networks and analyse how they have been operationalized in the European Community. What we need to know is how to distinguish empirically between different types of networks that exist in the real world – i.e., within the Community, within nation-states, and within regions. Our consideration of networking within the European Community is based on an operative definition of a 'network' that is itself based on the existence of at least some minimum criteria.[8] The minimum elements for a network to exist as expressed in graph theory are 'objects' or 'nodes' in the system – e.g., points on a graph – and 'relationships' – e.g., lines joining the points. In our most obvious case of transregional networking the objects being networked are regional or other local government institutions and the relationships consist of formal agreements to cooperate in the pursuit of common policy objectives. However, we recognize that networks can be used to bring together other subjects on the basis of other goals as will be evident in the discussion below.

The type of policy networks that are of interest here are those that can provide a potential contribution to the Community's policy planning and implementation process, and these in our opinion must contain five basic elements: (1) the objects being networked, (2) the content or interactive form of the linkage, (3) the policy area covered, (4) the territory over which the network operates, and (5) the timespan over which the network remains operative. The existence of a network assumes a shared, repeated, routinized and predictable set of behaviours among members over time. Putting these five elements together, we can define a policy network within the Community as an agreement for collective action based on a common set of objectives, resources and instruments for the purpose of planning and managing a service, product or sector within a defined territorial space.

From this perspective, transregional networks are an agreement operationalized through a series of relationships that permits the subjects (in our case regional institutions) to take action and to be present in the determination of decisions and implementation of policies outside their immediate territorial jurisdiction. Thus, for the network to become operative and institutionalized on a European-wide basis, it is important to determine: (a) its level of institutionalization (will the Mediterranean network be just a temporary agreement to act in unison or a formal contract among institutions designed to create permanent policy processes and active agencies capable of taking autonomous action in the pursuit of the contracting regions' interest?); (b) its territorial presence (how many regions will be involved and how will they interact?); and (c) its reach (will it be mono- or multi-sectorial in nature?). In the Single Market regional networks can operate throughout the Community, but in practice the territorial presence of the network is defined by its membership, scope and capacity to undertake effective policy-making and implementation.

The second important element to be considered in discussing networks is the potential pool of members or actors that will be effectively involved in the operation of a particular network. If we look at existing *ad hoc* network systems that have sprung up spontaneously in the Community to deal with the coordination of law enforcement issues or the cooperation among national airline pilots' associations, businesses and trade unions, we see that networks can be created to involve a wide variety of subjects which range from individuals and firms to voluntary groups and governmental units, but the number of transregional networks involving regional governments is still quite limited. Existing Community programmes such as Euro-partnership, BC-NET, LEDA and others already constitute explicit network systems among certain individuals and entities throughout the Community. However, they are limited on a number of other dimensions, such as 'density' – i.e., the variety of subjects involved is very low in comparison to the potential pool of actors present in the twelve member states.

In addition to being sparse, current EC networks are not yet diverse in terms of functions or levels of operation. Each network tends to operate at one level, sector, or type of participant, and the impact that it has on effectively reorienting individual/institutional decisions and plans is still low. In fact, the present approach to networking relegates the Commission-initiated networks mainly to the role of supplying information, creating communication links, and bringing entrepreneurs together. The dynamic generated by the preparation for the Single Market requires the regions to reconsider their role as the exigency for managing economic policy at the European level and taking a more active and direct role in the operation of networks.

The third element characterizing networks is the nature of the interaction. This interaction can be limited to the mere exchange of information or can extend all the way up to the joint management of important policy sectors. Thus, a telephone communication system is a network for the purpose of distributing information in the same way that the post office is the territorial network for the distribution of written correspondence.[9] Both service networks are organized so that they can penetrate all the way down to the local level: to individual families, houses and even rooms. Governmental administrative systems are also networks and so are individual firms or, as in the USA, inter-state authorities such as the Tennessee Valley Authority (TVA) or the New York Port Authority.

The purposes of these latter types of networks are not simply to transmit information but also to implement decisions and manage societal resources.

The US or Canadian examples of multiregional agencies for the management of services and resources are involved in complex activities that cover both the private and public sectors. One of the more interesting aspects of comparative work on subnational institutions inside and outside Europe is the extraordinary similarity in the pattern of responses to social welfare and economic growth formulated by local and regional governments. In a number of cases, what one observes taking place in Europe is also underway in other institutional and political settings in North America and Asia.

Networking in Europe can be seen as a first informal step toward the creation of formal, institutionalized arrangements in the form of European agencies and institutions capable of tackling economic and social problems from a Community perspective. Accordingly, networks organized on a transregional basis would be in a position to assume policy initiatives, formulate programmes for intervention, mobilize resources, administer programmes, and conduct programme oversight and verification on a Community-wide basis and as an alternative to the creation of separate national agencies.

Finally, networks can be designed to resolve specific problems that are not manageable by existing institutions and structures. Once the initial problem is resolved, the network might, in fact, move on to cover other spheres of activity. This was the case of the TVA which went from its initial task of land reclamation and flood control to the production of atomic energy. As a consequence, networks can be seen as flexible policy-making and administration structures that evolve over time in response to shifting needs.

In the changing institutional structure of the post-1993 Union, networks can be conceived of as 'pre-institutions' or a stepping stone on the way to reassembling institutions above and beyond the present boundaries drawn by the nation-state. One of the rationales behind the Community's present experimentation with area-wide networks is that after 1993 regional networks will help fill the institutional vacuum that will develop once the nation-state loses its exclusionary rights over the activities of subnational political, economic and social institutions.[10]

11.6   Linkage networks as alternative economic structures

As defined above, networks are interactive systems that create relationships and the basis for collective action across a variety of institutional levels and economic sectors. One of the fundamental aspects of our discussion of the potential change in the post-1993 institutional structure is the role played by networks in bringing together network nodes or 'actors' (individuals, institutions, associations, etc.) that find themselves in different geographic, sectoral and institutional settings. The territorial scope of the network is of fundamental importance because the potential for networking on a Union-wide basis is considerably enhanced with the creation of the Single Market.

Piore and Sabel (1984) were among the first to understand that the industrial districts present in the northern and central part of Italy were, in effect, linkage networks bringing together not only different manufacturers based on a horizontal division of labour but also networks that grew out of a partnership of local entrepreneurs with local and regional governments. In this regional configuration of networking, the local governments supply the industrial parks, social infrastructure (all-day schools, nurseries, and day care centres) and public infrastructure (roads, electrical hook-ups, etc.) while the regional governments provide the economically targeted professional education programmes, access to credit, and support services necessary for a diffused model of enterprise. In other words, diffused forms of enterprise based on small and medium-sized companies thrive where (or may be based on the existence of) macro- and meso-networking exist across a variety of institutions and groups – i.e., private as well as public institutions, groups, and actors. From this perspective, the existence of regionally based and functioning institutionalized networks may be seen as a prerequisite for the creation of a territorially diffused, Union-wide system of networks oriented toward the promotion and consolidation of small and medium-sized enterprise systems in the context of the realization of the single market.

Ever since the end of the 1980s, the Community has emphasized the role of networks in the implementation of its policies and programmes at the European level. These experiments have largely been focused in the areas of small and medium enterprise, research and development, information and communication technologies, industrial technologies, biotechnologies, Structural Funds, and vocational and university-level education.

The model of networking advanced by the Community is one that emphasizes the grassroots or 'from the bottom-up' approach. In its formulation of networks the Community has predominantly focused on the *horizontal* sectorial and individual networks that contain a minimal vertical component. Second, the EC has stressed in the majority of its initiatives the bringing together of *micro*-level actors – e.g., individuals, firms, universities, local action groups, local governments, etc. – to exchange information and share experiences in order to improve their individual performance and forging horizontal, one-on-one contractual arrangements. Networking in these contexts is conceived by the Community as predominantly either a technical link (such as the BRE communications system linking advisers and users of BC-NET or the ones being promoted in TELEMATIQUE, LEADER, and EUROFORM programmes) or the forging of mutually beneficial contacts between individuals and firms who were previously not in contact. In the first instance, the Community supplied the hardware and software that made links possible, and in the latter the Community operated as an 'incubator' for micro-interpersonal networks to take place.

The networks managed by DG XXIII and some of those promoted by the Structural Funds and the Framework Programmes operate for the purpose of facilitating contacts and developing opportunities for cooperation on a transregional basis between individuals and companies who would otherwise not be able to search for partners outside their immediate vicinity (CEC, 1990). In these cases, networking operates to compensate for the lack of a 'vertical dimension' similar to that enjoyed by large, multinational corporations that can afford to establish a presence in a variety of national settings and thereby facilitate exchanges within various national branches of the company and with other enterprises in the pursuit of common interests. A current example is the differentiation that is taking place in the organizational structure and plans for research and development undertaken by IBM which is moving towards a much greater decentralized and 'networked' structure.

The new generation of Structural Funds networks moves the Community's focus away from the micro and more toward macro forms of networking described as it pursues the establishment of intersectorial, interfunctional and intergovernmental networks. Along these lines, DG XVI has operationalized Article 10 of the ERDF regulation 4254/88 on the promotion of pilot projects among regions and cities of the Community by launching the RECITE programme to stimulate cooperation among subnational administrative entities in the pursuit of common objectives such as the improvement of administrative efficiency, achievement of economies of scale by sharing costs of common programmes, transfer of know-how between less and more developed parts of the Community, and improvement of the overall economic performance of less-favoured regions.

The network in the RECITE example would consist of the participants in a co-financed project, but the emphasis remains, once again, on the horizontal component of the link. The only vertical aspect of the network is conceived of as the periodic exchange of information between the Community and the 'contact person' representing the pilot project. The minimum size necessary for the establishment of a RECITE cooperation scheme is two participants from different member states, while the maximum number is ten. Even in the latter case, the network among the participants in a specific pilot project remains small. What is of great interest in the RECITE programme is that it is one of the first Community sponsored network programmes to make the jump to the third level of horizontal networking – i.e., the networking of governmental bodies at the subnational level. In fact, one of the requisites for participation is that the members of the authority have to be 'elected by universal suffrage'.

It is still too early to tell whether the RECITE programme will encourage regions and cities to link-up over a variety of policy areas, whether it will stick to its initial sector-by-sector approach, or whether the project-specific networks will be encouraged to link-up with each other. The most recent call for proposals suggests that a broader view will be applied. Pilot projects to be funded by the programme have to be concerned with the issue of economic development and improvement of the administrative efficiency of regional and local governments.

Conceivably, after the two-year experimental phase, the programme might venture down the road toward the creation of transregional networks with the objective of jointly managing policy programmes, but that still is far off in terms of the Community's ability to either conceptualize or operationalize such entities. In most cases these programmes are geared toward the transition period involved in the realization of the Single Market and the decision on what to do with the Structural Funds after 1993. The Mediterranean regions can use such initiatives as a means of advancing their candidacy for the management of Mediterranean-wide programmes as will be discussed in detail below.

Other Structural Funds programmes also hold out the prospect for the evolution of more complex, Mediterranean-wide networks. A case in point is the LEADER programme that posits two networking tasks. First, the goal is to network the rural area through the Local Action Group financed by the programme in an attempt to bring together various types of enterprises – e.g., agricultural, service, and industrial ones – for the purposes of coordinating development strategies and making use of common services such as marketing, market research, telecommunications systems, information on development opportunities, etc. Second, the LEADER programme envisions the networking of various LEADER groups throughout the national and Union territory in the prospect of sharing information, strategies and even markets in order to develop fully their prospects for growth.

11.7   Conclusions: a Mediterranean development network

The analysis presented above suggests that in creating a Mediterranean network of regions that could turn this peripheral area of the Union into one of Europe's cores the network should bring together regional institutions with active programmes of interpenetration with other institutions, associations, and sectoral groups at the subregional level. These regions need to be included (or, in fact, may be conceived as the necessary building blocks) in the launching of transregional networks because: (1) they have the political infrastructure ('political linkages') in forming regionally based policy communities around specific economic problems or goals among public and private operators; and (2) they have the administrative structures ('administrative linkages') to do the basic groundwork involved in the planning, coordination, and implementation of transregional schemes as pilot projects initiated and run at the regional level.

These considerations make it clear that the creation of the Mediterranean network for the pursuit of the objective of becoming an alternative European core area must have two fundamental characteristics. Without excluding the micro networks, the transregional networks that need to be created must be macro ones – that is, they must not only be formal networks but they must also directly involve the participation of regional governments. They cannot be construed as top-down initiatives of a Community administrative structure or the product of an informal agreement among regional officials. Instead, the network needs the active participation of regional authorities based on publicly sanctioned agreements. This type of network is important for the consolidation of a Single Market that offers opportunities to small and medium-sized enterprises and to the less-developed regions. Macro networks not only help to rationalize and expand the impact of development strategies taken by various components of the region's economy but also to increase the potential of achieving greater economic and social cohesion among the regions, thereby realizing one of the major objectives of the EU.

Macro transregional networks are important for the Single Market because they can help to rationalize development efforts undertaken by various components of the regional economy, and they will be a vital element in mobilizing collective action for the pursuit of economic growth. Regions active in the promotion of endogenous development have already undertaken a series of *ad hoc* initiatives to stimulate sectors fundamental to the health of the regional economy. Officials either at the regional or national level not accustomed to interfunctional and intergovernmental networks in their own contexts are not the logical candidates for experimenting with macro transregional networks at the Union level.

The above analysis highlights the need to distinguish among different types of networks and the dangers in mistaking one kind of network for another. A private micro network operated by institutional actors, such as regional government officials brought together by personal bonds, may assume the formal trappings of a macro network, but if it is not sustained by formal institutionalized commitments dealing with substantial policy areas it is difficult to perpetuate the network on a continuous and creative basis. In these cases, the micro network is more interested in the distribution of individual rather than collective or institutional gains. Once the individuals involved or their autonomy to act are removed, the network collapses and a vacuum is created at the institutional level.

The formulation of a Mediterranean transregional network is important to the Union. Caution must, of course, be exercised in integrating the regions and localities into a Mediterranean-wide policy making system. Integration must not lead to a drop in policy-making efficacy and administrative efficiency – i.e., an adjustment downwards. At the present time across the Union we find widely divergent levels of administrative efficiency in governmental organs at the subnational levels, and Community policy has not been overly concerned with the need to improve in a sustained manner administrative as well as economic performance at the regional and local levels.

In order to break the cycle of dependence on national structures that are not fine-tuned to the exigencies of regional economies and social demands or to the lack of sensitivity to the principles of additionality, subsidiarity and partnership on the part of national administrations, the Mediterranean network needs to emphasize its role in the upgrading of technical expertise of subnational administrative personnel, administrative structures, and policy-implementation procedures.

It should be remembered that the Mediterranean network will arch across Objective 1 as well as non-Objective 1 areas. The economic weakness of the Objective 1 areas should not be used to allocate to them subordinate political roles in the network nor to separate their needs from a common Mediterranean effort. If the network were to be constituted solely among the Objective 1 regions it would not have the initial economic and political power to propose itself as a strong, alternative area of development in Europe.

What are the policy areas in which the Mediterranean transregional network can operate? The most logical candidates are those areas of policy-making where a European approach makes the most sense and which are already emerging at the Union level. Three objectives come readily to mind when we consider the types of regional planning exercises that are already underway.

The first objective should be to fundamentally change the Community's Europe 2000 land use planning programme that divides the Mediterranean into two halves: a developed half that runs from the Straits of Gibraltar to Lazio and an underdeveloped half that starts from Campania and reaches into the Aegean. Such a plan leaves the southern part of Italy outside a Mediterranean network system, thereby leaving the less-developed but also high-potential-for-growth regions outside of the scheme. The foci for a *Mediterranean 2000 Plan* should be the role of tourism as a tool for economic development and the role of small and medium-sized firms that occupy the area between tourism, artisanry, service sector and industry. The Mediterranean 2000 Plan needs to build policy proposals from the ground up based on a clear understanding of the social and economic characteristics of the area. To operationalize such a plan, the regions need to establish a Joint Committee of Mediterranean Regions that can sustain a working secretariat. The secretariat needs to put together a database on the Mediterranean regions which can be drawn upon during the course of policy-making and formulation of Mediterranean-wide projects. Once the data set is operational the secretariat can begin formulating, for example, Mediterranean tourism programmes based on a network of marinas stretching from Portugal to Greece. Upon this network, other tourist attractions or programmes can be added, for example a network of European archaeological sites, Greco-Roman museums, etc. or even agri-tourism centres. The combinations are endless. What needs to be constituted is a working group that can generate these ideas for the Joint Committee of Mediterranean Regions to deliberate and operationalize.

The second objective should be to formulate a Mediterranean transportation plan. At the present time, the Mediterranean has good road as well as sea connections, but it is not at all well linked by rail or air links. A case in point is the current plans for the European TGV network that leaves significant gaps in the system. Similarly, the area is missing interactive linkages by airlines. It is practically impossible to travel east–

west across the Mediterranean; with few exceptions air links in the Mediterranean are north–south. In all the member states, the national capitals (Rome and Athens) linked with other national capitals (Paris and Madrid) perform the task as hubs for cross-Mediterranean air travel. If airports on the major Mediterranean islands (such as Sicily, Sardegna, Majorca, Crete, etc.) or major coastal airports (such as Pisa, Nice, Barcelona, Malaga) could be linked directly by regularly scheduled airline service, the map of air travel in Europe would change substantially and the prospects for the emergence of a Mediterranean core area would receive a significant boost in the short run.

A third objective of the Mediterranean network should be to participate as a group in Mediterranean ecological programmes such as MEDSPA. A region or country-specific approach will not suffice to tackle the problems of industrial and urban pollution of the Mediterranean, the destruction of its coastline, or the use of its resources. The Mediterranean regions need to cooperate in the formation of a Mediterranean Environmental Authority (MEA) that can assume the responsibility of managing and overseeing the Mediterranean Sea and coastline. MEA should be given the responsibility for evaluating the ecological impact of coastal development, overseeing the installation of water-purification plants for all urban centres along the coast, monitoring the dumping of petrol and chemical and industrial waste in the Mediterranean by coastal industries as well as cargo ships, and enforcing Union policies that impact on the quality of land developments, seawater and air along the Mediterranean coast.

There are many other objectives or task that one can envision for the Mediterranean regions. What needs to be done now is to bring the regions together for a common discussion of issues and the forging of the initial ties that will make the creation of Mediterranean-wide networks a reality. There is no shortage of problems that can be effectively tackled by such structures. What might be missing at the present on the part of the Mediterranean regions is the vision and will to think ambitious political thoughts on a Mediterranean-wide basis. But what is also missing is a vanguard region which can ignite the spark to begin the Mediterranean networking process. We believe that the region with the fundamental characteristics to undertake this task is Tuscany.

Notes

1. For example, the conferences organized by the German *Länder* to discuss the role of the regions in the new Community context: 'The Role of the Regions in the European Union', College of Europe, Bruges, 3–5 September 1992 and 'Toward European Union: The contribution of the German *Länder* and Italian regions', Villa Vigoni, Como, 1–4 October 1992.
2. The provisions made in the Maastricht Treaty for the creation of a consultative Committee of European Regions represents another step in the direction of institutionalizing the regions' role in EC decision-making. For a

discussion of the significance of the opening of regional offices in Brussels, see Marks, Nielsen and Salk (1993).

3. The revolutionary changes that have also taken place in Eastern Europe and the Soviet Union seem to be going in the opposite direction: larger markets are breaking down into smaller ones in response to nationalist fervour, and the consequence seems at first blush to be a drastic cut in economic production, trade, and social well-being (*Economist*, 320(7725), 21 September 1991).

4. A case in point here is the need to go beyond the nationally oriented networking arrangements found in national vocational programmes, such as the JET network in France, and to new Community-oriented networks such as PETRA.

5. Although we do accept the notion advanced by the Cecchini Report (1988) that the creation of the Single Market will represent a net economic benefit for citizens as well as entrepreneurs, we are not completely convinced that the main benefit of the internal market will be derived from the encouragement of economies of scale *within* the corporation and greater access to information (Siebert, 1989).

6. A first conceptualization of this phenomenon as applied to the Italian regions appears in Nanetti (1987).

7. Another way of expressing this relationship is in terms of 'distance' between policy-making centres in the system. The existence of networks is based on the achievement of 'institutional autonomy' of the policy-making bodies that permits policy initiatives to surface from the subnational level. Institutions that are not able to sustain the creation of networks must, by definition, seek to remain close to or dependent on the source of vital resources such as finances, legal adjudication and political power provided by central government elites, administration and policy-making structures. For a discussion of autonomy as a central concept in regional institutionalization, see Putnam, Leonardi, Nanetti, and Pavoncello (1984) and Israel (1987).

8. For a preliminary discussion of network theory in the study of social and political phenomenon see Berkowitz (1982) and Knoke (1990).

9. The BRS communication system linking advisers in the BC-NET system is the physical representation of the 'most' developed network presently in existence in the European Community. The BC-NET system brings together public as well as private entities that have joined the system as 'advisers' which constitute the principal access point. Among these advisers we find a conspicuous presence of Euro Info Centres (EICs) making sure that there is consistency in the Community's policies toward SMEs.

10. See the 'Report on European Union' presented by the Commission to the European Parliament on 27 February 1991, SN 1311/1/91 REV. 1.

References

Berkowitz, S.D., *An Introduction to Structural Analysis: The Network Approach to Social Research*, Toronto, Butterworths, 1982.

Cappellin, R., 'The European Internal Market and the Internationalization of Small and Medium Size Enterprises', *Built Environment*, 16(1), 1990.

CEC, *EC Research Funding* (2nd edn), Luxembourg, Office for Official Publications of the European Communities, 1990.

Cecchini, P., *1992: The European Challenge*, Aldershot, Gower, 1988.

Israel, A., *Institutional Development: Incentives to Performance*, Baltimore, Johns Hopkins University Press, 1987.

Knoke, D., *Political Networks: The Structural Perspective*, Cambridge, Cambridge University Press, 1990.

Leonardi, R., *Convergence, Cohesion and Integration in the European Union*, London, Macmillan, 1994.

Marks, G., Nielsen, F. and Salk, J., 'Regional Mobilization in the European Union', paper presented at the conference on 'EC Cohesion Policy and National Networks' Nuffield College, Oxford, 2–5 December 1993.

Nanetti, R.Y., 'The Strategy of Regional-Specific Development', *Geoforum*, 1, pp. 81–8, 1987.

Piore, M. and Sabel, C., *The Second Industrial Divide: Possibilities for Prosperity*, New York, Basic Books, 1984.

Putnam, R.D., Leonardi, R., Nanetti, R.Y. and Pavoncello, F., 'Explaining Institutional Success: The Case of Italian Regional Government', *American Political Science Review*, March, pp. 55–74, 1984.

Siebert, H. (ed.), 'The Completion of the Internal Market: Symposium 1989', mimeo, Kiel Institute of World Economics, Kiel, 1988.

Index